PSA Schedule of Rates for
Landscape Management

SECOND EDITION 2001

London: The Stationery Office Ltd

© Carillion 2000

Applications for reproduction should be made in writing to The Stationery Office
Limited, St Crispins, Duke Street, Norwich NR3 1PD.

The information contained in this publication is believed to be correct at the time
of manufacture. Whilst care has been taken to ensure that the information is
accurate, the publisher can accept no responsibility for any errors or
ommissions or for changes to the details given. Every effort has been made to
trace copyright holders and to obtain permission for the use of copyright
material. The publishers will gladly receive any information enabling them to
rectify any errors or omissions in subsequent editions.

First published 2000

ISBN 0 11 702515 1

Printed in the United Kingdom for The Stationery Office by Deanprint Ltd, Stockport, Cheshire
TJ3140 C5 12/00

This is the Second Edition of The Schedule of Rates for Landscape Management and is the latest in a line of Schedules dating back to 1840, now produced by Carillion Services.

Carillion Services has many years of experience in compiling Schedules of Rates for use by professionals in both the private and public sectors. This derives from origins within the Property Services Agency where a comprehensive portfolio of publications was developed to meet the needs of the Government Estate.

Carillion Services provide a range of additional Schedule of Rates related services including:

- **Bespoke Schedules of Rates**
  Schedules tailored to *your* requirements; sections not required can be removed and/or additional items can be included, and the rates can be easily amended to reflect particular resource costs and/or allowances.

- **Computerised Estimating and Term Contract Administration Systems**
  Advice on systems utilising The Schedules of Rates.

  A number of firms have been granted licences to reproduce PSA Schedules of Rates in a computerised form.

- **Measured Term Contract advice**
  Contract action, tender evaluation and post-contract administration.

- **Training**
  Schedules of Rates and Term Contracting generally.

To obtain advice and information please contact:

Carillion Services Limited
Westlink House
981 Great West Road
Brentford, Middlesex
TW8 9DN

Telephone: 087 0128 5220
Facsimile: 020 8380 5050
E.mail: scheduleofrates@carillionplc.com

www.carillionplc.com

Adjustments to the rates in these Schedules can be made using the "Updating Percentages – Adjustments for Measured Term Contracts" produced by the Department of Environment, Transport and the Regions and published by:

Tudorseed Construction
Unit 3, Ripon House
35, Station Lane
Hornchurch
Essex RM12 6JL

Telephone: 01708 444678
Facsimile: 01708 443002
E.mail: tudorseed@fdn.co.uk

Whilst all reasonable care has been taken in the compilation of this Schedule of Rates, Carillion Services will not be under any legal liability of any kind in respect of any misstatement, error or omission contained herein, or for the reliance any person, company or authority may place thereon.

Contents

GENERALLY

Format

Apart from this General Directions Section, this document is structured in accordance with the "Common Arrangement of Work Sections For Building Works" 2nd Edition, published in 1998 by the Building Project Information Committee as part of the initiative towards Co-ordinated Project Information.

Preambles

Preambles which apply to all Sections are contained in this General Directions Section.

Preambles which apply only to specific Sections and Sub-Sections are contained within the particular Section.

Tender documents

The Conditions of Contract and all other tender documents are to be read in conjunction with this Schedule.

Legislation

Comply with all relevant legislation at the time of execution of the work.

PRELIMINARIES

All Inclusive Rates

The Rates in this Schedule are all inclusive and, as such, include for Preliminaries.

Significant preliminary items

When assessing any adjustment to be tendered to the level of the Rates, consideration must be given to any unique preliminary items which could be encountered. The following list gives examples only and does not limit the actual requirements encountered.

    Establishment charges, overheads and profit.
    Nature and location of the Works.
    Liabilities and insurances.
    Access to the Works.
    Existing services.
    Plant, tools, vehicles and transport.
    Site organisation, security, health and safety
    Water, lighting and power.
    Temporary works: eg hardstandings,
       accommodation, storage, telephones,
       fencing, footways and gantries.
    Statutory obligations.

Value of old Items

Unless specifically agreed otherwise, all old items for disposal will become the sole property of the Contractor.

Removing and depositing arisings

Unless specifically agreed otherwise, all arisings for removing and depositing will become the sole property of the Employer.

Materials and Workmanship

Where not particularly specified, materials and methods of working are at the Contractor's discretion and must be entirely suitable and of good practice for the work in hand.

PRELIMINARIES

Agreed rates for materials

Where using a "fixing only" or "laying only" rate for materials paid for by the Contractor or where the Contractor is supplying only materials, reimburse--ment of the cost of materials, unless the Conditions of Contract state otherwise will be made on the basis of agreed current market or invoice rates delivered to site or store (after the deduction of all discounts obtainable for cash, insofar as they exceed 2½ per cent, and of all trade discounts, rebates and allowances) with the addition of 5 per cent to cover profit and all other liabilities. Such reimbursement shall not be subject to further adjustment.

Sub-Contractors and Suppliers

In the case of work ordered to be placed with a Sub-Contractor or Supplier, the Contractor, unless the Conditions of Contract state otherwise, will be reimbursed the net agreed amount of their account (after the deduction of all discounts obtainable for cash, insofar as they exceed 2½ per cent, and of all trade discounts, rebates and allowances) with the addition of 5 per cent to cover profit and all other liabilities. Such reimbursement shall not be subject to further adjustment.

Asbestos removal

Observe all statutory requirements and Health and Safety Executive guidance. A Licensed Contractor must be appointed for removal of asbestos-based products.

ENVIRONMENTAL PROTECTION

Generally

All operations are to be strictly controlled to avoid contamination of soil, ground water, waterways, wildlife habitats, etc.

Comply with all legislative controls and regulations.

Fire risk

Take all appropriate actions to avoid risk of fire.

During periods of high fire risk, ensure that any activity carried out does not increase that risk.

PLANT, EQUIPMENT AND TOOLS

Generally

To be approved type, appropriate to the work ordered and maintained and operated in accordance with the manufacturers instructions and relevant Codes of Practice.

Follow guidance in BS 7370: Part 1.

Maintenance

Carry out refuelling and servicing of machines on paved, not grassed, bitumen or tarmac areas.

Clean up spilled fuel, oil, etc. immediately with suitable solvents.

Immobilise or remove from site all machines at the end of each working day.

Tractors

When used for grass cutting, maintenance work or where otherwise specified, tractors are to be fitted with grassland tyres. Do not operate on sloping ground with a gradient exceeding that recommended by the vehicle manufacturer.

"Ride-on" self powered equipment

Do not operate on sloping ground with a gradient exceeding that recommended by the manufacturer.

Measurement rules

This Schedule stands alone. Where not self-evident from the Item descriptions, the rules of measurement are stated.

Every effort has been made to adhere to the Standard Method of Measurement of Building Works: Seventh Edition (SMM7), but by the very nature of the Schedule's uses some expansion and changes are necessary.

Measurement

Measure work net as executed or fixed in position unless otherwise stated.

Where Rates are quoted as per 100 m, per 100 m² or per hectare: take dimensions used in calculating quantities to the nearest 500 mm.

All other Rates: take dimensions used in calculating quantities to the nearest 10 mm.

Linear or superficial work on sloping or undulating sites:
Measure on the surface of the ground.

Excavating and subsequent disposal:
Measure the bulk before excavating and make no allowance for any subsequent variations in bulk.

Filling:
Measure as equal to the void filled.

Measure thickness after compaction.

Billing

Bill all quantities to the nearest two decimal places of the billing unit for each particular item.

Voids

Unless otherwise stated, minimum deductions for voids refer only to openings or wants within the boundaries of the measured work.

Always deduct openings or wants at the boundaries of measured work, irrespective of size.

Do not measure Items for widths not exceeding a stated limit where these widths are caused by voids.

Nominal sizes

All sizes are nominal unless otherwise stated.

Size ranges

Sizes expressed as " .... to .... " , are to be read as "exceeding .... but not exceeding ....".

Base Date

The Rates in this Schedule reflect the costs of resources as at the third quarter 2000.

Multiplying factors

Where two or more multiplying factors are to be applied to a Rate, the factors are first to be multiplied together and not added.

Rates expressed per unit of thickness, etc.

Rates per unit of thickness, width, girth, or the like:
Pay for part of a unit as a whole unit.

Rates expressed as per unit of weight, or of volume, per unit of area (e.g. per tonne per hectare, per m³ per hectare):
Calculate the Rate proportionally for the actual weight or volume.

Work in confined or isolated areas

Where the unit of measurement is the hectare (except for Stone Picking (Items D20.067 and D20.068) and litter clearance (Item D20.174)):

Multiply the appropriate Rates by 1.50.

Rates throughout exclude (except where otherwise stated)

Drawings:
Preparing drawings.

Rates throughout include (except where otherwise stated)

All Rates:
For preliminaries, labour, waste and lost time.

For supplying and delivering materials, unloading and getting into store or other approved position.

For storage of materials.

For assembling, fitting and fixing materials in position.

For carrying out work in any circumstances, unless otherwise stated. It is assumed that work carried out in disadvantageous circumstances (e.g. work in occupied buildings, alterations, repairs or extensions) will be offset by work carried out in advantageous circumstances.

For working at any height unless otherwise stated.

For providing scaffolding or working platforms not exceeding 4.50 metres above the base of any scaffolding.

For carrying out the work in accordance with the requirements of the Specification clauses whether or not these are repeated elsewhere.

For executing in sections as necessitated by the nature of the work or to suit the chosen method of working.

For any break in working after the continuity of the work has been interrupted by any temporary obstruction not specifically stated in this Schedule.

For providing all equipment, implements and tools.

For multiple handling materials and items.

For providing samples and tests.

For protecting old and new works from damage.

For square cutting.

For fixing to new or old backgrounds.

For keeping the site free from all surplus materials, rubbish and debris arising from the execution of the Works.

For leaving the site clean and tidy on completion of the Works.

Taking out, taking up or the like:
For breaking up, cutting away, stripping or the like.

For work incidental to alterations but not for the complete demolition of a structure.

For taking out from any background unless otherwise stated.

For getting out from the interior to the exterior of the building and lowering or hoisting to ground level as necessary by means of barrows and wheeling gangways, chutes, bagging, bucketing or hoists.

For removing off the site to a chute or other place of disposal including payment of any charges in connection therewith.

For removing to stack or other place of storage on site as ordered.

For carefully taking out all materials ordered to be stacked or removed to store for re-use.

For carefully taking out all fixings both from the background and from the item removed.

For all necessary cleaning of materials removed to store in preparation for re-use.

For providing all necessary dust sheets and tarpaulin coverings.

For laying dust by adequate sprinkling with water.

For all necessary dismantling of bulky fittings or the like preparatory to removing to stack or store.

Fixing only or laying only:
For fixing only or laying only new items or items previously set aside for re-use.

For taking delivery, storing and sending back returnable packings.

For obtaining from stack or other place of storage on site.

For handling, loading, unloading, protecting, transporting to the site of the work, hoisting, lowering, assembling and fixing complete.

For all fixing or jointing materials required.

Resecuring:
For fixing in position loosened components or materials.

For removing and renewing damaged or defective fixing or jointing materials as required.

Work in repairs:
For removing any existing work.

For new work to match existing.

For all preparatory work and making good.

For jointing new to existing work.

For work of any width.

Composite items:
For assembling, breaking down into suitable sections for transport and installation and subsequent reassembly and any adjustment necessary for fixing.

Plugging:
For providing and fixing approved proprietary plugs or, at the Contractor's discretion, for fixing by approved mechanical means.

Work to crossfalls:
For intersections.

Removing and depositing
For collecting, loading and transporting within the boundary of the site and depositing.

Burning:
For burning on site where directed and providing all supervision.

Disposing:
For collecting, loading and transporting to a place of disposal outside the boundary of the site including payment of any charges in connection therewith.

Work involving the use of wheeled equipment:
For manoeuvering to clear obstructions.

Work executed by means other than tractors:
For work to sloping ground, banks and traverses except where specifically indicated in the Rates.

Work executed with tractors:
For work to sloping ground having a gradient not exceeding 18° from the horizontal.

DEFINITIONS

Project Manager (PM)

The person employed in that capacity and appointed by the Employer as his representative.

Approved or ordered

Approved or ordered by the PM.

Or equivalent Alternative

Alternative articles and materials to those described and approved by the PM in writing.

BS

The latest British Standard (published by the British Standards Institution) referred to by its serial number, including any amendments, revisions or replacements.

Site

The land or place where work is to be executed and any adjacent land or place which may be used to carry out work.

Store

A permanent or temporary structure providing security and weather protection for storage purposes within or in close proximity to the site.

Masonry (as a background for fixing)

Includes concrete, brick, block or stone.

Timber (as a background for fixing)

Includes all forms of timber and manufactured building board, etc.

Large stones

Stones and clay balls exceeding 50 mm in any dimension.

Obstructions

Airfield lights, manhole covers, trees or the like.

Small area

Area not exceeding 2500 m².

Large area

Area exceeding 2500 m².

Confined area

Area of work not exceeding 2500 m² bounded on three or more sides by obstructions which will not permit machines and equipment to manoeuvre freely.

Isolated area

Area of work not exceeding 2500 m² which requires the separate transportation of equipment

A36: EMPLOYER'S REQUIREMENTS FOR TEMPORARY WORKS

TEMPORARY SCREENS, HOARDINGS AND FENCING

Notes

Screens, hoardings and fencing:
Pay for only where specifically ordered in addition to the Contractor's Obligations described in the "General Directions".

Rates for the following include

Generally:
For use and waste of timber.

For putting together, erecting, fixing to any background, maintaining, adjusting, striking, removing and making good.

For all necessary bolts, holes, dogs, spikes and folding wedges.

For dismantling and removing within a period of six calendar months. Where specifically ordered in writing to be left in position for a longer period than six calendar months, pay an additional 10 per cent for each additional calendar month or part of a month. When payment has been made for use and waste for a total period of twelve months, the whole of the materials will become the property the Employer.

Item A36	Square Metre	£
	Screen: dust proof: sealing joints and edges with masking tape	
001	polythene sheet: draped	2.53
	timber frame	
	polythene sheet lining	
002	one side	12.06
003	both sides	14.59
	insulation board lining	
004	one side	15.19
005	both sides	20.85
	hardboard lining	
006	one side	15.23
007	both sides	20.94
008	Screen: weather proof: timber frame: insulation board lining one side: waterproof lining other side	17.76
	Each	
009	Extra over Items A36.004 to A36.008 for single access door not exceeding 1.00 m wide: rebates, stops and ironmongery	29.69
	Metre	
010	Hoarding: next main thoroughfare: 2.00 m high: constructed of any suitable material	39.91

A36: EMPLOYER'S REQUIREMENTS FOR TEMPORARY WORKS

TEMPORARY SCREENS, HOARDINGS AND FENCING

Item A36		£
	Each	
	Extra over Item A36.010 for	
011	single access gate not exceeding 1.00 m wide: rebate, stops and ironmongery	21.24
012	pair of access gates 1.00 to 2.50 m wide: rebate, stops and ironmongery	55.07
	Metre	
	Fencing: chestnut pale or similar	
013	1.05 m high	11.57
014	1.50 m high	20.18
	Each	
015	Extra over Items A36.013 and A36.014 for access gate and posts not exceeding 1.00 m wide: suitable hangings and fastenings	40.56

EMERGENCY COVERINGS TO EXISTING BUILDINGS

Notes

Tarpaulins:
Pay for only where specifically ordered as *emergency* coverings to existing buildings not provided for in the Contractor's Obligations described in the "General Directions".

Pay for each tarpaulin up to a maximum total period of eight weeks. Make no further payment for tarpaulins retained for periods exceeding eight weeks.

Rates for the following include

Generally:
For providing tarpaulins and all battens, ropes, weights or the like at any height and in any position so as to completely protect the works covered.

For maintaining.

For taking down and removing from site.

		1	2
		First week or part	Each additional week or part
	Each	£	£
	Tarpaulin		
016	not exceeding 20 m²	26.86	10.87
017	20 to 30 m²	28.79	12.08
018	30 to 40 m²	30.73	13.28

C: Demolition, Alteration and Renovation

C20: ALTERATIONS

GENERALLY

Specification

Support of existing structure: support existing existing structure as necessary during cutting of new openings or replacement of structural parts. Do not allow new work to be overstressed when removing supports.

Notes

Filling in openings:
Pay for at the Rates in the relevant Section.

Demolition of complete structures:
Pay for at Rates agreed between the PM and the Contractor.

Method of measurement

Concrete, brickwork, blockwork or stonework:
Measure overall including the thickness of finishings except for finishings ordered to be removed separately. Measure such finishings separately.

Forming or enlarging openings in concrete, brickwork, blockwork or stonework:
Measure the net finished size of the opening required with such additions as necessary to accommodate new lintels or the like. Deduct the areas of any existing openings incorporated in the new opening.

C20: ALTERATIONS

CONCRETE

Rates for the following include

Generally:
For cutting to line at boundary of work.

For cutting reinforcement in reinforced concrete.

Item C20	*Cubic Metre*	1 Plain £	2 Reinforced £
	Taking out		
001	bed	82.72	111.77
002	slab	99.10	136.43
	Cutting to form or enlarge opening through		
003	slab	299.96	400.47

	Square Metre	£
004	Cutting to reduce thickness of concrete: trimming surface: not exceeding 25 mm thick	13.65
005	ADD *for each additional 25 mm of thickness*	10.43
006	ADD where reinforcement exposed and protected	4.95

C20: ALTERATIONS

BRICKWORK AND BLOCKWORK

Notes

Making good jambs or the like:
Pay for at the Rates in Section F10.

Cleaning and stacking old bricks:
Count only serviceable stacked bricks approved as suitable for re-use.

Rates for the following include

Taking down, cutting or the like:
For work of any description in any type of mortar.

For taking down concrete or stone lintels, copings, band courses, dressing or the like when taken down in conjunction with the brickwork or blockwork.

Cleaning and stacking old bricks:
For bricks of any description previously built in lime or cement-lime mortar.

For cleaning off mortar and dirt and stacking where directed.

Item **C20**	*Square Metre - per 25 mm of thickness*	£
007	Taking down brickwork	1.34
008	Taking down reinforced brickwork	1.77
	Cutting to form or enlarge opening through	
009	brickwork	3.17
010	reinforced brickwork	4.60

	Each - per 25 mm of depth	
011	Cutting pocket or hole for needle or shore not exceeding 0.10 m² section area in existing brickwork	1.03

	Thousand	
012	Cleaning and stacking old bricks for re-use	90.85

	Square Metre - per 25 mm of thickness	
013	Taking down blockwork	1.04
014	Cutting to form or enlarge opening through blockwork	2.01

C20: ALTERATIONS

STONEWORK

Notes	**Rates for the following include**
Stone dressings taken down in conjunction with brickwork: Pay for at the Rates for taking down brickwork.	*Generally:* For stone of any description in any mortar.

Item C20	*Cubic Metre*	£
015	Taking down rubble walling	31.67

METAL STAIRS, WALKWAYS AND BALUSTRADES

	Kilogramme	£
016	Taking down mild steel or cast iron section: any description	0.43

	Metre	£
017	Taking down steel tubular handrail, baluster or the like and fittings: any weight: any diameter	3.01

C20: ALTERATIONS

Rates for the following include

Generally:
For breaking through for insertion of ducts, pipe lines or the like.

Breaking up bituminous bound materials:
For black top surfacing to concrete roads or pavings.

Item C20		£
	Metre	
	Taking up including any haunching: any size	
	precast concrete	
018	kerb	4.02
019	edging	2.17
020	channel	4.02
	granite	
021	kerb	2.17
022	sett string course - *per row*	2.17
	brick	
023	edging	2.17
	Cubic Metre	
	Taking up sub-base or roadbase	
024	hardcore or granular material	23.85
025	concrete or other cement bound material	50.92
	Breaking up road	
026	plain concrete	51.17
027	reinforced concrete	64.88
	Square Metre	
028	Breaking up bituminous bound materials: not exceeding 75 mm total thickness	3.50
029	ADD *for each additional 25 mm of thickness*	1.07
030	Taking up stone or concrete flag paving: not exceeding 75 mm thick	2.86
031	Taking up granite sett paving: not exceeding 150 mm thick	6.60
	Taking up cobblestone paving: not exceeding 130 mm thick	
032	hoggin base	7.39
033	concrete base	10.14
034	Taking up brick paving: not exceeding 125 mm thick	5.03

C20: ALTERATIONS

DRAINAGE BELOW GROUND

Notes

Excavation and reinstatement:
Measure separately.

Rates for the following include

Generally:
For all cutting or otherwise disconnecting as required unless otherwise stated.

		1	2	3	4
		Diameter of drain not exceeding			
Item C20	*Metre*	100 mm £	150 mm £	225 mm £	300 mm £
035	Taking up concrete or clay pipework and fittings	0.97	1.21	1.58	2.01
036	Taking up concrete, clay or plastics land drain pipework and fittings	0.84	1.07	1.43	1.85
037	Taking up plastics or pitch fibre pipework and fittings	0.49	0.73	0.85	0.97
038	Taking up iron pipework and fittings	1.47	1.93	3.54	5.32
	ADD where				
039	with shingle or gravel bed	0.73	0.85	1.09	1.33
040	with shingle or gravel covering	1.09	1.28	1.64	2.01
041	with concrete bed and haunching	3.35	3.90	5.02	6.26
042	with concrete bed and covering	6.04	6.99	9.11	11.16
043	Taking up suspended iron pipework: fittings: supports	7.09	7.97	9.02	10.63
044	Taking up clay channel with concrete bed	2.69	3.35	4.65	5.92
	Each				
	Taking up gully with concrete surround				
045	not exceeding 600 mm deep	2.69	2.98	3.64	4.19
046	exceeding 600 mm deep	3.90	4.47	5.49	6.42
047	Taking off cast iron fresh air inlet: any pattern: cutting or burning out lead joint	3.00	3.63	-	-
048	Burning out caulked lead joint: for disconnection of cast iron pipe or fitting (applicable only where pipe or fitting to be re-used or renewed)	3.63	6.03	7.56	9.07

14

DRAINAGE BELOW GROUND - *continued*

Item C20	*Each*	£

Plugging end of disused drain with concrete: any mix:
for a length of at least 300 mm

049	not exceeding 100 mm diameter	5.88
050	150 mm diameter	6.46
051	225 mm diameter	7.79
052	300 mm diameter	9.99
053	375 mm diameter	12.17
054	450 mm diameter	14.37

	Square Metre	
055	Breaking up concrete wall of manhole: not exceeding 100 mm thick	9.14
056	ADD *for each additional 25 mm of thickness*	1.91
057	Breaking up reinforced concrete wall of manhole: not exceeding 100 mm thick	11.17
058	ADD *for each additional 25 mm of thickness*	2.35

Breaking up brick wall of manhole

059	half-brick thick	8.04
060	one-brick thick	14.57
061	one-and-a-half-brick thick	20.97
062	Breaking up concrete benching, channels and branches: 150 to 450 mm thick	14.84
063	Breaking up concrete bed to manhole: not exceeding 100 mm thick	3.82
064	ADD *for each additional 25 mm of thickness*	0.99
065	Breaking up reinforced concrete cover slab to manhole: not exceeding 100 mm thick	8.02
066	ADD *for each additional 25 mm of thickness*	1.71

	Cubic Metre	

Filling disused manhole

067	with selected excavated material	9.15
068	with approved granular material	51.33
069	with concrete: grade 20N/mm² 20 mm aggregate	115.59

C40: REPAIRING AND RENOVATING BRICK AND STONE

RE-FACING EXISTING BRICKWORK

Notes

Number of bricks:
Calculate the actual number of bricks required and add 10 per cent for waste.

Rates for the following include

Cutting out:
For brickwork built in any mortar.

Re-facing:
For everything except the cost of bricks.

For new or old bricks.

Common bricks:
For work in any mortar.

Facework:
For finishing joints fair.

Facing bricks:
For facework one side to match existing.

Facing bricks Column A:
For jointing and pointing in cement or cement--lime mortar.

Facing bricks Column B:
For jointing and pointing in white or coloured cement or cement-lime mortar or with coal ash substituted for sand as ordered.

Item C40	Square Metre	1 Re-facing in Common Bricks £	2 Facing bricks A £	3 B £
	Cutting out decayed, defective or cracked work and re-facing: any bond: in patches			
070	exceeding 1.00 m²	77.55	105.37	110.36
071	0.10 to 1.00 m²	89.24	119.59	125.61
072	ADD for facework one side to match existing	5.49	-	-
	Each			
073	isolated brick or bricks in group not exceeding 0.10 m²: facework one side to match existing	2.01	2.69	2.78

C40: REPAIRING AND RENOVATING BRICK AND STONE

RE-POINTING EXISTING BRICKWORK OR BLOCKWORK

Rates for the following include

Generally:
For brickwork or blockwork of any description.

For brushing and cleaning down to remove dust,
dirt, flaking paint or the like.

For wetting joints.

Item C40	*Square Metre*	1 Existing brickwork £	2 Existing blockwork £
	Raking out lime, cement-lime or decayed cement mortar joints 20 mm deep: pointing		
074	in cement or cement-lime mortar	12.50	8.53
075	in white, coloured or coal ash cement or cement-lime mortar	14.41	-
	Metre		
076	isolated joint of door or window frame or the like	1.63	1.63
077	ADD for pointing in mastic instead of mortar	4.84	4.84

RE-FACING EXISTING STONEWORK

Rates for the following include

Cutting out:
For stonework built in any mortar.

Re-facing:
For everything *except* the cost of stone.

For jointing and pointing in cement or cement-
-lime mortar to match existing.

		1 Bath £	2 Portland £	3 York £
	Square Metre - per 25 mm of depth			
	Cutting out decayed, defective or cracked work and refacing in patches			
078	exceeding 1.00 m²	12.78	15.66	18.12
079	0.10 to 1.00 m²	15.66	19.28	22.36
	Each - per 25 mm of depth			
080	not exceeding 0.10 m²	2.34	2.90	3.30

C40: REPAIRING AND RENOVATING BRICK AND STONE

RE-POINTING AND RE-DRESSING EXISTING STONEWORK

Rates for the following include

Generally:
For brushing and cleaning down to remove dust,
dirt, flaking paint or the like.

Mortar:
For coloured mortar, or substituting for sand,
crushed stone or stone dust of the same type as
the stone used.

Item C40	*Square Metre*	£
	Raking out decayed mortar joints: pointing in cement or cement-lime mortar	
081	ashlar: to a depth of 10 mm	5.90
082	squared rubble or squared rubble brought to courses: to a minimum depth of 13 mm	9.04
083	random rubble or random rubble brought to courses: to a minimum depth of 13 mm	12.46

	Metre	
084	isolated joint: to a minimum depth of 13 mm	1.77

	Square Metre	
085	Re-dressing decayed face of existing stonework with picked face to hard freestone: any type: re-pointing: in cement or cement-lime mortar	54.81

D11: SOIL STABILISATION

STABILISING MESH

Specification

Mesh and fixing pins or pegs: obtain from an approved manufacturer.
a. Polypropylene/wire mesh:
   1. mesh size: 8 No 8 mm threads per 100 mm.
   2. weight: 0.20 kg/m²
   3. fixing pins: 203 mm long.
b. Polyethylene composite mesh in four layers:
   1. weight: 0.45 kg/m²
   2. fixing pegs: 280 mm long.

Lay:
a. Polypropylene/wire mesh:
   1. side and end laps: 80 mm.
   2. fixing pins: at 500 mm centres along all edges.
b. Polyethylene composite mesh in four layers:
   1. side and end laps: 100 mm.
   2. fixing pins: at 1000 mm centres along all edges.

Drive pegs well into ground so that no projections will interfere with mowing.

Bury edge of mesh:
a. where abutting retaining walls or the like: turn down edge and bury 150 mm deep into ground: secure with fixing pins or pegs.
b. at perimeter: turn down edge and bury 250 to 300 mm deep into ground: secure with fixing pins or pegs.

Notes

Covering mesh with topsoil:
Where ordered, pay for at the appropriate Rates in Section D20.

Grass cutting prior to laying mesh:
Where ordered, pay for at the appropriate Rates in Section Q35.

Rates for the following include

Generally:
For work to banks, slopes, traverses, etc.

For laps.

For cutting to slope or profile.

For the use of ladders and planks on slopes exceeding 50° from horizontal.

Turning down and burying edge of mesh:
For all necessary excavation, temporary storage of spoil, backfilling, levelling and consolidation.

STABILISING MESH - *continued*

Item D11	*Square Metre*	1 Poly-propylene/ wire mesh £	2 Polyethylene composite mesh £
	Stabilising mesh: on grassed or soil area		
001	on surfaces not exceeding 30° from horizontal	5.03	6.06
	on surfaces 30° to 50° from horizontal		
002	not exceeding 2 m high	5.17	6.21
003	2 to 5 m high	5.32	6.43
004	5 to 10 m high	5.46	6.65
005	exceeding 10 m high	5.61	6.86
	on surfaces exceeding 50° from horizontal		
006	not exceeding 2 m high	5.90	7.15
007	2 to 5 m high	6.05	7.23
008	5 to 10 m high	6.19	7.44
009	exceeding 10 m high	6.34	7.66
	Turning down and burying edge of mesh		
010	at abutments to retaining walls or the like	0.98	1.13
011	at perimeter	0.98	1.13

RETAINING WALLS

	Each	£
	Gabion retaining walls: galvanized mesh: filling with broken stone: securely wired: on grassed or soil area	
012	2.00 x 1.00 x 0.50 m	90.73
013	2.00 x 1.00 x 1.00 m	162.63
014	3.00 x 1.00 x 0.50 m	129.16
015	3.00 x 1.00 x 1.00 m	239.13

D20: EXCAVATING AND FILLING

GENERALLY

Specification

Safety: ensure the safety of all personnel working in and around excavations.

Protection: protect excavations against frost.

Water disposal:
a. keep excavations free of water at all times;
b. remove water so that it does not enter construction work.
c. where pumping is necessary form sumps clear of excavations for permanent work.

Obstructions: report to the PM details of any underground obstructions.

Excavations taken too wide or too deep: backfill as ordered at the Contractor's own expense.

Foundation bottoms:
a. excavate the last 150 mm of trenches immediately prior to laying concrete;
b. inform the PM and obtain his instructions if natural bearing bottom cannot be found at the prescribed depths because solid rock is encountered, the ground is made up or is otherwise unsuitable for building upon;
c. obtain approval before laying concrete.

Definition of terms

Ground level: ground, stripped or reduced level.

Rock: a material which in the opinion of the PM can only be removed by means of wedges, special plant or explosives.

Ground water: excludes spring or running water.

Notes

Excavation below ground water level:
If ground water is encountered in the course of excavation, the water level will be established by the PM before pumping is commenced (in tidal conditions this will be the average of the mean high and low levels), and the level PM established will be taken as the water level throughout the period of the execution of the order notwithstanding any changes.

Depths stated:
Relate to ground level.

Method of measurement

Excavating and disposal:
Measure the void to be occupied by, or vertically above the permanent work. Make no allowance for variations in bulk or for the extra space for earthwork support.

Working space:
Measure additional excavation up to a maximum of 600 mm from faces of formwork, rendering, tanking or protective walls which are less than 600 mm from the face of the excavation.

Do not adjust if more or less space is actually required.

Rates for the following include

Excavating, disposal and filling:
For multiple handling unless specifically ordered.

Curved earthwork support:
For any extra costs of curved excavation.

D20: EXCAVATING AND FILLING

SITE CLEARANCE

Specification

Site features: before starting work verify with PM which existing trees, shrubs, hedges and other site features are to be removed and which are to be retained.

Method of measurement

Tree:
Measure girth 1.00 m above ground.

Tree stump:
Measure girth at top.

Notes

Supplying imported filling material:
Pay for separately.

Rates for the following include

Removing, clearing:
For grubbing up roots.

For disposing of materials off site.

For filling voids with selected material obtained from elsewhere on the site, or approved imported material, as ordered.

VEGETATION

Specification

Large roots: pull or grub up and dispose of large roots without undue disturbance of soil and adjacent areas.

Chipping or shredding on site of materials arising from the work will not be permitted.

Method of Measurement

Clearing grass, etc. on or against fencing:
Measure the length of the fence.

Rates for the following include

Clearing site
For removing hedges, trees and saplings not exceeding 150 mm girth where in massed growth or within an area of bushes, scrub or undergrowth

Item D20	100 Square Metres	1 £	2 ADD for burning arisings £	3 ADD for disposing arisings £
	Clearing site: removing and depositing arisings: cultivating surface to even gradient and medium tilth			
001	bracken, light undergrowth or the like	34.32	3.50	10.55
002	bushes, scrub and undergrowth	172.29	10.51	42.19
003	ADD for grubbing up roots: filling voids	135.95	2.34	7.04
004	Cutting down brambles: pulling or grubbing up roots: removing and depositing arisings	28.50	2.92	8.81

D20: EXCAVATING AND FILLING

VEGETATION - *continued*

Item D20	*Metre*	1	2 ADD for burning arisings	3 ADD for disposing arisings
		£	£	£
	Clearing grass and other vegetation growing on or against fencing: pulling or grubbing up roots: removing and depositing arisings			
005	one side of fence	0.70	0.06	0.17
006	both sides of fence	1.16	0.09	0.28

	Square Metre	£
007	Lifting turf for preservation: minimum 40 mm thick: removing not exceeding 50 m: stacking	4.45

EXCAVATING

Rates for the following include

Excavating:
For excavating by hand or machine any material encountered (including hardcore) except where otherwise stated.

For keeping the excavations free of surface water.

Excavating below ground water level:
For keeping excavations free of ground water.

	Square Metre	£
008	Topsoil for preservation: 150 mm average depth	0.44
009	ADD or DEDUCT *for each 25 mm variation in depth*	0.05

	Cubic Metre	1	2	3
		Maximum depth not exceeding		
		0.25 m	1.00 m	2.00 m
		£	£	£
010	To reduce levels	2.95	2.86	2.97
011	Pit	9.63	8.52	9.73
012	Trench not exceeding 0.30 m wide	12.15	11.96	12.17
013	Trench exceeding 0.30 m wide	8.63	8.68	9.21

EXCAVATING - *continued*

Item D20	Cubic Metre	£
014	ADD to Items D20.010 to D20.013 where starting over 0.25 m below ground level - *for each 1.00 m below*	2.81
015	Extra over excavation irrespective of depth for excavating below ground water level	2.42
	Extra over excavation irrespective of depth for breaking out	
016	rock	32.95
017	concrete	30.55
018	reinforced concrete	46.19
019	brickwork, blockwork or stonework	16.56

	Square Metre	
020	concrete paving - *per 25 mm of thickness*	0.64
021	reinforced concrete paving - *per 25 mm of thickness*	0.89
022	concrete or stone flag paving: not exceeding 75 mm thick	0.78
023	brick paving: not exceeding 125 mm thick	0.93
024	stone sett or cobble paving: not exceeding 150 mm thick	1.40
025	coated macadam or asphalt paving - *per 25 mm of thickness*	0.53

026	Where hand excavation is specifically ordered, price at the foregoing Rates *multiplied by 2.00.*	

	Metre	
	Extra over excavation irrespective of depth for excavating	
027	next to existing service or group of services	7.61

	Each	
028	around existing service or group of services crossing excavation	22.33

EARTHWORK SUPPORT

Definition of terms

Unstable ground: running silt, running sand, loose gravel or the like.

Earthwork support next to roadway or existing building: earthwork support which, in the opinion of the PM, is required to protect any adjacent roadway or building from movement or damage.

Method of measurement

Earthwork support:
Measure the full depth to all vertical and sloping earthwork faces exceeding 45° from horizontal, whether or not support is required, except to faces not exceeding 0.25 m high.

Earthwork support below ground water level or in unstable ground:
Measure from the commencing level of the excavation to the full depth.

Distances between opposing faces:
Classify with adjoining work at intersections, corners or ends of trenches or the like.

Rates for the following include

Generally:
For providing everything to uphold the sides of excavation by whatever means necessary including sheet steel piling unless this is ordered as a specific design requirement.

		1	2
		Maximum depth not exceeding	
Item		1.00 m	2.00 m
D20	*Square Metre*	£	£
	To face of excavation: distance between opposing faces		
029	not exceeding 2.00 m	3.56	4.14
030	2.00 to 4.00 m	3.81	4.64
031	exceeding 4.00 m	6.62	8.54
	ADD where		
032	curved	2.07	2.36
033	below ground water level	6.26	6.89
034	in unstable ground	4.88	5.31
035	next to roadway	3.92	4.64
036	next to existing building	3.42	3.75

D20: EXCAVATING AND FILLING

DISPOSAL

Rates for the following include

Generally:
For any type of excavated or broken out material.

Item **D20**	Cubic Metre	£
	Excavated material	
037	off site	18.41
038	on site not exceeding 25 m and depositing	4.93
039	ADD *for each additional 50 m*	0.44

FILLING

Specification

Earth filling: approved readily compacted subsoil, free from harmful contaminants or vegetable matter and suitable for the location.

Granular filling: gravel, sandy soil or other approved material free from fines, clay or other harmful matter.

Spread filling: in layers; compact and consolidate each layer before spreading the next.

Hardcore: hard stone, concrete, coarse gravel, sound slag or hard broken brick, free from rubbish or other deleterious matter, capable of passing in every direction a ring of diameter not greater than two thirds thickness of bed, subject to a maximum diameter of 150 mm and graded so that when compacted, filling is dense and without voids.

Spread hardcore: in layers and compact:
a. with mechanical plant until all movement in the hardcore ceases;
b. until all voids are full and surface is smooth and even.

Approval: backfill only with approval.

Method of measurement

Filling generally:
Measure as equal to the void filled.

Measure the average thickness after compaction.

Rates for the following include

Topsoil filling:
For lightly compacting, digging over and leaving for planting free of weeds, large stones and debris.

Filling of any material except topsoil:
For compacting in layers not exceeding 150 mm thick.

Hardcore obtained from the excavations or demolitions:
For selecting for re-use and breaking to required sizes.

FILLING - *continued*

Item D20	*Cubic Metre*	1 Selected excavated material arising from excavations on site £	2 Imported material Earth £	3 Granular £	4 Hardcore Obtained from the excavations or demolitions £	5 Imported £
	Filling to excavation					
040	not exceeding 0.25 m average thick	11.61	17.65	28.28	15.09	27.78
041	exceeding 0.25 m average thick	9.67	15.71	26.35	12.58	25.26
	Filling to make up levels					
042	not exceeding 0.25 m average thick	12.93	18.96	29.60	16.81	29.49
043	exceeding 0.25 m average thick	10.77	16.81	27.44	14.00	26.68
	Square Metre					
044	Surface packing: to vertical or battered face exceeding 15° from horizontal	2.13	2.13	2.13	3.19	3.19

SURFACE TREATMENTS

	Square Metre	£
	Levelling or grading to falls and slopes not exceeding 15° from horizontal: compacting	
045	ground	0.76
046	earth or granular filling	0.76
047	hardcore filling	1.14
048	bottom of excavation	0.35
049	Blinding surface of hardcore with approved fine material	1.51
050	Trimming sloping surface exceeding 15° from horizontal	1.22
051	Trimming bottom or side of excavation in rock to falls, slopes or cambers	14.33

D20: EXCAVATING AND FILLING

SOIL PREPARATION

Specification

Standards: carry out the work to approved agricultural and horticultural standards.

Timing: time all stages of work to obtain optimum effect, giving full regard to the season, weather and soil condition.

Cultivate soil to depths stated or as otherwise ordered. Carry out the work using ploughs, disc harrows, rotary cultivators, rigid or spring tined harrows or other equipment as ordered. Produce a coarse friable soil condition to the full working depth suitable for blade grading.

Subsoiling to break up deep panning may be carried out as part of the soil cultivation if ordered.

Blade grading will normally follow cultivation. Obtain approval to the work before proceeding with the final stage of preparation.

Break up compacted subsoil or plough pan on arable or grassland by subsoiling not exceeding 750 mm deep as directed.

Ploughs: suitable for the depth of cultivation ordered.

Depth and type of ploughing: as ordered.

Furrows: of even depth and uniform finish with vegetation turned in and buried.

Harrow with the equipment ordered to produce a coarse crumb structure to the depth required or to produce a fine crumb tilth as directed.

Note

Clearing vegetation:
Pay for separately.

Rates for the following include

Generally:
For work executed using equipment mounted on or towed by tractor, unless otherwise stated.

For clearing obstructions to the use of equipment before commencing work.

For disposing roots and all weeds.

For stone picking except where work is paid for at Rates per 100 Square Metres or per Hectare when Items D20.065 to D20.068 shall be paid in addition.

For work on any type of soil.

Ploughing:
For ploughing arable, stubble or grassland.

Ploughing, cultivating, harrowing and rolling:
For once over the area ordered.

SOIL PREPARATION - *continued*

Item D20	*Hectare*	1 Type of soil Light £	2 Type of soil Heavy £
	Ploughing		
052	2 furrows	27.91	30.70
053	4 furrows	33.49	37.68
054	6 furrows	39.07	44.66

	Hectare	£
	Harrowing: using	
	tractor mounted equipment	
055	chain or light flexible spiked harrow	13.10
056	standard disc harrow	22.57
057	heavy disc harrow	31.09
058	spring tined harrow	23.83
059	heavy rotary cultivator	48.00

	100 Square Metres	
	pedestrian operated self-powered cultivator or rotavator	
060	100 mm deep	12.75
061	300 mm deep	15.77

D20: EXCAVATING AND FILLING

CULTIVATING TOPSOIL

Rates for the following include

Digging and raking:
For collecting undesirable material brought to the surface including large stones, roots, weeds, tufts of grass and foreign matter: disposing and leaving area tidy.

Item D20	Square Metre	£
062	Hand digging with fork or spade to an average depth of 230 mm: leaving rough	0.29
063	Hand digging with fork or spade to an average depth of 230 mm: breaking down lumps: leaving surface with a medium tilth	0.33
064	Hand raking dug or graded soil: breaking down lumps to a fine tilth: leaving surface smooth and even	0.08

STONE PICKING

Definition

Other undesirable material:
Anything lying on the surface which might damage grass cutting equipment or vehicle tyres, or which might be a hazard to aircraft.

Rates for the following include

Removal:
For collecting undesirable material including large stones and foreign matter: disposing and leaving area tidy.

		1	2	3
		Size of stones		
		10 to 25 mm	25 to 50 mm	Exceeding 50 mm
	100 Square Metres	£	£	£
	Removal of large stones and other undesirable material: gathering into heaps: removing and depositing on site			
	by hand			
065	not exceeding 0.5 m³ per hectare	14.54	10.90	5.81
066	0.5 to 1 m³ per hectare	17.44	13.08	6.98

Item		Hectare	£
067	by machine: mechanical stone rake or the like		138.46
068	ADD for disposing off site - *per m³ per hectare*		18.40

TOPSOIL

Specification

Imported soil (where ordered):
Quantity and quality ordered.

Obtain from an approved supplier.

Excavated top soil: keep separate from excavated top soil. Do not remove topsoil from below the spread of trees to be retained.

Handling topsoil: minimize disturbance, trafficking and compaction. Take care that soil is not spilt on roadways or the like. Clean up as necessary.

Keep different grades of topsoil separate from each other when handling and stockpiling.

Definition

Spoil heaps:
Soil deposited not exceeding six months prior to the execution of the order and includes:
a. material from a source other than the excav--ation.
b. material deposited under a separate order or contract.
c. material from the excavations which, in the opinion of the PM, is impossible to deposit in readiness for spreading and levelling.

Note

iImported soil (where ordered):
Pay for separately.

Rates for the following include

Generally:
For hand or machine work except where otherwise stated.

Item D20	*Cubic Metre*	£
	Excavating: topsoil	
	for preservation: 150 mm average depth	
069	by machine	1.97
070	by hand	6.94
	from spoil heaps	
071	by machine	0.95
072	by hand	4.75
	Disposal: topsoil	
	deposited on site	
	by machine: transporting a distance not exceeding 25 m	
073	in permanent spoil heaps	0.87
074	ADD for each additional 25 m	0.58
075	spread on site	2.90
076	ADD for each additional 25 m	0.51

TOPSOIL - *continued*

Item D20	*Cubic Metre*	£
	Disposal: topsoil	
	deposited on site	
077	by hand: wheeling a distance not exceeding 25 m: in wheel barrows: spread on site	21.85
078	ADD for each additional 25 m	4.37
	removed from site	
079	uncontaminated	10.94
080	contaminated	14.85
	Filling to make up levels: topsoil	
	selected preserved or imported	
	by machine	
081	not exceeding 0.25 m average thick	1.26
082	exceeding 0.25 m average thick	1.22
	by hand	
083	not exceeding 0.25 m average thick	6.21
084	exceeding 0.25 m average thick	4.93
	ADD for passing through mechanical screen of approved gauge: removing and depositing screenings	
085	by machine	1.51
086	by hand	3.65
087	ADD for disposal of screenings: transporting a distance not exceeding 25 m	1.09
088	ADD for each additional 25 m	0.73

FILLING EXTERNAL PLANTERS

	Each	£
	Filling external planter with soil: drainage layer	
089	50 litre planter	0.65
090	75 litre planter	0.87
091	100 litre planter	1.09

D20: EXCAVATING AND FILLING

POWER PUMPING

Notes

Generally:
When not in connection with removing surface water or ground water encountered during excavations, working time only (ie the actual hours of pump running time) will be paid for the use of pumps as ordered.

Rates for the following include

Generally:
For bringing to and removing from the site.

For moving about the site as required.

For hoses.

For operating.

For disposal of water.

For attendance.

Item D20	Hour	£
	Single diaphragm pump	
092	75 mm	4.30
093	100 mm	6.23
	Double diaphragm pump	
094	75 mm	4.76
095	100 mm	6.56
	Self-priming centrifugal pump	
096	50 mm	4.27
097	75 mm	6.04
098	100 mm	7.30
099	150 mm	9.89

E: In situ Concrete

E10: IN SITU CONCRETE

SPECIFICATION

Generally

British Standards: concrete is to comply with BS 5328 and BS 8110 unless otherwise specified.

Constituent materials

Ordinary and rapid-hardening Portland cement: to BS 12 and manufactured by a BSI Registered Firm.

Sulphate-resisting Portland cement: to BS 4027 and manufactured by a BSI Registered Firm.

Do not use pulverised fuel ash, ground granulated blast furnace slag and/or any other cementitious materials or admixtures.

Aggregates: from natural sources to BS 882. Do not use marine aggregates or aggregates which contain chlorides unless approved.

Water: to be clean and uncontaminated. Obtain approval for other than mains supply.

Admixtures: do not use without prior approval.

Definitions

Standard mixes: in accordance with Section 4 of BS 5328 Part 2.

Designed mixes: in accordance with Section 5 of BS 5328 Part 2.

Ready mixed concrete

Obtain from approved suppliers.

Quality control of concrete

Provide PM with any information required in the prescribed form regarding the concrete and constituent materials before commencing concreting.

Testing

Testing and sampling:
a. constituent materials: to the appropriate BS, or as ordered;
b. concrete, fresh or hardened: to BS 1881, or as ordered.

Test equipment and facilities: provide and maintain as necessary.

Test laboratory: submit to PM name and address of independent test laboratory proposed. Obtain approval before arranging tests.

Packing and transport of samples: pack and transport samples to selected or nominated testing laboratory.

Test certificates: instruct laboratory to send two copies of each certificate to PM.

Workmanship

Generally:
British Standards: comply with BS 8000 Part 2 in respect of:
a. materials handling and preparation (Section 2.1, sub-section 2);

b. weather conditions (Section 2.1, sub-section 3);

c. site mixing of concrete (Section 2.1, sub-section 4);

d. transporting concrete on site (Section 2.1, sub-section 5).

SPECIFICATION - *continued*

Concrete production

Handling and storage of constituent materials:
a. cement: obtain in sealed bags or containers, store in dry enclosed conditions on a raised platform separating different types of cement. Use in order of delivery.

b. aggregates: store on a hard, clean base which permits free drainage keeping different types and sizes separate. Protect from frost and contamination by deleterious materials.

Batching and mixing: comply with Section 13 of BS 5328. Do not use frozen or frost covered materials. Ensure workability of concrete is such that:
a. it can be readily worked into corners and angles of forms and around reinforcement.

b. constituent materials do not segregate and free water does not collect at the surface during placing.

Placing and compacting

Avoidance of contamination: avoid contamination, segregation or loss of ingredients, by cleaning transporting equipment immediately after use or whenever cement or aggregate is changed. Remove free water.

Placticity: place concrete whilst it is still sufficiently plastic for full compaction to take place. Record time and date of all concrete pours.

Compaction: compact concrete thoroughly around reinforcement, duct formers, inserts and into corners of formwork. Ensure full compaction and amalgamation with previous batches. Do not allow segregation.

Construction joints: lightly roughen entire face to expose coarse aggregate. Thoroughly wire brush to remove all loose material. Ensure face is clean and damp before fresh concrete is placed.

Cold weather workings: do not place concrete when air temperature is below 6°C:

a. do not cast against frozen surfaces;

b. maintain temperature of placed concrete at not less than 7°C for at least five days after placing by covering with mineral wool or glass fibre insulation or any other;

c. do not use water spraying or wet coverings when freezing temperatures are likely;

d. cover concrete surfaces with an insulating material when temperature reaches 10°C and is falling.

Frost damage: remove and replace concrete damaged by frost.

Curing concrete

Curing period: not less than 7 days unless otherwise ordered.

Curing method: as directed and either:

a. waterproof sheeting kept in close contact; or

b. absorbent material kept damp; or

c. a curing compound.

Curing compounds: of proprietary manufacture and:

a. approved before use;

b. having a minimum efficiency of 90 per cent when tested to BS 7542.

c. containing solvent based resin and fugitive dye.

Application of curing compound:

a. apply immediately after finishing operations;

b. apply uniformly at manufacturer's recommended rate and in accordance with manufacturer's instructions;

c. do not place or store any building materials on concrete surfaces before end of curing period;

d. remove any remaining traces of compounds by steam cleaning or other suitable, non abrasive method.

E10: IN SITU CONCRETE

GENERALLY

Definition of terms

Foundations: includes attached column bases and attached pile caps.

Bed: includes blinding beds, plinths and thickening of beds.

Slab: includes attached beams and beam casings whose depth is not exceeding three times their width (depth measured below the slab) and column drop heads.

Walls: includes attached columns and piers and kickers.

Staircase: includes landings and strings.

Upstand: excludes kickers.

Method of measurement

Concrete volume:
Measure net but make no deductions for the following:
a. reinforcement;
b. steel sections of area not exceeding 0.05m²;
c. cast in accessories;
d. voids not exceeding 0.05 m³.

Thickness range:
Exclude projections and recesses.

Rates for the following include

Concrete generally:
For Standard or Designated Mixes.

For ordinary Portland cement unless otherwise stated.

For medium or high workability.

For hand compacting or mechanically vibrating.

For curing.

For protecting concrete by any means when poured on or against earth or unblinded hardcore.

Bed:
For laying in bays where ordered.

E10: IN SITU CONCRETE

IN SITU CONCRETE: 20 N/mm²: 20 mm AGGREGATE

Item E10	*Cubic Metre*	1 Plain Thickness not exceeding 150 mm £	2 150 to 450 mm £	3 exceeding 450 mm £	4 Reinforced not exceeding 150 mm £	5 150 to 450 mm £	6 exceeding 450 mm £
001	Bed	97.16	90.81	87.15	100.84	94.49	90.83
002	Wall	107.16	100.44	96.01	121.05	110.82	103.95

		1 Plain £	2 Reinforced £
003	Foundation	92.52	98.78
004	Isolated foundation	96.38	101.49
005	Staircase	118.93	139.85
006	Upstand	109.41	125.82

Cubic Metre	£
ADD to the foregoing Rates for beds, slabs or the like where	
007 sloping not exceeding 15° from horizontal	4.35
008 sloping exceeding 15° from horizontal	8.71

ADJUSTMENT TO FOREGOING RATES FOR OTHER MIXES AND CEMENTS

Item E10	Cubic Metre	1 Plain or reinforced Ordinary cement £	2 Rapid-hardening cement £	3 Sulphate-resisting cement £
	ADJUST for Standard or Designated Mix			
	10 N/mm²			
009	40 mm aggregate	-7.02	-5.84	-4.50
010	20 mm aggregate	-3.97	-2.64	-1.12
	20 N/mm²			
011	40 mm aggregate	-2.36	-0.86	0.85
012	20 mm aggregate	0.00	1.61	3.45
013	10 mm aggregate	3.57	5.38	7.44
	30 N/mm²			
014	20 mm aggregate	4.79	6.73	8.95
015	10 mm aggregate	9.20	11.40	13.91

E10: IN SITU CONCRETE

FLEXIBLE SHEET MEMBRANES

Specification

Waterproof building paper:
a. to BS 1521;
b. loose lay in a single layer with minimum
   150 mm laps.

Polythene sheet:
a. translucent or black opaque;
b. loose lay in a single layer with minimum
   150 mm laps.

Definition of terms

Horizontal:
Includes slopes not exceeding 10° from horizontal.

Method of measurement

Generally:
Measure area in contact with the base. Make no deduction for voids not exceeding 1.00 m².

Rates for the following include

Generally:
For all cutting, holing, notching and bending.

For extra material for laps.

Item E10	*Square Metre*	1 Waterproof building paper: grade AIF £	2 BIF £
016	Sheeting: horizontal: on ground, filling, sub-base or the like	2.16	1.50

		1	2	3	4	5
		Polythene sheet: gauge				
		250	500	1000	1200	2000
		£	£	£	£	£
017	Sheeting: horizontal: on ground, filling, sub-base or the like	0.65	0.78	0.93	1.07	1.65

E20: FORMWORK FOR IN SITU CONCRETE

SPECIFICATION

Materials

Materials: wood, plywood, metal or plastic sheet material of sufficient strength, rigidity and durability and capable of providing the formed finish ordered.

Release agents: neat oil plus surfactant or mould cream emulsion.

Workmanship

Construct in accordance with Section 6.9 of BS 8110 Part 1 and ensure that formwork:
a. is accurately placed in correct position, true to line and level, dimensionally correct and grout tight;
b. faces in contact with concrete are clean and either well wetted without an accumulation of surplus water at bottom or treated with a release agent.

Propping: provide adequate propping before and after striking formwork to prevent construction loads causing excessive deflection or damage to structure.

Retention: retain formwork in position for not less than the periods shown below unless otherwise ordered:
a. vertical faces: 7 days;
b. soffits of slabs: 14 days;
c. soffits of beams: 21 days.

Striking: strike formwork without damaging concrete.

Formed finishes

Basic finish: rub down prominent irregularities, make good voids, honeycombing and any large defects with cement-sand mortar (1:3).

Plain finish:
a. ensure that formwork, concrete and concrete placing produces surfaces:
   1. free from voids, honeycombing and other large defects;
   2. with tie holes in a regular pattern;
   3. even and to required profiles;
   4. free from discolouration due to contamin--ation or grout leakage.

b. do not allow deviation to exceed:
   1. abrupt irregularities: 5 mm;
   2. gradual irregularities expressed as maximum permissible deviation from 3000 mm straight edge: 10 mm.

c. make good blow holes and tie holes with cement-sand mortar (1:3) of matching colour.

d. rub down any projecting fins.

GENERALLY

Method of measurement

Generally:
Measure to concrete surfaces of the finished structure which require temporary support during casting.

Rates for the following include

Formwork generally:
For basic finish.

For all curved and raking cutting on linear and enumerated items.

For vertical or horizontal formwork as appropriate.

41

E20: FORMWORK FOR IN SITU CONCRETE

SIDES EDGES OR THE LIKE

Definition of terms

Foundation: includes bases.

Method of measurement

Passings of ground beams:
Make no deductions.

Item E20		1 Exceeding 1.00 m high	2 Not exceeding 250 mm high	3 250 to 500 mm high	4 500 mm to 1.00 m high
		Square Metre	Metre		
		£	£	£	£
018	Side of foundation	21.85	6.50	10.83	20.61
019	Side of ground beam or edge of bed	23.40	7.05	12.11	21.71

WALLS

Definition of terms

Wall: includes isolated columns and column casings whose length on plan exceeds four times their thickness.

Method of measurement

Voids:
Make no deduction for voids not exceeding 5.00 m².

Wall kickers:
Make no deductions for area of wall kickers.

Area of walls exceeding 3.00 m high:
Include the area below 3.00 m high.

	Square Metre	£
020	Vertical wall	26.75
021	Battered wall	30.59
	ADD where wall	
022	interrupted	1.76
023	exceeding 3.00 m high	4.45

E20: FORMWORK FOR IN SITU CONCRETE

RECESSES, NIBS AND REBATES

Item E20	*Metre - per 25 mm of girth*	£
	Extra over formwork for	
024	recess, rebate or the like	0.86
025	nib or the like	1.19

STAIRFLIGHTS

Method of measurement	**Rates for the following include**
Stairflight: Measure length between top and bottom nosings.	*Stairflight:* For formwork to soffit, risers and strings.
Measure width overall.	For waist of any thickness.
	For risers and strings of any type and size.

	Metre	£
026	Stairflight: 1000 mm wide	100.67
027	ADD or DEDUCT *for each 100 mm variation in width*	6.90

ADJUSTMENTS TO THE FOREGOING RATES

Square Metre

Formwork other than basic finish: price at the foregoing Rates
multiplied by the following factors:

028	plain finish	multiply by 1.125

E20: FORMWORK FOR IN SITU CONCRETE

ADJUSTMENTS TO THE FOREGOING RATES - *continued*

Item E20	*Square Metre*	
	Curved formwork of any shape: price at the foregoing Rates multiplied by the following factors:	
029	not exceeding 2.00 m radius	multiply by 1.75
030	2.00 to 3.00 m radius	multiply by 1.50
031	3.00 to 5.00 m radius	multiply by 1.25
032	5.00 to 15.00 m radius	multiply by 1.05
033	exceeding 15.00 m radius	no adjustment

034   Formwork left in: price at the foregoing Rates for basic finish multiplied by 1.50.

MORTICES AND HOLES

Definition of terms

Hole: those not exceeding 5.00 m².

Rates for the following include

Mortice:
For any shape.

For dishings, pockets, sinkings or the like.

		1	2	3
		Depth		
		not exceeding 250 mm	250 to 500 mm	500 mm to 1.00 m
	Each	£	£	£
	Mortice			
035	not exceeding 500 mm girth	5.77	7.13	12.56
036	500 mm to 1.00 m girth	9.70	11.32	22.17
037	ADD *for each additional 1.00 m of girth*	8.17	9.73	14.97
	Hole			
038	not exceeding 500 mm girth	8.71	9.58	15.38
039	500 mm to 1.00 m girth	14.05	16.13	31.78
040	ADD *for each additional 1.00 m of girth*	11.38	15.20	20.69

E30: REINFORCEMENT FOR IN SITU CONCRETE

SPECIFICATION

Materials

Supply: obtain all steel bar and fabric reinforcement:

a. from firms belonging to the UK Certification Authority for Reinforcing Steels (CARES) Scheme for firms of approved capability;

b. ensuring that it is traceable to its parent casts;

c. cut and bent by a CARES Licensee in accordance with the requirements of BS 4466.

Tying wire soft iron 1.6 mm diameter.

Cover spacers: 10 mm aggregate concrete, cement-sand (1:2) mortar or plastic of approved type.

Chairs: provide as necessary to support reinforcement in position.

Workmanship

British Standard: comply with BS 8000: Part 2, Section 2.2 in respect of:
a. materials handling and preparation (sub-section 2);
b. reinforcement (paragraph 3.2.1.6 and sub-section 4).

Inspection and rejection: inspect and reject bends and hooks showing signs of cracking or brittleness.

Accuracy: check information on bar bending schedules for compatibility with drawings, report and discrepancies to the PM and obtain his instructions.

Site operations: provide on-site facilities and:

a. confine cutting and bending by non CARES Licensees to minor adjustments and cutting of random lengths of secondary reinforcement made on site;

b. comply with BS 4466.

Cold bending: bend bars on approved machines.

Hot bending: hot bend only with approval.

Rebending: do not rebend, bend after fixing or straighten any bars without approval.

Hooks: do not provide hooks unless shown on the bar bending schedule.

Position of reinforcement: secure reinforcement and maintain in proper positions with the correct cover shown in the drawings by means of approved temporary or permanent chairs, spacers etc and ample use of tying wire. Bend back all ends of tying wire well clear of the formwork.

Placed concrete: do not insert any bars into placed concrete.

E30: REINFORCEMENT FOR IN SITU CONCRETE

GENERALLY

Definition of terms

Straight: without bends or hooks.

Notes

Spacers and chairs:
Measure only where not at the discretion of the Contractor and pay for at the Rates for links.

Method of measurement

Bar reinforcement:
Make no allowance in weight for surface treatments or rolling margin.

Fabric reinforcement:
Measure the area covered with no allowance for laps. Make no deductions for voids not exceeding 1.00 m².

Rates for the following include

Generally:
For obtaining test certificates as required or ordered.

For tying wire.

For spacers and chairs which are at the discretion of the Contractor.

For horizontal, sloping or vertical bars of any length.

For laps not exceeding 225 mm in fabric.

Fixing only reinforcement:
For everything *except* the cost of bars or fabric.

HOT ROLLED HIGH YIELD STEEL (GRADE 460) DEFORMED BARS TO BS 4449 OR COLD WORKED STEEL DEFORMED BARS TO BS 4461

		1	2	3	4
		Supplying and fixing		Fixing only	
Item E30	Kilogramme	Straight bars £	Curved or bent bars £	Straight bars £	Curved or bent bars £
	Bars other than links				
041	6 mm diameter	1.08	1.24	0.61	0.70
042	8 mm diameter	0.94	1.09	0.51	0.60
043	10 mm diameter	0.83	0.98	0.42	0.51
044	12 mm diameter	0.77	0.92	0.37	0.47
045	16 mm diameter	0.73	0.81	0.33	0.37
046	20 mm diameter	0.63	0.72	0.24	0.28
047	25 mm diameter	0.63	0.71	0.24	0.28
048	32 mm diameter	0.59	0.67	0.19	0.24
049	40 mm diameter	0.56	0.66	0.19	0.24

E30: REINFORCEMENT FOR IN SITU CONCRETE

HOT ROLLED MILD STEEL (GRADE 250) ROUND BARS TO BS 4449

Item E30	Kilogramme	1 Supplying and fixing £	2 Fixing only £
	Bars other than links: straight, curved or bent		
050	6 mm diameter	1.19	0.65
051	8 mm diameter	1.04	0.56
052	10 mm diameter	0.94	0.47
053	12 mm diameter	0.88	0.42
054	16 mm diameter	0.79	0.36
055	20 mm diameter	0.70	0.26
056	25 mm diameter	0.71	0.26
	In links or the like: bent		
057	6 mm diameter	1.68	0.79
058	8 mm diameter	1.45	0.65
059	10 mm diameter	1.32	0.55

STEEL FABRIC TO BS 4483: LONG MESH FABRIC: 100 X 400 mm MESH

		1	2	3	4
		Nominal mass per m²			
	Square Metre	2.61 kg £	3.41 kg £	4.34 kg £	6.72 kg £
060	Fabric	3.54	4.16	4.84	6.99
	Metre				
	Fabric: with main bars along the length				
061	strip not exceeding 300 mm wide	1.49	1.68	1.94	2.72
062	strip 300 to 450 mm wide	1.88	2.25	2.61	3.68
063	Bending	1.42	1.60	1.88	2.33
064	Raking cutting	2.67	3.09	3.50	4.21
065	Curved cutting	3.93	4.58	5.18	6.27

E40: DESIGNED JOINTS IN IN SITU CONCRETE

Specification

Formwork: wood, plywood, metal or plastic sheet that will:
a. result in all joints showing a straight line;
b. accommodate any projecting reinforcement without bending or displacement.

Construct formwork for designed joints:
a. ensuring faces are clean prior to assembly and placing of concrete;
b. straight, vertical or horizontal as ordered;
c. with rigid stop ends;
d. fixed with top edge true to line at joints in floor slabs.

Formwork gaps and voids: do not allow concrete to enter formwork gaps and voids.

Timing: do not place concrete simultaneously on both sides of joints.

Minimum retention period: retain formwork in position for not less than 7 days unless otherwise ordered.

Joint filler: waterproof, compressible, non-extruding pre-moulded filler with high recovery factor after compression at temperatures below 50°C.

Fix joint filler accurately in position ensuring correct space is left for sealant.

Sealants: approved joint sealant.

Sealing: ensure that joint surfaces are clean, dry, smooth, undamaged and, where required, primed.

Notes

Construction joints located at the discretion of the Contractor:
Do not measure.

Rates for the following include

Joints generally:
For all necessary formwork.

For continuity of reinforcement as required.

For rounded arrises where required.

Ordinary joint:
For lightly roughening entire face to expose coarse aggregate, thoroughly wire brushing to remove all loose material, cleaning and wetting face before fresh concrete is placed against it.

Bitumen coated joint:
For coating face with bitumen.

Watertight joint:
For lightly roughening face to expose coarse aggregate by mist-spraying or lightly chipping by approved mechanical means, wire brushing and wetting to achieve complete watertightness.

Filled joint:
For pre-moulded joint filler 25 mm thick and all cutting.

E40: DESIGNED JOINTS IN IN SITU CONCRETE

DESIGNED JOINTS

Item E40	*Metre*	1 Ordinary £	2 Bitumen coated £	3 Watertight £	4 Filled £
	Formed joint: width or depth				
066	not exceeding 150 mm	6.53	7.79	8.13	9.99
067	150 to 300 mm	10.50	11.45	12.10	14.43
068	300 to 450 mm	17.45	19.06	20.02	24.17
069	ADD where formwork notched and fitted around reinforcement	7.32	7.32	7.32	10.98

	Metre	£
	Joint at boundary of the work against existing abutment: existing face cleaned, roughened and coated with cement slurry: width or depth	
070	not exceeding 150 mm	2.97
071	150 to 300 mm	4.42
072	300 to 450 mm	5.81
073	Forming surface groove: any shape: any size	0.65
	Sealant: 25 x 25 mm	
074	bitumen compound	3.70
075	polysulphide compound	19.42

E41: WORKED FINISHES AND CUTTING TO IN SITU CONCRETE

Specification

Tamped finish:
a. general requirement: do not wet surface of concrete to assist surface working;
b. method: tamp surface with edge of a board or beam to give an even texture of parallel ribs.

Wood float finish: use a wood float to give an even texture within specified deviations.

Steel float finish: use a steel float to produce a smooth even surface free from float marks within specified deviations.

Power float finish: allow concrete to stiffen sufficiently to be properly worked. Produce smooth even surface free from pitting, grooving and indentation within specified deviations.

Power grinding:
a. power grind within the period 24 to 36 hours after placing;
b. employ a trained and skilled operator;
c. hand finish areas inaccessible to power grinder;
d. produce a smooth even finish within specified deviations.

Permissible deviation of floated and ground finishes to be:
a. abrupt irregularities: nil;
b. gradual irregularities from 3000 mm straight edge: 3 mm.

Scored finish:
a. general requirement: do not wet surface of concrete to assist surface working;
b. metal comb finish: scratch with a metal comb to give a slightly roughened even surface;
c. brush finish: scratch surface with a stiff brush to give a slightly roughened even surface.

Rates for the following include

Worked finishes:
For producing by hand or mechanical means.

Making good:
For making good to match adjacent surface.

Cutting:
For cutting set or existing concrete.

Mortice:
For any shape.

For dishings, pockets, sinkings or the like.

Mortars:
For any mix.

E41: WORKED FINISHES AND CUTTING IN IN SITU CONCRETE

WORKED FINISHES

Item E41	Square Metre	£
076	Tamped ribbed finish	0.73
077	Rolled pattern finish	1.60
078	Power floated finish to smooth, even surface	1.82
079	Even textured finish: scraping with straight edge and medium coarse fibre broom	2.91
	ADD to the foregoing Rates where	
080	sloping	0.73
081	to falls	0.36
082	to crossfalls	0.58
083	Grinding	2.92
084	Scoring	2.81
	Hacking	
085	new concrete	3.63
086	old concrete: plain or painted	5.45
087	ADD to the foregoing Rates where to soffits	0.87

	Metre	1 Straight £	2 Curved £	3 ADD for making good £	4 ADD where in reinforced concrete £
088	Cutting chase: not exceeding 100 mm girth	4.72	6.18	2.68	3.63
089	ADD for each additional 50 mm of girth	2.36	3.09	1.15	1.82
090	Cutting rebate: not exceeding 100 mm girth	4.00	5.45	2.39	3.63
091	ADD for each additional 50 mm of girth	2.00	2.73	0.96	1.82
092	Cutting chamfer: not exceeding 100 mm girth	3.27	4.72	2.61	3.63
093	ADD for each additional 50 mm of girth	1.64	2.36	0.96	1.82

WORKED FINISHES - *continued*

		1	2	3	4	5	6	7
		Not exceeding 100 mm deep	100 to 200 mm deep	200 to 300 mm deep	ADD for making good	ADD where in reinforced concrete	ADD for grouting with mortar	ADD for caulking with lead
Item E41	*Each*	£	£	£	£	£	£	£
	Cutting mortice							
094	not exceeding 2500 mm²	4.15	11.78	17.96	0.66	1.74	1.78	4.24
095	2500 to 5000 mm²	4.55	12.91	19.45	1.06	2.18	2.23	5.15
096	5000 to 7500 mm²	4.95	14.40	21.30	1.41	2.73	3.04	6.26
097	7500 to 10000 mm²	5.39	15.93	23.19	1.81	3.63	3.79	7.43
	Cutting hole							
098	not exceeding 2500 mm²	7.27	10.90	18.17	0.81	1.96	1.54	3.82
099	ADD *for each additional* 2500 mm²	1.09	1.82	2.54	0.58	1.64	1.23	2.80

F10: BRICK AND BLOCK WALLING

GENERALLY

Specification

Constituent materials for mortar:
a. cement: to BS 12, BS 146 or BS 4027 and manufactured by a BSI Registered Firm;
b. masonry cement: to BS 5224;
c. sand: to BS 1200 Table 1;
d. hydrated lime powder and lime putty: to BS 890;
e. ready mixed lime/sand mix: to BS 4721 Section 2.

f. plasticizer: to BS 4887 Part 1 and manufactured by a BSI Kitemark Licensee;
g. pigments for coloured mortar: to BS 1014;
h. water: clean and uncontaminated. Obtain approval for other than mains supply.

Mix Proportions: mix constituent materials in proportion by volume as the following Table:

Mortar Types

Type No.	BS Mortar Designation	A Cement-sand	B Cement: ready mixed lime/sand (proportions of lime and sand as given in brackets)		C Cement-sand with plasticizer	D Masonry cement-sand
1	(i)	1:3	1:3	(1:12)	-	-
2	(II)	-	1:4½	(1:9)	1:3-4	-
3	(iii)	-	1:6	(1:6)	1:5-6	1:4-5
4	(iv)	-	1:9	(1:4½)	1:7-8	1:5½-6½
5	(v)	-	1:12	(1:4)	1:8	1:6½-7

Coloured Portland cement mortars: added pigments must not exceed 10% of the weight of the cement used, except for carbon black which must not exceed 3% by weight of cement.

Ready mixed mortar: to BS 4721 Part 3, mortar designation as specified for the Type No scheduled in Table. Do not use for structural masonry without approval.

Site mixed mortar: mix in the proportions by volume as specified for the Type No scheduled in Table.

Setting time: use mortars containing cement within two hours of mixing unless retardants have been added. Discard unused mortar.

Cold weather: do not mix mortar unless precautions are taken to ensure that it has a minimum temperature of 4°C when laid.

Finishing of mortar joints not visible: strike off with trowel as work proceeds joints not visible in finished work.

Definition of Terms

Composite work: walls, etc built of more than one type of brick or block in the thickness of the wall.

Isolated pier: isolated walls whose length on plan is not exceeding four times their thickness, except where caused by openings.

Projection: attached piers (whose length on plan is not exceeding four times the thickness of projection), plinths, oversailing courses or the like.

Notes

Work generally:
Vertical unless otherwise stated.

Method of measurement

Generally:
Measure brickwork and blockwork on the centre line of the material unless otherwise stated. Make no deductions for:

a. voids not exceeding 0.10 m²;

b. flues, lined flues and flue blocks where voids and work displaced are together not exceeding 0.25 m².

Measure deductions for string courses, lintels, sills, plates and the like as regards height to the extent only of full brick or block courses displaced and as regards depth to the extent only of full half-brick beds displaced.

Building against other work and bonding to other work:
Measure where the other work is existing or consists of a differing material.

Extra over for facework:
Measure on the exposed face.

Arch:
Measure the mean girth or length on face.

Rates for the following include

Generally:
For English or Flemish bond, or stretcher bond in the case of half-brick walls or blockwork, unless otherwise stated.

For rough cutting new work except rounded or chamfered angles.

For fair straight, raking or splay cutting new work.

For rough horizontal chases in new work.

For raking out joints of brickwork to a depth of 13 mm as the work proceeds as key for plaster or render coatings, or for the use of grooved bricks at the Contractor's option.

For labour in eaves filling.

For centering.

Cement mortar:
For any of the mortars in Type 1 of the Mortar Type Table.

Cement-lime mortar:
For any of the mortars in Types 2, 3, 4 or 5 of the Mortar Type Table.

Any mortar:
For any mortar in the Mortar Type Table including mortar incorporating sulphate-resisting cement.

Curved work:
For extra material.

Building against other work:
For bedding in mortar.

Bonding to other work:
For extra material for bonding.

Bonding end of new wall to existing:
For any approved method of bonding to suit the particular circumstances.

For extra material for bonding and for cutting sockets.

F10: BRICK AND BLOCK WALLING

GENERALLY - *continued*

Facework:
For selecting bricks and blocks with undamaged arrises and flat surfaces.

For finishing joints with flush, concave, weathered or recessed joint as the work proceeds, unless otherwise stated.

Fair angle:
For vertical, raking or horizontal angles.

Arch:
For all cutting to arch and wall.

For ends.

Sill, threshold or coping:
For angles and ends.

Fair cutting brickwork:
For cutting not exceeding half-brick deep.

Making good existing facework:
For pointing to match existing.

COMMON BRICKWORK: LAYING ONLY: GENERALLY

Notes

Number of bricks:
Calculate from the following Table:

Number of common bricks per square metre including waste.		
Thickness of wall	65 mm and 67 mm	73 mm
Half-brick stretcher bond	65	59
Half-brick honeycomb bond	39	35
One-brick	128	116
One-brick honeycomb bond	78	70
One-and-a-half brick	191	173
ADD *for each additional half-brick* *thickness*	63	57
One-brick curved not exceeding 2 m radius	140	127
One-brick curved exceeding 2 m radius	134	122

For linear items calculate the actual number of bricks required and add 10 per cent for waste.

Rates for the following include

Generally:
For everything *except* the cost of bricks.

For laying new or old bricks of any of the following types:

1. Clay common bricks to BS 3921;

2. Calcium silicate common bricks to BS 187;

3. Approved common bricks as ordered, nominal size 219 x 105 x 67 or 73 mm.

F10: BRICK AND BLOCK WALLING

COMMON BRICKWORK: LAYING ONLY: IN CEMENT - LIME MORTAR

		1	2	3	4
		Brick thickness			
		Half	One	One-and-a-half	ADD *for each additional half-brick*
Item F10	*Square Metre*	£	£	£	£
001	Wall	23.17	42.90	53.20	16.00
002	Wall: in honeycomb bond: one third area void	21.79	35.13	-	-
	ADD where				
003	in filling existing opening	7.94	14.44	21.78	5.44
004	building overhand	7.94	14.44	21.78	5.44
005	building against other work	3.95	3.95	3.95	-
	bonding to other work				
006	forming pockets	2.97	2.97	2.97	-
007	cutting pockets: in existing brickwork or blockwork	6.74	6.74	6.74	-
008	cutting pockets: in existing stonework	19.25	19.25	19.25	-
	curved on plan				
009	not exceeding 2 m radius	14.13	22.56	26.81	12.46
010	exceeding 2 m radius	10.04	17.03	24.25	7.22
011	curved bricks: not exceeding 2 m radius	17.60	28.13	-	-
012	Isolated pier	-	53.15	74.48	21.42
013	Isolated casing	27.81	45.94	64.24	18.66
014	Chimney stack	-	53.15	74.48	21.42

	Square Metre - per half-brick thickness	£
	ADD where	
015	in cement mortar	1.54
016	sulphate-resisting cement used instead of ordinary cement	0.13

COMMON BRICKWORK: LAYING ONLY: IN CEMENT - LIME MORTAR - *continued*

	1	2	3	4
	Brick projection			
	Half	One	One-and-a-half	ADD *for each additional half-brick*
Item F10 *Metre - per half-brick width*	£	£	£	£
Projection				
017 vertical	3.34	5.73	7.70	2.35
018 horizontal	3.34	5.73	7.70	2.35
ADD where bonding to other work				
019 forming pockets	2.97	5.07	6.76	1.67
020 cutting pockets: in existing brickwork	3.79	5.89	7.58	1.85

	£
ADD where	
021 in cement mortar	0.17
022 sulphate-resisting cement used instead of ordinary cement	0.01

Square Metre

	£
Extra over for facework	
023 exceeding half-brick wide	5.03
024 exceeding half-brick wide: building overhand	7.65
025 exceeding half-brick wide: curved on plan: not exceeding 2 m radius	5.54
026 exceeding half-brick wide: curved on plan: exceeding 2 m radius	5.29

Metre

027 not exceeding half-brick wide	1.14
028 Fair chamfered or rounded external angle: any girth	4.12

Each

029 end or mitre	0.92

F10: BRICK AND BLOCK WALLING

COMMON BRICKWORK: LAYING ONLY: IN CEMENT - LIME MORTAR - *continued*

Item F10	*Metre*	1 One ring £	2 Two ring £
	Rough brick on edge arch: any type: through		
030	half-brick wall	4.88	8.61
031	one-brick wall	9.63	14.41
032	one-and-a-half brick wall	14.50	22.40
033	two-brick wall	19.37	29.02

COMMON BRICKWORK: LAYING ONLY: IN ANY MORTAR

Rates for the following include

Generally:
For facework to exposed faces.

	Metre	£
034	Flat arch: brick on end: one-brick high on face: half-brick wide soffit	22.52
035	ADD for cambered soffit	1.97
	Segmental or semi-circular arch: two half-brick rings: one-brick high on face	
036	half-brick wide soffit	30.07
037	one-brick wide soffit	45.55

		1 Half £	2 One £	3 One-and-a-half £
		Brick width		
	Sill, threshold or coping: raking or horizontal: square or rounded external angles: set level or weathering			
038	brick on edge	-	13.23	17.48
	ADD where curved on plan			
039	not exceeding 2 m radius	-	1.28	2.61
040	exceeding 2 m radius	-	0.69	1.31
041	brick on end	11.95	-	-
	ADD where curved on plan			
042	not exceeding 2 m radius	1.03	-	-
043	exceeding 2 m radius	0.51	-	-

F10: BRICK AND BLOCK WALLING

COMMON BRICKWORK: SUNDRIES

Rates for the following include

Generally:
For everything *including* bricks.

For work in any mortar.

Making good existing facework:
For work to common brickwork or facing brickwork.

Item F10	*Square Metre*	1 New brickwork £	2 Existing brickwork £
044	Rough cutting	Incl	19.68
	Metre		
	Rough cutting rounded or chamfered angle		
045	not exceeding 75 mm wide/girth	2.92	5.75
046	75 to 150 mm wide/girth	3.89	7.05
	Fair cutting		
047	to curve	5.72	11.44
048	straight	Incl	4.47
049	raking or splayed	Incl	8.59
050	birdsmouth angle	5.72	-
051	squint angle	6.30	-

	Metre	1 Thickness Half-brick £	2 One-brick £	3 One-and-a-half brick £	4 Not exceeding 300 mm hollow £	5 ADD where making good existing facework - per side £
052	Preparing top of existing wall for raising	1.37	2.76	4.15	3.01	-
053	Bonding end of new wall to existing	6.67	12.99	19.08	14.00	2.27
054	Making good with new brickwork: pockets in existing wall where old wall removed	10.86	17.62	21.58	20.88	-
055	ADD for facework to new brickwork: to match existing	2.27	3.69	5.11	4.38	-
056	Making good with new brickwork: plain jamb of opening cut in existing wall: bonding new to existing	11.69	22.72	33.77	-	5.09
057	ADD for rebated jamb	-	11.32	13.83	-	-
058	Making good with new brickwork: half-brick thick: plain jamb of opening cut in existing hollow wall: closing cavity: not exceeding 75 mm wide: bonding new to existing	-	-	-	26.41	5.09
059	ADD for rebated jamb	-	-	-	9.71	-

COMMON BRICKWORK: SUNDRIES - *continued*

Item F10	*Metre*	£
	Closing cavity: not exceeding 75 mm wide: with brickwork	
060	half-brick thick: vertical	6.49
061	one-brick thick: vertical	7.12
062	one course deep: horizontal	7.60

FACING BRICKWORK AND COMPOSITE WORK: LAYING ONLY: GENERALLY

Rates for the following include

Generally:
For everything *except* the cost of bricks.

For laying new or old bricks of any of the following types:

1. Clay facing bricks to BS 3921;
2. Calcium silicate facing bricks to BS 187;
3. Approved facing bricks as ordered, nominal size 219 x 105 x 67 or 73 mm.

For additional labour where facings of more than one type or colour are used in association.

For the even distribution of multi-coloured facings throughout the finished work.

Column A:
For jointing and pointing in cement-lime mortar.

Column B:
For jointing and pointing in white or coloured cement-lime mortar or with coal ash substituted for sand as ordered.

Column C:
For jointing in cement-lime mortar, raking out to a depth of 20 mm as the work proceeds and pointing with a weathered or recessed joint as the scaffolding is struck in white or coloured cement or cement-lime mortar or with coal ash substituted for sand as ordered.

FACING BRICKWORK: LAYING ONLY

Notes

Number of bricks:
Calculate from the following Table:

Number of facing bricks per square metre including waste.		
Thickness of wall	65 mm and 67 mm	73 mm
Half-brick stretcher bond	62	56
Half-brick in English bond with snapped headers	62	56
One-brick	122	110

For linear items calculate the actual number of bricks required and add 5 per cent for waste.

Rates for the following include

Arch, sill, threshold or coping:
For facework to exposed faces.

		1	2	3
		A	B	C
Item F10	*Square Metre*	£	£	£
	Wall: half-brick thick			
	stretcher bond			
063	facework one side	33.33	36.34	38.80
064	facework both sides	36.85	39.50	41.36
	English bond			
065	snapped headers: facework one side	39.20	42.70	45.07
066	snapped headers: building against other work: facework one side . . .	39.98	43.79	46.24
	ADD where			
067	in cement mortar	1.54	1.54	1.54
068	in filling existing opening	8.91	8.91	8.91
	Wall: one brick thick			
069	garden wall bond: facework both sides	60.40	62.45	70.90
070	English bond: facework both sides	60.63	62.78	71.20
071	Flemish bond: facework both sides	60.86	63.13	71.43
	ADD where			
072	in cement mortar	3.18	3.18	3.18
073	in filling existing opening	14.44	14.44	14.44
	Metre			
	Extra for fair return			
074	not exceeding half-brick wide	1.56	1.56	1.81
075	half-brick to one-brick wide	2.33	2.33	2.59

FACING BRICKWORK: LAYING ONLY - *continued*

Item F10		1	2	3
		A	B	C
	Metre	£	£	£
076	Fair chamfered or rounded external angle: any girth	4.12	4.12	4.12
	Each			
077	end or mitre	0.92	0.92	0.92
	Metre - per half-brick width			
	Projection: facework to face and margins - *per half-brick projection from face of wall*			
078	vertical	4.78	5.28	5.63
079	horizontal	4.78	5.28	5.63
	ADD where bonding to other work			
080	forming pockets	4.36	4.36	4.36
081	cutting pockets: in existing brickwork	4.80	4.80	4.80
	Metre			
082	Flat arch: brick on end: one-brick high on face: half-brick wide soffit	22.97	23.11	26.77
083	ADD for cambered soffit	1.97	1.97	1.97
	Segmental or semi-circular arch: two half-brick rings: one-brick high on face			
084	half-brick wide soffit	19.90	19.96	31.12
085	one-brick wide soffit	30.66	30.88	48.54
	Brick on edge sill, threshold or coping: raking or horizontal: square or rounded external angles: set level or weathering			
086	one-brick wide	14.95	15.15	18.81
	ADD where curved on plan			
087	not exceeding 2 m radius	1.54	1.54	1.54
088	exceeding 2 m radius	0.82	0.82	0.82
089	one-and-a-half brick wide	21.30	21.61	25.28
	ADD where curved on plan			
090	not exceeding 2 m radius	2.95	2.95	2.95
091	exceeding 2 m radius	1.49	1.49	1.49
	Brick on end sill, threshold or coping: raking or horizontal: square or rounded external angles: set level or weathering			
092	half-brick wide	13.85	13.93	17.59
	ADD where curved on plan			
093	not exceeding 2 m radius	1.42	1.42	1.42
094	exceeding 2 m radius	0.70	0.70	0.70

F10: BRICK AND BLOCK WALLING

COMPOSITE WORK: LAYING ONLY: EXTRA OVER COMMON BRICKWORK IN CEMENT LIME MORTAR FOR FACING BRICKWORK

Notes

Number of bricks:
Calculate from the following Table:

Number of facing bricks per square metre including waste.		
Bond	Facing bricks and DEDUCT Common bricks	
	65 mm and 67 mm	73 mm
English bond	92	82
English bond with snapped headers	62	56
Flemish bond	81	73
Flemish bond with snapped headers	62	56
ADD where curved on plan not exceeding 2 m radius	8	8
ADD where curved on plan exceeding 2 m radius	4	4

For linear items calculate the actual number of facing bricks required and add 5 per cent for waste. DEDUCT the same number of common bricks.

Method of measurement

Generally:
Measure on the exposed face.

Rates for the following include

Column B
For the extra cost of providing Column B type mortar through the full thickness of the faced wall.

Band:
For ends and angles.

Item F10	Square Metre	1 A £	2 B £	3 C £
	Facework: exceeding half-brick wide			
095	English bond	12.25	15.54	18.49
096	Flemish bond	12.77	15.89	19.03
097	English or Flemish bond with snapped headers	13.64	16.75	19.63
	ADD where			
098	building overhand	3.58	3.72	4.42
099	curved on plan: exceeding 2 m radius	1.25	1.28	1.65
100	curved bricks: not exceeding 2 m radius	4.99	5.12	6.60
	Metre			
101	Facework: not exceeding half-brick wide	2.05	2.88	3.18
	Plain band: horizontal: not exceeding 300 mm wide on face: facework to face and margins - *per 75 mm of height*			
102	sunk not exceeding half-brick width from face of wall	2.77	3.21	3.65
103	projecting not exceeding half-brick width from face of wall	4.84	5.22	5.71

F10: BRICK AND BLOCK WALLING

COMPOSITE WORK: LAYING ONLY: EXTRA OVER COMMON BRICKWORK IN CEMENT LIME
MORTAR FOR FACING BRICKWORK - *continued*

Item F10	Metre	1 A £	2 B £	3 C £
	Brick on end band: horizontal: one-brick high on face: facework to face - *per 75 mm of height*			
104	flush	13.69	14.27	14.94
105	sunk not exceeding half-brick width from face of wall: facework to margins	16.43	17.08	18.12

FACING BRICKWORK AND COMPOSITE WORK: SUNDRIES

Rates for the following include

Generally:
For everything *including* bricks.

For work in any mortar.

	Metre	£
	Fair cutting	
106	to curve	9.15
107	birdsmouth angle	9.61
108	squint angle	10.16

F20: NATURAL STONE RUBBLE WALLING

GENERALLY

Specification

Stone for random rubble walling:
irregular shaped stones supplied with at least one bonder for each square metre of finished wall.

Preparation of stone:
roughly shape stones to suit walling.

Mortar materials and mix proportions:
as specified in Section F10.

Mortar types:
use the following mortar types detailed in the Mortar Type Table in Section F10 unless otherwise ordered:

Granite, quartzite or similar	Type 1
Dense sandstone and cast stone	Type 3
Limestone and porous sandstone	Type 4 or 5

Notes

Work generally:
Vertical unless otherwise stated.

Method of measurement

Generally:
Measure mean dimensions. Make no deductions for:

a. voids not exceeding 0.10 m²;

b. flues, lined flues and flue blocks where voids and work displaced are together not exceeding 0.25 m².

Bonding to other work:
Measure where the other work is existing or consists of a differing material.

Rates for the following include

Generally:
For everything except the cost of stone.

For any kind of stone of any profile.

For rough and fair square cutting.

For fair returns, ends, angles or the like on superficial items.

For ends, angles or the like on linear items.

For labour in eaves filling.

Mortar:
For the use of coloured mortar, or substituting for sand, crushed stone or stone dust of the same type as the stone used.

Laying only stone previously set aside for re-use:
For cleaning off beds and joints and stacking prior to use.

Pointing:
For finishing joints by striking off flush as the work proceeds.

Bonding to other work:
For extra material for bonding.

Bonding end of new wall to existing:
For extra material for bonding and for cutting pockets.

F20: NATURAL STONE RUBBLE WALLING

STONEWORK: LAYING ONLY

Item F20	*Square Metre*	1 Laying only new stonework £	2 Laying only stonework previously set aside for re-use £
109	Wall: random uncoursed: not exceeding 300 mm thick	44.95	48.93
110	ADD *for each additional 50 mm of thickness*	3.39	3.63
	ADD where		
	bonding to other work		
111	forming pockets	29.92	29.92
112	cutting pockets: in existing stonework	30.93	30.93
113	bringing to courses at average 750 mm vertical intervals - *per side*	4.04	4.04
114	pointing - *per side*	4.11	4.11
	Metre		
115	Coping: not exceeding 300 x 300 mm: horizontal: pointing exposed faces: levelling rubble walling	36.74	39.95
	ADD for		
116	*each additional 50 mm of width*	5.16	5.61
117	*each additional 50 mm of height*	4.48	4.86
118	Bonding end of new wall to existing: not exceeding 300 mm thick	7.57	7.57
119	ADD *for each additional 50 mm of thickness*	1.34	1.34
120	Rough raking or circular cutting: not exceeding 300 mm thick	13.73	13.73
121	ADD *for each additional 50 mm of thickness*	2.29	2.29
122	Fair raking or circular cutting: not exceeding 300 mm thick	32.95	32.95
123	ADD *for each additional 50 mm of thickness*	5.49	5.49

DAMP PROOF COURSES

Specification

Bitumen damp proof course: to BS 6398 Type E.

Polyethylene damp proof course: to BS 6515.

Pitch polymer damp proof course: from an approved manufacturer.

Lead damp proof course: to BS 743 Code 4, bitumen coated both sides.

Slate damp proof course: to BS 743.

Method of measurement

Generally:
Measure the area covered with no allowance for laps. Make no deduction for voids not exceeding 0.50 m².

Rates for the following include

Generally:
For bedding in cement mortar.

For pointing exposed edges.

Sheet damp proof course:
For laying in single layer.

For laying with 150 mm laps in length and full lap at angles.

For dressing projecting edges up or down as ordered.

Slate damp proof course:
For laying in two courses breaking joint.

Curved work:
For all necessary cutting.

DAMP PROOF COURSES - *continued*

Sheet damp proof courses

Item **F30**	*Square Metre*	1 Horizontal or stepped Bitumen £	2 Poly-ethylene £	3 Pitch polymer £	4 Lead £	5 ADD where vertical £
	On surface					
124	not exceeding 225 mm wide	17.98	9.84	16.49	57.33	3.86
125	exceeding 225 mm wide	17.56	9.51	16.15	55.96	3.69

Slate damp proof courses

	Square Metre	1 Horizontal or stepped £	2 Add where vertical £
	On surface		
127	not exceeding 225 mm wide	62.99	6.82
128	exceeding 225 mm wide	62.19	6.49

Sheet or slate damp proof course

129	Where curved on plan: price at the foregoing Rates multiplied by 1.20.	

F30: ACCESSORIES AND SUNDRY ITEMS FOR BRICK, BLOCK AND STONE WALLING

JOINT REINFORCEMENT

Specification

Mesh Reinforcement: galvanised to BS 729 and coated with bitumen.

Method of measurement

Generally:
Measure the length covered with no allowance for laps.

Rates for the following include

Generally:
For 225 mm laps.

For folding at corners.

Item F30	Metre	£
	In wall	
130	100 mm wide	1.93
131	112.5 mm wide	2.53
132	225 mm wide	3.03

WEATHER AND ANGLE FILLETS

Rates for the following include

Generally:
For angles and ends.

	Metre	1 Hacking off £	2 Cement mortar £
	Weather or angle fillet: straight or curved: trowelling smooth: width on face		
133	not exceeding 50 mm	0.60	1.70
134	50 to 75 mm	0.73	2.17
135	75 to 100 mm	0.91	2.61
136	100 to 150 mm	1.04	3.13
137	150 to 200 mm	1.21	3.92
138	200 to 250 mm	1.45	4.67

L: Windows, Doors and Stairs

L30: STAIRS, WALKWAYS AND BALUSTRADES

GENERALLY

Specification

Steel: to BS EN 10025.

Machine screws and nuts: to BS 4183.

Rivets: to BS 4620.

Holing: form holes to BS 5950: Part 2.

Bimetallic corrosion: prevent metallic contact of dissimilar metals, likely to cause bimetallic corrosion, by insulation at contact points.

Welding: comply with BS 5135 and execute in the fabrication workshop unless otherwise ordered.

Balustrades: to BS 6180.

Notes

Mortices for lugs in concrete:
Pay for at the Rates in Section E20 or E41.

Mortices for lugs in brickwork or blockwork:
Pay for at the Rates in Section F30.

Rates for the following include

Generally:
For any size or section shape unless otherwise stated.

For lugs for building in, bolts or screws for fixing as appropriate.

Welding:
For leaving as laid unless otherwise stated.

STEEL CAT LADDERS, GRILLES OR THE LIKE

Specification

Steel access ladders: to BS 4211: Class A galvanised to BS 729 after fabrication.

Rates for the following include

Cat ladder, grille or the like:
For flat metal strings or frames.

For round bars or rungs.

For all curved work to ends of cat ladders.

For all supports, lugs and fixings.

For drilling holes.

Item L30	Kilogramme	1 Supplying and fixing £	2 Fixing only £
001	Cat ladder, grille or the like: steel: framed: riveting or welding and finishing smooth	7.73	0.54

L30: STAIRS, WALKWAYS AND BALUSTRADES

STEEL ISOLATED BALUSTRADES AND HANDRAILS

Rates for the following include

Generally:
For balustrades or railings consisting of handrail or core rail, balusters between handrail or core rail and bottom rail and standards with fanged, forged or flattened ends for building in or bolting.

For balustrades or railings with balusters with fanged, forged or flattened ends for building in or bolting where bottom rail is omitted.

For countersunk set screwing, riveting or welding members and finishing smooth.

For drilling holes.

For framed work.

For ends, angles and intersections of balustrades or railings.

Item L30	Kilogramme	1 Supplying and fixing £	2 Fixing only £
002	Handrail, core rail or bottom rail	4.21	1.25
003	Intermediate rail	4.32	1.25
004	ADD where curved in plane of bar	0.55	-
005	Baluster or standard	5.08	1.25
	Each		
	Extra for		
006	ramp	10.67	-
007	wreath	13.14	-
008	scroll	20.53	-
009	quadrant bend in plane of bar	16.42	-

STEEL ISOLATED TUBULAR BALUSTRADES AND HANDRAILS

Specification

Steel tubes: to BS 1387.

Galvanising: hot dip to BS 729.

Screwed fittings: malleable cast iron to BS 143 and 1256.

Clamp type fittings:
from an approved manufacturer.

Method of measurement

Handrail, baluster or the like:
Measure over all fittings.

STEEL ISOLATED TUBULAR BALUSTRADES AND HANDRAILS - *continued*

Item L30		1	2	3	4	5	6
		Light weight				Medium weight	
		Black		Galvanised		Galvanised	
		Nominal size					
		40 mm	50 mm	40 mm	50 mm	40 mm	50 mm
	Metre	£	£	£	£	£	£
010	Handrail, baluster or the like	10.84	13.25	13.53	17.27	14.64	18.76
	Each						
	Extra for						
011	made bend	9.85	13.14	-	-	-	-
012	made bend: re-galvanising	-	-	11.98	15.38	13.62	17.03
	Extra for welded joint finished smooth						
013	mitred angle	2.97	3.69	-	-	-	-
014	intersection	2.38	2.97	-	-	-	-
	Extra for screwed fitting						
015	straight connector	6.66	8.70	7.15	9.57	7.15	9.57
016	elbow	7.51	9.37	8.24	10.50	8.24	10.50
017	tee junction	12.21	16.74	13.16	18.35	13.16	18.35
018	double tee junction	19.55	26.73	21.41	29.64	21.41	29.64
019	flange floor plate: screwing to timber	9.16	10.83	10.48	12.56	10.48	12.56
020	flange floor plate: bolting	9.43	11.38	10.76	13.10	10.76	13.10
	Extra for clamp type fitting						
021	straight coupling	7.13	8.92	5.05	6.67	5.05	6.67
022	elbow	8.07	14.53	5.98	12.34	5.98	12.34
023	side outlet elbow or two socket tee	10.95	13.46	8.88	11.24	8.88	11.24
024	three socket tee	10.01	16.57	7.93	14.37	7.93	14.37
025	two socket cross	9.52	14.71	7.43	12.52	7.43	12.52
026	side outlet tee	10.75	18.59	8.66	16.40	8.66	16.40
027	four socket cross	15.32	20.50	13.26	18.31	13.26	18.31
028	light flange: screwing to timber	8.25	10.30	6.16	8.08	6.16	8.08
029	railing standard flange: bolting	10.42	17.04	8.32	14.84	8.32	14.84
	Extra for fitting with welded joints finished smooth						
030	6 mm flange plate: drilling and screwing to timber	6.02	6.38	-	-	-	-
031	6 mm flange plate: drilling and bolting	6.48	6.83	-	-	-	-

M60: PAINTING AND CLEAR FINISHING

SPECIFICATION

Materials generally

Obtain materials from approved suppliers and inform PM of selected supplier.

Container sizes: obtain coating materials other than spray, bituminous and textured masonry paints in containers with a maximum capacity of 5 litres.

Finishing systems: obtain all coats of each system from the same supplier.

Primers and sealers

Select primers and sealers appropriate to the surface to be decorated in accordance with the following Tables.

Table of primers

Surface	Primer	Notes	Reference
Softwood generally	Low lead primer for wood		BS 5358 Type A
	Water thinned primer for wood		BS 5082
Hardwood, resinous softwood and copper naphthenate treated softwood.	Aluminium primer for wood		BS 4756
Iron and steel generally	Red lead primer	(1)	BS 2523 Type B
	Zinc phosphate primer (low lead)	(2), (9)	An approved proprietary type
	Red oxide of iron/zinc chrome primer	(3)	An approved proprietary type
	Metallic zinc rich primer	(4)	BS 4652
Zinc and galvanised surfaces generally	One pack primer for galvanised steel (low lead)	(5), (9)	An approved proprietary type
	Etching primer plus zinc chrome primer	(6)	An approved proprietary type
	Etching primer plus zinc phosphate primer	(7)	An approved proprietary type
Aluminium and sprayed aluminium coatings	Zinc chrome primer		An approved proprietary type
Smooth and polished aluminium	Etching primer plus zinc chrome primer		An approved proprietary type
Smooth and polished copper Smooth lead	Etching primer	(8)	An approved proprietary type

SPECIFICATION - *continued*

Notes to Table of primers;

(1) For site application but slow drying. Not to be used in areas of domestic use and/or where public has access. Do not use when a lower lead primer is equally suitable.

(2) General purpose primer for new and maintenance priming of blast or manually cleaned steel. Has an equivalent performance to lead based primers. Should be used on steel in preference to lead primers in locations where lead paint may be a health hazard. On galvanised surfaces, etch prime.

(3) For interior or sheltered exterior use. Dries overnight. May be used in domestic buildings.

(4) Epoxy resin-based two pack product. For factory priming blast-cleaned structural steelwork or for touching-in damaged areas of galvanised or zinc-sprayed coatings. Frequent stirring is necessary and applications should be by brush or spray as appropriate.

(5) Preferred primer for galvanised steel where oil-based finishing paints are specified. Replaces calcium plumbate primer.

(6) On galvanised surfaces, etch prime first.

(7) Equivalent to (6).

(8) For non-ferrous metal pre-treatment/priming.

(9) Lead content to be within the limits given in BS 4310.

Table of sealers

Surface	Finish	Sealer	Reference
Dry plaster Dry concrete Dry asbestos cement Dry fibre-cement	Oil paint	Alkali-resisting primer-sealer	An approved proprietary type
Concrete or plaster not fully dried out Porous wall surfaces generally	Emulsion paint	Emulsion paint (thinned)	BS 7719
Asbestos-free fibre reinforced boards	Oil paint	Alkali-resisting primer-sealer	An approved proprietary type
Bituminous paint Old creosote	Oil paint	Aluminium primer	An approved proprietary type
Cementitious surfaces	Textured masonry paint (oil base)	Alkali-resisting primer-sealer	An approved proprietary type

Ancillary materials

White spirit: to BS 245: Type A.

Knotting: to BS 1336.

Stopping for woodwork: ready mixed emulsion polymer or oil based type, suitable for internal or external use as appropriate.

Stopping and filler for woodwork to receive clear finishes: ready mixed and tinted to match timber species.

Rust remover: phosphoric acid type.

Paint remover: to BS 3761 Type 1.

Fungicidal solution: proprietary product from an approved manufacturer.

Detergents: approved proprietary types.

Workmanship generally

British Standards: comply with BS 8000: Part 12.

Lead at work regulations: comply with the Control of Lead at Work Regulations 1980 where applicable.

Approval of sample areas: obtain approval of representative sample areas of each type of coating before carrying out the remainder of the work.

Preparation of new surfaces

Preparing new timber and plywood: rub down with with medium glasspaper to a smooth surface and:
a. remove resinous exudations and apply two coats of knotting to resinous timber, bluish sapwood and all knots, extending cover 25 mm beyond affected areas;
b. wipe down hardwoods with an excess of natural oil with white spirit, immediately before priming;
c. after priming, stop nail holes and similar depressions, finishing flush and priming all stopping.

Filling timber surfaces: after priming and stopping fill pore and grain irregularities with filler, brush or knife applied. Remove surplus when dry and rub down to leave a smooth, even surface.

Pre-primed timber surfaces: remove any areas of defective primer and patch prime. Wipe down primed surfaces with white spirit to remove dirt and grease.

Stopping timber surfaces for clear finishes: stop nail holes and similar depressions with stopping to match the colour of the timber, finishing flush.

Preparing new iron and steel surfaces: mechanically clean or blast clean to remove contamination.

Preparing new non-ferrous metal surfaces:
a. copper surfaces: clean with white spirit to remove dirt and grease. For small areas only, rub down with abrasive paper in lieu of etch priming. Remove copper dust before priming;
b. zinc and galvanised surfaces: clean with white spirit to remove dirt and grease and wash with detergent solution to remove corrosion products; if zinc coating is defective, obtain instructions before painting.

Preparation of existing decorated surfaces

Asbestos cement surfaces: do not dry scrape; dry abrade, or wire brush asbestos cement surf--aces. Use wet methods of surface preparation only. Collect residues before they dry out and remove from site.

Removal of existing paint from timber:
a. burn off existing coating. Scrape, abrade or plane any scorched areas and rub down smooth; or
b. solvent strip existing coating. Swab off residue of stripper with water, allow to dry and rub down smooth.

Preparing painted timber:
a. rub down sound paintwork with abrasive paper or block used wet;
b. scrape back or rub down loose or defective material to a firm edge;
c. rinse down and allow to dry;
d. prime bared surfaces as new work and bring forward with undercoating;

e. inform the PM of the presence of any rotten or infested timber and await instructions.

Preparing painted iron and steel:
a. wash down sound paintwork with detergent and warm water to remove dirt. Rinse with clean water;
b. chip, scrape or wire brush rusted areas back to bare metal;
c. rub down all surfaces with abrasive paper or block used wet and rinse with clean water;
d. prime bared areas as for new work and bring forward with undercoating.

Preparing painted non-ferrous metals:
a. wash down with detergent and warm water to remove dirt. Rinse with clean water;
b. remove loose and defective material and corrosion products with fine abrasive paper; Do not damage protective coatings;
c. wipe down with white spirit;
d. prime bared areas as for new work and bring forward with undercoating.

Preparing clear finished surfaces:
a. wash down intact varnished finishes, not requiring removal, with detergent and warm water to remove dirt;
b. solvent strip existing defective varnished surfaces, swabbing off residues with water. Allow to dry and rub down;
c. wipe down oiled surfaces with a cloth moistened with warm detergent solution, followed by clean water, then leather off and prepare for new work;
d. brush down exterior wood stained surfaces with a stiff fibre brush and wash down to remove any remaining dirt;
e. wash down wax polished surfaces with white spirit to completely remove polish, dry off, then rub down with abrasive paper to remove stain (if any) and prepare as for new work;
f. inform the PM of the presence of rotten or infested timber and await instructions.

Preparation of paint and clear wood finishes

Stirring:
a. stir before use to an even consistency throughout the container unless otherwise recommended by the manufacturer;
b. stir at intervals during use where recommended by the manufacturer.

Thinning: do not thin any paints or varnishes unless recommended by the manufacturer and/or permitted by the PM and:
a. do not thin oil paints in excess of 5% by volume of thinner;
b. thin emulsion paint in accordance with the manufacturer's recommendations for the method of application and the porosity of the background to which it is to be applied. Do not exceed 10% by volume of water without approval.

Mixing:
a. do not mix different materials or like materials of different manufacture;
b. mix etching primer in sufficient quantity for use within eight hours;
c. mix two-pack materials in accordance with manufacturer's recommendations.

Paint application

Sealing: consult PM where the adequacy of specified sealer to suit porosity of surface is doubted, or if one full coat of sealer or emulsion paint is insufficient to satisfy the porosity of the surface, or surfaces may be harmful to subsequently applied paint systems.

Priming generally: apply priming coats by brush unless other methods are specifically permitted and:
a. work primer into surface, joints, angles and end grain;
b. prime surfaces of joinery that will be hidden from view before joinery is fixed in position;
c. ensure that priming coats are of adequate thickness especially on sharp edges. Thin slightly if necessary to suit surface porosity;
d. ensure that any primed surfaces which have deteriorated on site or in transit are cleaned and touched up or rubbed down and reprimed.

Priming iron and steel: allow minimum drying times of:
a. seven days for priming paint to BS 2523 before applying undercoating;
b. two days between successive coats of priming paint to BS 2523;
c. 24 hours for zinc phosphate priming paint.

SPECIFICATION - *continued*

Surface preparation between coats:
a. lightly rub down priming and undercoats with abrasive paper to remove surface nibs;
b. dust off before applying next coat;
c. do not rub down lead based primers;
d. avoid reducing film thickness.

External timber doors: paint bottom edges before fixing with paint system ordered for external timber.

Brush application: apply in a wet, even film over all surfaces, avoiding brush marks, sags, runs, "orange-peel" and other defects. Ensure adequate edge protection.

Metallic paint coverage rate: avoid excessive brushing out. Coverage must not exceed 18 m² per litre.

Roller application: use rollers with coverings of type recommended by the roller or paint manufacturer. Use brushes for cutting-in.
Do not apply with rollers:
a. priming coats;
b. work not of a plain character.

Spray painting generally: use approved equipment. Mask all adjoining surfaces and take all necessary precautions to prevent contamination of adjoining areas by spray mist and accumulation of vapour. Do not apply by spray:
a. priming paints for wood;
b. lead paints within the meaning of the Control of Lead at Work Regulations 1980.

Painting acoustic surfaces: spray coating material thinly at an angle of 30° to the surface.

Application of clear wood finishes

Oil staining: apply stain to give an even colour and penetration over entire surface.

Exterior wood staining: brush apply the coating system in accordance with the manufacturer's recommendations. Allow the correct drying interval between each coat.

Varnishing:
a. apply first coat by brush avoiding uneven thicknesses at edges and angles;
b. brush well into the surfaces;
c. apply subsequent coats by brush in full even coats free of sags and other defects;
d. ensure good even protection of edges, etc.

Wax polishing: apply pre-polishing oil with a circular rubbing motion at a rate or 22 m² per litre, and wipe dry. Allow at least 48 hours to elapse, then wax polish to approved finish.

Oiling: apply oil as ordered with a flannel, well rubbed in.

Proprietary finishes: apply first coats in joinery shop where practicable. Do not allow deterioration of first coats before application of subsequent coats.

Fire precaution: carefully dispose of rags, swabs, etc. soaked in flammable solvents or varnishes, to avoid fire risk.

GENERALLY

Definitions

General surfaces: All surfaces not otherwise described.

Floors: Includes landings.

Wood: Includes softwood, plywood, hardwood or the like.

Soft building board: Includes fibreboard, chip--board, hardboard or the like where there is a high rate of initial absorption or a sealant is required.

Hard building board: Includes plasterboard, laminboard or the like where there is a minimal rate of absorption.

M60 PAINTING AND CLEAR FINISHING

Irregular: corrugated, fluted, carved or ornamental.

Plain open railing, fence or gate: Includes plain post and wire, post and rail, cleft pale, palisade and metal bar.

Close railing, fence or gate: Includes close boarded and corrugated.

Method of measurement

Generally:
Measure the area or girth covered and make allowance for the extra girth of edges, mouldings, panels, sinkings, corrugations, flutings, carvings, enrichments or the like unless otherwise stated. Make no deduction for voids not exceeding 0.50 m².

When divided into panes of more than one size, average the sizes.

Measure the work to associated linings and sills as general surfaces.

Frame (including linings, architraves and the like): Measure the girth separately each side irrespective of whether the same treatment is to be applied to both sides.

Plain open railing, fence or gate:
Measure individual members.

Close railing, fence or gate:
Measure each side overall.

Structural metalwork:
Measure over all fittings, plates and the like.

Rates for the following include

Generally:
For external work.

For any areas or girth unless otherwise stated.

For work in any location or at any height unless otherwise stated.

For schemes of decoration involving any number of colours unless otherwise stated.

For the use of dust sheets, tarpaulins, etc. to protect adjacent works.

For all necessary preparatory work described for the respective surfaces, except additional preparatory work under Items M60.001 to M60.005 which will be paid separately where specifically ordered.

For filling cracks not exceeding 4 mm wide.

For application by brush, roller or spray.

For carrying out work on members before fixing either on or off site when required.

For work to flagstaffs when lowered. *(Pay for lowering or painting in position at agreed Rates).*

For taking off any ironmongery or the like necessary for the proper execution of the work and for cleaning and refixing.

For decorating surface conduit or the like in with the surface to which it is attached and for any additional area so resulting.

Isolated areas:
For work of any girth.

General surfaces:
For work on butts and fastenings attached to doors, frames and linings.

Structural metalwork:
For work to attached hookbolts, clips, connecting plates, end plates, fittings and the like.

Gutters:
For work to gutter brackets.

Services:
For work to saddles, pipehooks, holderbats, conduit boxes and other components for fixing.

Cutting in edge:
For marking line with chalk or pencil.

For masking tapes and the like.

M60 PAINTING AND CLEAR FINISHING

ADDITIONAL CLEANING

Notes

Generally:
Pay for only where specifically ordered.

Specification

Blast cleaning: to BS 7079, preparation grade Sa2.

Item **M60**	*Square Metre*	1 Cleaning with mechanical wire brush £	2 Cleaning with mechanical chisels £	3 Blast cleaning to BS 7079 £
001	General surfaces: metal	3.49	4.36	21.98

	Metre			£
002	Cleaning out old gutters prior to repainting: staunching joints with mastic or bituminous composition: externally			2.08

REMOVING PAINT: FROM METAL OR WOOD

Notes

Generally:
Pay for only where specifically ordered.

Where removing paint is measured, pay for repainting at the Rates for new work.

	Square Metre	1 Burning off £	2 Solvent stripping £	3 Hot air blowers £
003	General surfaces			
	exceeding 300 mm girth	6.06	9.43	12.15
	Metre			
004	isolated surfaces not exceeding 300 mm girth	3.03	4.72	6.08
	Each			
005	isolated areas not exceeding 0.50 m²	5.87	8.79	11.78

M60 PAINTING AND CLEAR FINISHING

EMULSION PAINTING

Specification

Eggshell finish emulsion paint, exterior quality:
an approved proprietary type.

| Item **M60** | *Square Metre* | 1 Painting one coat emulsion paint on | 2 | 3 ADD for each additional coat |
		new or old untreated work	old emulsion painted work	
		£	£	£
	General surfaces			
006	concrete, brickwork or render	2.16	1.80	1.44
007	blockwork	2.75	2.20	1.66
008	roughcast render	4.07	3.08	2.10

FINE TEXTURED MASONRY PAINTING

Specification

Fine textured masonry paint: an approved proprietary water or solvent thinned type.

| | *Square Metre* | 1 Painting one coat fine textured masonry paint on old painted work | 2 Painting one coat primer-sealer and one coat fine textured masonry paint on | 3 | 4 ADD for each additional coat of fine textured masonry paint |
			new or old untreated work	old painted work	
		£	£	£	£
	General surfaces				
009	concrete, brickwork or render	3.38	6.31	5.85	2.92
010	blockwork	4.17	7.51	7.03	3.53
011	roughcast render	5.02	8.36	7.87	4.29

ALKYD GLOSS AND EGGSHELL FINISH PAINTING: MASONRY, RENDER, ETC.

Specification

General use paint: undercoat and finish: to BS 7664.

Item **M60**	*Square Metre*	1 Painting one coat primer-sealer, one undercoat and one finishing coat on new or old untreated work £	2 ADD for each additional undercoat £	3 DEDUCT where no finishing coat £
	General surfaces			
012	concrete, brickwork or render	8.07	1.89	2.17
013	blockwork or soft building board	10.24	2.03	2.29
014	plaster	6.58	1.76	2.03

		1 Painting one finishing coat on old oil painted work £	2 ADD for each additional undercoat £	3 DEDUCT where no finishing coat £	4 ADD for one coat primer-sealer on old oil painted work £
	General surfaces				
015	concrete, brickwork, blockwork or render	2.95	1.89	2.19	2.34
016	plaster, soft building board or hard building board . .	2.47	1.85	2.13	2.34

		£
017	ADD where finishing coat stippled.	1.30

M60 PAINTING AND CLEAR FINISHING

BITUMINOUS EMULSION PAINTING

Specification

Bituminous finish emulsion paint: an approved proprietary type.

		1	2
		Painting one coat bituminous emulsion paint	ADD for each additional coat
Item **M60**	*Square Metre*	£	£
018	General surfaces: concrete, brickwork or blockwork: new or old	2.39	1.89

WATER REPELLENT PAINTING

Specification

Water repellent coating: an approved proprietary type.

	Square Metre	£
019	Painting one coat water repellent coating: general surfaces: brickwork: new or old	2.24
020	ADD for additional coat	1.62

M60 PAINTING AND CLEAR FINISHING

ALKYD GLOSS AND EGGSHELL FINISH PAINTING: METAL

Specification

General use paint: undercoat and finish: to
BS 7664.

Item M60		1 Painting one undercoat and one finishing coat on new work delivered primed	2 Painting one coat primer, one undercoat and one finishing coat on new work	3 Painting one finishing coat on old painted work	4 ADD for each additional undercoat	5 DEDUCT where no finishing coat	6 ADD for one coat etching primer	7 ADD for one coat rust inhibitor
	Square Metre	£	£	£	£	£	£	£
	General surfaces							
021	exceeding 300 mm girth	4.09	6.75	3.31	1.77	2.01	2.07	1.65
	ADD where to							
022	perforated floor - *per side*	1.25	2.04	1.00	0.54	0.61	0.60	0.41
023	exceeding 300 mm girth: irregular	4.24	7.05	3.39	1.84	2.06	2.15	1.72
	Metre							
024	isolated surfaces not exceeding 300 mm girth	1.63	2.75	1.35	0.69	0.81	0.82	0.67
	Each							
025	isolated areas not exceeding 0.50 m²	2.77	4.62	2.24	1.19	1.36	1.37	1.11

ALKYD GLOSS AND EGGSHELL FINISH PAINTING - *continued*

Specification

General use paint: undercoat and finish: to BS 7664.

		1	2	3	4	5	6
		Painting one undercoat and one finishing coat on new work delivered primed	Painting one coat primer, one undercoat and one finishing coat on new work	Painting one finishing coat on old painted work	ADD for each additional undercoat	ADD for one coat etching primer	ADD for one coat rust inhibitor
Item **M60**	*Square Metre*	£	£	£	£	£	£
	Plain open railings, fences or gates						
026	exceeding 300 mm girth	4.92	8.16	3.97	2.01	2.32	1.90
	Metre						
027	isolated surfaces not exceeding 300 mm girth	1.76	2.92	1.43	0.72	0.83	0.68
	Each						
028	isolated areas not exceeding 0.50 m²	2.98	4.91	2.39	1.20	1.37	1.14
	Square Metre						
029	Close railings, fences or gates	4.62	7.66	3.72	1.87	2.18	1.76

M60 PAINTING AND CLEAR FINISHING

ALKYD GLOSS AND EGGSHELL FINISH PAINTING: BITUMEN COATED METAL

Specification

General use paint: undercoat and finish: to BS 7664.

Item M60	*Square Metre*	£
	Painting one coat aluminium primer, one undercoat and one finishing coat: services	
030	exceeding 300 mm girth	7.45
	Metre	
031	isolated surfaces not exceeding 300 mm girth	2.68
	Each	
032	isolated areas not exceeding 0.50 m²	4.49

BITUMINOUS PAINTING: METAL

Specification

Bituminous paint: black bitumen solution for cold application to BS 6949 Type 1.   Not suitable for contact with potable water.

	1	2	3
	Painting one coat bituminous paint on old bitumen painted work	Painting one coat primer and one coat bituminous paint on new or old untreated work	ADD for each additional coat of bituminous paint
Square Metre	£	£	£
General surfaces			
033 exceeding 300 mm girth	2.48	4.09	1.57
ADD where to			
034 perforated floor - *per side*	0.76	1.30	0.48
035 exceeding 300 mm girth: irregular	2.59	4.20	1.64
Metre			
036 isolated services not exceeding 300 mm girth	0.94	1.54	0.59
Each			
037 isolated areas not exceeding 0.50 m²	1.58	2.62	1.00

M60 PAINTING AND CLEAR FINISHING

BITUMINOUS PAINTING: METAL - *continued*

Specification

Bituminous paint: black bitumen solution for application to BS 6949 Type 1. Not suitable for use in contact with potable water.

Item M60	*Square Metre*	1 Painting one coat bituminous paint on old painted work	2 Painting one coat primer and one coat bituminous paint on new or old untreated work	3 ADD for each additional coat of bituminous paint
		£	£	£
	Plain open railings, fences or gates			
038	exceeding 300 mm girth	2.98	4.84	1.86
	Metre			
039	isolated surfaces not exceeding 300 mm girth	1.06	1.71	0.66
	Each			
040	isolated areas not exceeding 0.50 m²	1.74	2.78	1.09
	Square Metre			
041	Close railings, fences or gates	2.83	4.60	1.77

ALUMINIUM PAINTING: METAL

Specification

Aluminium paint: an approved proprietary type.

	Square Metre	1 Painting one coat aluminium paint on old painted work	2 Painting one coat primer and one coat aluminium paint on new or old untreated work	3 ADD for each additional coat of aluminium paint
		£	£	£
	General surfaces			
042	exceeding 300 mm girth	3.03	4.15	1.89
	ADD where to			
043	perforated floor - *per side*	0.91	1.27	0.58
044	exceeding 300 mm girth: irregular	3.18	4.42	1.98
	Metre			
045	isolated surfaces not exceeding 300 mm girth	1.14	1.59	0.70
	Each			
046	isolated areas not exceeding 0.50 m²	1.82	2.43	1.11

M60 PAINTING AND CLEAR FINISHING

ALUMINIUM PAINTING: METAL - *continued*

Specification

Aluminium paint: an approved proprietary type.

Item M60	*Square Metre*	1 Painting one coat aluminium paint on old painted work £	2 Painting one coat primer and one coat aluminium paint on new or old untreated work £	3 ADD for each additional coat of aluminium paint £
	Plain open railings, fences or gates			
047	exceeding 300 mm girth	3.61	4.95	2.24
	Metre			
048	isolated surfaces not exceeding 300 mm girth	1.30	1.75	0.78
	Each			
049	isolated areas not exceeding 0.50 m²	2.16	2.95	1.34
	Square Metre			
050	Close railings, fences or gates	3.37	4.60	2.09

MICACEOUS IRON OXIDE PAINTING: METAL

Specification

Micaceous iron oxide: an approved proprietary type.

Item	*Square Metre*	1 Painting one coat micaceous iron oxide on old painted work £	2 Painting one coat primer and one coat micaceous iron oxide on new or old untreated work £	3 ADD for each additional coat of micaceous iron oxide £
	General surfaces			
051	exceeding 300 mm girth	4.34	5.88	2.81
	ADD where to			
052	perforated floor - *per side*	1.33	1.83	0.88
053	exceeding 300 mm girth: irregular	4.49	6.09	2.90
	Metre			
	General surfaces or services			
054	isolated surfaces not exceeding 300 mm girth	1.58	2.14	1.02
	Each			
055	isolated areas not exceeding 0.50 m²	2.60	3.55	1.67

MICACEOUS IRON OXIDE PAINTING: METAL - *continued*

Specification

Micaceous iron oxide: an approved proprietary type.

Item **M60**	*Square Metre*	1 Painting one coat micaceous iron oxide on old painted work	2 Painting one coat primer and one coat micaceous iron oxide on new or old untreated work	3 ADD for each additional coat of micaceous iron oxide
		£	£	£
	Plain open railings, fences or gates			
056	exceeding 300 mm girth	5.18	7.02	3.35
	Metre			
057	isolated surfaces not exceeding 300 mm girth	1.86	2.54	1.20
	Each			
058	isolated areas not exceeding 0.50 m²	3.07	4.17	1.98
	Square Metre			
059	Close railings, fences or gates	4.86	6.58	3.16

ALKYD GLOSS AND EGGSHELL PAINTING: WOOD

Specification

General use paint: undercoat and finish: to BS 7664.

	Square Metre	1 Painting one coat primer, one undercoat and one finishing coat on new work	2 Painting one finishing coat on old painted work	3 ADD for each additional undercoat	4 DEDUCT where no finishing coat
		£	£	£	£
060	General surfaces				
	exceeding 300 mm girth	6.18	2.70	1.50	1.90
	Metre				
061	isolated surfaces not exceeding 300 mm girth	2.27	0.98	0.54	0.66
	Each				
062	isolated areas not exceeding 0.50 m²	3.69	1.64	0.88	1.12

ALKYD GLOSS AND EGGSHELL PAINTING: WOOD - *continued*

Specification

General use paint: undercoat and finish: to BS 7664.

Item **M60**	*Square Metre*	1 Painting one coat primer, one undercoat and one finishing coat on new work £	2 Painting one finishing coat on old painted work £	3 ADD for each additional undercoat £
	Plain open railings, fences or gates			
063	exceeding 300 mm girth	7.53	3.33	1.82
	Metre			
064	isolated surfaces not exceeding 300 mm girth	2.71	1.20	0.67
	Each			
065	isolated areas not exceeding 0.50 m²	4.47	1.98	1.08
	Square Metre			
066	Close railings fences or gates	6.94	3.09	1.69

PRESERVATIVE PAINTING: WOOD

Specification

Creosote for brush application: to BS 144.

	Square Metre	1 Painting one coat creosote externally on new or old untreated work £	2 old treated work £	3 ADD for each additional coat of creosote £
067	General surfaces: exceeding 300 mm girth	2.04	1.86	1.69
068	Plain open railings, fences or gates: exceeding 300 mm girth	2.50	2.34	2.07
069	Close railings, fences or gates	2.32	2.18	1.96

PRESERVATIVE PAINTING: WOOD - *continued*

	1	2	3
	Painting one coat creosote externally on		ADD for each additional coat of creosote
	new or old untreated work	old treated work	
Item **M60** *Metre*	£	£	£
General surfaces or plain open railings, fences or gates			
070 isolated surfaces not exceeding 300 mm girth	0.92	0.86	0.76
Each			
071 isolated areas not exceeding 0.50 m²	1.45	1.35	1.19

OILING: WOOD

Specification

Raw linseed oil for hardwood: to BS 6900.

Mineral oil for teak: an approved proprietary type.

	1	2
	Twice oiling new work	Washing down and twice oiling old work
Square Metre	£	£
072 General surfaces		
exceeding 300 mm girth	3.67	3.16
Metre		
073 isolated surfaces not exceeding 300 mm girth	1.21	1.07
Each		
074 isolated areas not exceeding 0.50 m²	2.05	1.81

M60 PAINTING AND CLEAR FINISHING

STAINING: WOOD: EXTERNALLY

Specification

Exterior wood stain: an approved proprietary type.

Item M60	*Square Metre*	1 Staining with one coat of exterior wood stain on old stained work £	2 Staining with two coats of exterior wood stain on new or old untreated work £	3 ADD for each additional coat £
075	General surfaces			
	exceeding 300 mm girth	2.16	3.68	1.53
	Metre			
076	isolated surfaces not exceeding 300 mm girth	0.78	1.29	0.53
	Each			
077	isolated areas not exceeding 0.50 m²	1.28	2.20	0.93

SEALER VARNISHING: WOOD

Specification

Sealer varnish: oleo-resinous sealer of an approved proprietary type.

	Square Metre	1 Varnishing with one coat sealer varnish on new or old untreated work £	2 ADD for each additional coat £
	General surfaces		
078	exceeding 300 mm girth	2.22	1.77
	Metre		
079	isolated surfaces not exceeding 300 mm girth	0.80	0.67
	Each		
080	isolated areas not exceeding 0.50 m²	1.33	1.14

POLISHING: WOOD

Specification

Wax polish: bleached beeswax and genuine turpentine, or an approved proprietary type.

	1	2	3	4
	Sealing and polishing new work	Cleaning and reviving old work	Stripping and repolishing old work	ADD for staining or bleaching old work
Item **M60** *Square Metre*	£	£	£	£
General surfaces				
081 exceeding 300 mm girth	6.29	4.83	12.43	1.95
Metre				
082 isolated surfaces not exceeding 300 mm girth	2.31	1.77	4.58	0.71
Each				
083 isolated areas not exceeding 0.50 m²	3.83	2.92	7.65	1.18

N: Furniture and Equipment

N15: SIGNS AND NOTICES

WALL OR FLOOR MARKING

Specification

Line marking paint: an approved proprietary type.

Rates for the following include

Generally:
For external work.

For preparatory work.

For setting out.

For painting to new or old surfaces of any kind.

For straight or curved work.

For clean cut edges.

Item N15	*Metre - per 25 mm of width*	1 Painting one coat line marking paint £	2 ADD for each additional coat £
001	Line	1.38	0.99
002	Letter, numeral or symbol	2.76	1.98
	Repainting existing		
003	line	1.19	0.79
004	letter, numeral or symbol	2.37	1.68

CARVING STONEWORK

Rates for the following include

Generally:
For plain sunk work executed in position.

	Each	1 Bath £	2 Portland £	3 York £	4 Granite £
005	Letter, numeral or symbol - *per 25 mm of height*	2.60	3.75	5.49	8.70
006	Stop, hyphen or comma	1.92	2.47	3.39	5.03

N15: SIGNS AND NOTICES

SIGNS OR THE LIKE

Rates for the following include

Fixing only:
For fixing to any background by any means.

Taking down:
For making good background *except* decorations and applied finishings.

Item N15	Each	1 Fixing only £	2 Taking down £
	Sign, name plate or the like		
007	not exceeding 0.25 m²	2.75	1.83
008	ADD *for each additional 0.25 m²*	0.46	0.31
009	Letter, numeral or symbol: any size	1.60	0.69
	Notice board		
010	not exceeding 1 m²	6.41	3.20
011	1 to 2 m²	7.32	3.66
012	2 to 3 m²	8.24	4.12
013	3 to 4 m²	9.15	4.58

P30: TRENCHES, PIPEWAYS AND PITS FOR BURIED ENGINEERING SERVICES

GENERALLY

Reference to other Sections: the Preambles to Sections D20, E10 and R12 apply equally to this Section where appropriate.

EXCAVATING TRENCHES

Specification

Excavating:
a. excavate trenches at least 300 mm wider than external diameter of pipeline;
b. ensure trench bottom provides a firm even pipe bed for full length of pipes.

Parallel ducts: allow 25 mm minimum clearance between ducts.

Backfilling: over services not requiring a structural surround, backfill and compact by hand in 100 mm layers to 300 mm above pipelines with approved selected fill, readily compacted, free from roots, vegetable matter, building rubbish, frozen soil, clay lumps retained on a 75 mm sieve and stones retained on a 25 mm sieve.

Warning tapes: lay above service at a depth of 300 mm except where road or pavement construction exceeds 300 mm total thickness when tape should be laid immediately below base construction.

Method of measurement

Parallel services:
Add together the nominal sizes plus clearance between services and treat as one service.

Rates for the following include

Service trenches:
For earthwork support, consolidating trench bottom, trimming excavations, backfilling and compacting and disposing of surplus excavated material off site.

For sifting and backfill and where cable covers are used for backfilling in two stages.

P30: TRENCHES, PIPEWAYS AND PITS FOR BURIED ENGINEERING SERVICES

EXCAVATING TRENCHES - *continued*

Item P30	Metre	1 not exceeding 200 mm £	2 200 to 250 mm £	3 250 to 300 mm £
		Nominal size of pipe, duct or cable		
	For service: average depth			
001	not exceeding 0.50 m	10.17	10.72	11.28
002	0.50 to 0.75 m	14.89	15.73	16.56
003	0.75 to 1.00 m	19.61	20.72	21.84
004	1.00 to 1.25 m	25.85	27.26	28.64
005	1.25 to 1.50 m	30.87	32.55	34.22
006	1.50 to 1.75 m	35.90	37.86	39.80
007	1.75 to 2.00 m	40.92	43.15	45.38

008   Where hand excavation is specifically ordered, price at the foregoing Rates multiplied by 2.00.

	Metre	£
009	Polythene warning tape with legend: 150 mm wide and 0.10 mm thick: laid in trench	0.32

UNDERGROUND DUCTWORK

Specification

Vitrified clay ducts and fittings: to BS 65 extra strength class with polyethylene sleeve joints and manufactured by a BSI Kitemark Licensee.

UPVC ducts and fittings: to BS 4660 with ring seal joints and manufactured by a BSI Kitemark Licensee.

Draw lines: nylon with a minimum breaking strength of 550 N.

Removable plugs: hardwood or plastics.

Alignment: provide alignment by drawing through a wooden mandrel 250 mm long and 7 mm less in diameter than the bore of the duct. Variations from alignment not to exceed 1 in 30 horizontally and 1 in 60 vertically.

Draw lines: thread nylon draw lines through each duct way during laying and leave 4000 mm longer than each respective duct.

Duct ends: plug duct ends immediately after laying to prevent entry of soil. Secure both ends of each draw line outside plugged ends of duct.

Rates for the following include

Generally:
For straight, horizontal or vertical ducts.

For proving alignment.

For draw lines.

P30: TRENCHES, PIPEWAYS AND PITS FOR BURIED ENGINEERING SERVICES

UNDERGROUND DUCTWORK - *continued*

Item P30	*Metre*	1 Vitrified clay Nominal size 100 mm £	2 150 mm £	3 UPVC 110 mm £	4 160 mm £
010	Duct	7.40	10.30	6.88	9.36
	Each				
	Extra for				
011	bend	13.87	21.35	15.28	31.79
012	bell mouth	15.26	26.65	14.62	16.57
013	split type conduit plug	2.87	4.47	2.87	4.47

P31: HOLES, CHASES AND COVERS FOR SERVICES

GENERALLY

Definition of terms

Duct: includes trays, trunking, gratings or the like.

Pipe: includes tubes, bars, cables, conduit or the like.

Rates for the following include

Mortar:
For mortar to match adjacent work unless otherwise stated.

Hole for duct:
For any profile.

Making good facework, facings and stonework:
For pointing to match existing.

HOLES

Rates for the following include

Hole through concrete:
For building in pipe sleeve (supplied).

Making good fair finish to concrete:
For making good to match adjacent finish.

Hole through brickwork and blockwork:
For building in pipe sleeve (supplied).

Hole for pipe exceeding 110 mm nominal size through brickwork:
For turning arch over.

For any centring required.

Cutting hole through roof covering and wall covering or cladding:
For cutting holes through any isolating membranes, underlays or vapour barriers.

Cutting hole through existing surface finishes:
For cutting holes through any associated membranes, underlays, beds or backings.

P31: HOLES, CHASES AND COVERS FOR SERVICES

HOLES - *continued*

Item P31	Each	1 For duct not exceeding 1.00 m girth £	2 ADD *for each additional 0.50 m of girth* £	3 For pipe not exceeding 55 mm nominal size £	4 55 to 110 mm nominal size £	5 exceeding 110 mm nominal size £
014	Cutting hole through set or existing concrete: not exceeding 100 mm thick	22.37	11.23	14.08	17.65	21.14
015	ADD *for each additional 25 mm of thickness*	5.03	2.57	3.17	3.97	4.76
	ADD for					
016	cutting reinforcement where ordered	11.44	5.72	4.58	9.15	13.73
017	making good fair face finish - *per face*	3.05	1.53	0.92	1.37	2.75
	Cutting hole through new or existing common brickwork					
018	half-brick thick	7.77	3.93	4.29	5.76	8.56
019	one-brick thick	14.77	7.48	8.15	10.75	16.26
020	one-and-a-half-brick thick	21.77	11.02	12.01	16.13	23.96
021	ADD for making good facework - *per side*	2.75	1.37	0.92	1.14	1.60
022	ADD for making good facework to facing brickwork - *per side*	4.12	2.06	1.37	1.71	2.40
023	Cutting hole through new or existing blockwork not exceeding 100 mm thick	4.98	2.29	1.84	2.26	2.96
024	ADD *for each additional 25 mm of thickness*	1.12	0.51	0.41	0.51	0.67
025	ADD for making good facework - *per side*	1.37	0.64	0.69	0.92	1.37
026	ADD where opening through cavity wall for sealing cavity not exceeding 75 mm wide around opening with slates in mortar	5.99	2.85	-	-	-
027	ADD for rendering around internally in mortar - *per 25 mm of wall thickness*	1.63	0.70	-	-	-

028   Cutting holes through new or existing engineering brickwork: price at the Rates for common brickwork multiplied by 2.00.

HOLES - *continued*

Item **P31**	*Each - per 25 mm of thickness*	1 For pipe not exceeding 55 mm nominal size £	2 55 to 110 mm nominal size £	3 exceeding 110 mm nominal size £
	Cutting hole through new or existing stonework in position: making good			
029	Bath	1.22	1.64	2.45
030	Portland	2.43	3.27	4.89
031	York	4.01	5.40	8.08
032	Granite	7.30	9.82	14.68

MORTICES

	Metre run of pipe	£
	Mortices: for supports for pipe or duct: not exceeding 55 mm nominal size: grouting with mortar (any mix): making good	
033	forming in unset concrete	2.02
034	cutting in set or existing concrete	4.76

	Each	
	Mortice: for support for pipe or duct: not exceeding 55 mm nominal size: grouting with mortar (any mix): making good	
035	forming in unset concrete	2.57
036	cutting in set or existing concrete	5.95

P31: HOLES, CHASES AND COVERS FOR SERVICES

SUNDRIES

Item P31	*Metre run of pipe*	1 Common brickwork £	2 Blockwork £	3 ADD for making good facework £	4 ADD for making good facework to facing brickwork £
037	Cutting and pinning ends of supports for pipe or duct: not exceeding 55 mm nominal size	2.29	1.56	0.46	0.50
	Each				
038	Cutting and pinning end of support for pipe or duct: exceeding 55 mm nominal size	.4.03	3.02	0.82	0.92

		1 Common brickwork	2	3 Blockwork	4
		Not exceeding 75 mm deep	ADD *for each additional 25 mm of depth*	Not exceeding 75 mm deep	ADD *for each additional 25 mm of depth*
	Each	£	£	£	£
	Cutting into or through work to release end of pipe, pipe support or the like: nominal size				
039	not exceeding 55 mm	4.58	1.92	3.48	1.28
040	55 to 110 mm	5.77	2.29	4.58	1.92
041	exceeding 110 mm	7.69	3.11	5.86	2.29

042   Items in engineering brickwork: price at the Rates for Items P31.037 to P31.041 (common brickwork) multiplied by 2.00.

P31: HOLES, CHASES AND COVERS FOR SERVICES

MAKING GOOD HOLES

		1	2	3	4	5	6
		Common brickwork		Blockwork		ADD for making good facework - per side	ADD for making good facework to facing brickwork - per side
		Not exceeding half-brick thick	ADD for each additional half-brick thickness	Not exceeding half-brick thick	ADD for each additional 25 mm of thickness		
Item P31	Each	£	£	£	£	£	£
	Making good hole after removal of						
	duct: girth						
043	not exceeding 1.00 m	12.40	3.76	9.66	2.83	3.02	4.30
044	1.00 to 2.00 m	22.75	7.28	16.54	5.32	5.49	7.78
	pipe: nominal size						
045	not exceeding 55 mm	4.76	1.56	3.71	1.15	1.56	1.83
046	55 to 110 mm	7.51	2.27	6.01	1.79	2.29	3.11
047	exceeding 110 mm	11.28	3.35	8.35	2.52	2.75	3.75

Q: Paving, Planting and Fencing

Q10: STONE AND CONCRETE KERBS, EDGINGS AND CHANNELS

PRECAST CONCRETE AND GRANITE KERBS AND EDGINGS

Specification

Precast concrete: to BS 7263: Part 1:
a. Kerbs, channels and edgings: any finish: natural colour;
b. Quadrants: to match adjacent kerbs.

Granite: to BS 435:
a. Kerbs: standard finish: fine picked, fair picked, single axed or nidged, or rough punched as ordered;
b. Quadrants: type X or Y as ordered: finish to match adjacent kerbs;
c. Setts: hand hewn finish.

Cement: ordinary or rapid-hardening Portland cement to BS 12 and manufactured by a BSI Registered Firm.

Sand: to BS 1200 Table 1.

Mortar: cement and sand (1:3).

Reinforcement dowels: 12 mm diameter mild steel bar (Grade 250) to BS 4449, 100 mm long.

Laying kerbs on foundation:
a. lay on a 10 to 15 mm mortar bed, aligned vertically and horizontally;
b haunch with concrete;
c. lay with movement joint coinciding with those in concrete road slab and extending through foundation and haunching;
d. fill movement joints with expansion joint filler and sealant.

Laying kerbs on concrete road slabs:
a. roughen surface of concrete slab to form key;
b. drive dowels into green concrete to a depth of 50 mm;
c. lay on a 10 to 15 mm mortar bed, aligned vertically and horizontally;
d. haunch with concrete;
e. form movement joints coinciding with those in slab;
f. fill movement joints with expansion joint filler and sealant.

Jointing kerbs dry: lay with dry vertical joints not exceeding 3 mm wide.

Jointing kerbs with mortar: joint with mortar 6 mm wide as the work proceeds. Neatly flush point.

Laying edgings: bed on concrete base, haunch with concrete and:
a. with vertical points close fitting, unpointed, not exceeding 3 mm in width;
b. to line and levels vertically and horizontally aligned within a tolerance of 3 mm.

Laying setts: bed on concrete base and grout in mortar. Finish flush with adjoining surfaces or as ordered.

Notes

Excavation work:
Pay for at the Rates in Section D20.

Rates for the following include

Generally:
For laying on new or old base.

For preparing base.

For cut angles.

For ends.

For cutting to length.

Setting to curve:
For curved units.

Q10: STONE AND CONCRETE KERBS, EDGINGS AND CHANNELS

PRECAST CONCRETE AND GRANITE KERBS AND EDGINGS - *continued*

Item Q10	*Metre*	1 Precast concrete 125 x 255 mm £	2 150 x 305 mm £	3 Fixing only: not exceeding 150 x 305 mm £	4 Granite Edge kerb: 150 x 300 mm £	5 Flat kerb: 300 x 200 mm £	6 Fixing only: not exceeding 300 x 200 mm £
001	Kerb: square bullnosed, full battered or half battered: dry jointing	7.24	11.68	5.43	47.60	52.98	10.06
	ADD for						
002	jointing with mortar	0.83	1.00	1.00	1.66	2.00	2.00
003	dowels driven into concrete at 450 mm centres	2.20	2.20	2.20	2.20	2.20	2.20
004	setting to curve: any radius	2.73	2.30	0.53	1.37	1.94	1.94
	Each						
	Extra for						
005	angle unit	7.33	7.33	1.62	26.80	28.98	4.85
	quadrant						
006	305 mm radius	10.66	-	1.62	-	30.39	7.68
007	455 mm radius	12.18	-	2.43	30.21	34.94	7.68

	Metre	1 Precast concrete 50 x 150 mm £	2 50 x 205 mm £	3 50 x 255 mm £	4 Fixing only: not exceeding 50 x 255 mm £
008	Edging: square, chamfered, rounded or bullnosed	4.21	5.11	5.62	3.29
009	ADD for setting to curve: any radius	0.79	0.94	1.34	0.70

	Metre	1 Granite 100 x 100 x 100 mm long £	2 100 x 125 x 200 mm long £	3 laying only: not exceeding 100 x 125 x 200 mm long £
	Sett string course			
010	single row	13.65	13.89	5.08
011	double row	26.61	27.09	9.46

Q10: STONE AND CONCRETE KERBS, EDGINGS AND CHANNELS

DRAINAGE CHANNELS

Specification

Polyester concrete drainage channel units and fittings: from an approved manufacturer:
a. Dimensions: 155 mm wide overall: 105 to 309 mm deep overall: 100 mm bore: channel with integral fall.
b. Joint type: in accordance with the manufacturers recommendations.
c. gratings: castiron slotted inlay gratings fixed with bolts and locking bars.
d. Lay on 100 mm concrete (20 N/mm²: 40 mm maximum size aggregate) base and haunch up with similar concrete both sides.

Precast concrete drainage channel units and fittings: from an approved manufacturer:
a. Dimensions: 310 mm wide overall: 230 mm deep: encasing 110 mm diameter PVC pipe.
b. Joint type: in accordance with the manufacturers recommendations.
c. inlets: single row of circular conical or straight slotted inlet apertures.
d. Lay on 100 mm concrete (20 N/mm²: 40 mm maximum size aggregate) base and haunch up with similar concrete both sides.

Laying channels: lay on a 10 to 15 mm mortar mortar bed on concrete base and:
a. lay with vertical points close fitting in mortar;
b. to line and levels vertically and horizontally aligned within a tolerance of 3 mm;
c. separated from raised kerbs with 10 to 15 mm layer of mortar.

Notes

Excavation work:
Pay for at the Rates in Section D20.

Rates for the following include

Generally:
For laying on new or old base.

Polyester concrete drainage channel units:
For units of any depth within manufacturers range.

Item Q10	*Metre*	£
012	Polyester concrete drainage channel: grating	54.53

	Each	
	Extra for	
013	end plate	5.77
014	end plate with 100 mm diameter PVC union	9.50
	PVC union: to suit knock out drainage point	
015	100 mm diameter: round	4.13
	150 mm diameter	
016	round	8.69
017	oval	9.11

DRAINAGE CHANNELS - *continued*

Item Q10	*Metre*	£
018	Precast concrete drainage units	59.88

	Each	
	Extra for	
019	junction or silt box: removable grating	234.99
020	rodding unit: lockable removable grating	38.17

		1	2
		Precast concrete	
		255 x 125 mm	Fixing only: not exceeding 255 x 125 mm
	Metre	£	£
021	Channel: square	7.95	3.91
022	ADD for setting to curve: any radius	2.57	0.81

BRICK EDGINGS: LAYING ONLY

		1	2	3
		Common Brickwork	Engineering Brickwork	Facing Brickwork
	Metre	£	£	£
	Edging: single course			
023	stretchers: half brick wide	7.86	9.64	8.92
	ADD where curved on plan			
024	not exceeding 2 m radius	0.75	0.75	0.75
025	exceeding 2 m radius	0.38	0.38	0.38
026	brick on edge: one brick wide	12.77	15.65	14.50
	ADD where curved on plan			
027	not exceeding 2 m radius	1.23	1.23	1.23
028	exceeding 2 m radius	0.67	0.67	0.67

Q10: STONE AND CONCRETE KERBS, EDGINGS AND CHANNELS

IN SITU CONCRETE AND FORMWORK

Reference to other Sections: the Preambles to Sections E10 and E20 apply equally to this Sub-Section.

Specification

Concrete: 20 N/mm²: 20 mm aggregate.

Formwork: basic finish.

Item Q10	Cubic Metre	£
029	Concrete foundation and haunching: formwork	142.76

MOVEMENT JOINTS

Specification

Movement joint filler and sealant:
a. knot-free softwood or waterproof, compressible non-extruding, premoulded filler with high recovery factor after compression at temperatures below 50°.
b. sealant to BS 2499 type A2.

	Each	£
	Movement joint: 25 mm thick filler: sealant: formwork	
030	through kerb and haunching: any size	8.23
031	through kerb, haunching and foundation: any size	13.55

Q20: HARDCORE BASES AND SUB-BASES TO ROADS AND PAVINGS

HARDCORE

Specification

Hardcore:
a. Hard stone, concrete, coarse gravel, sound slag or hard broken brick, free from rubbish or other deleterious matter, capable of passing in every direction, a ring of diameter not greater than two thirds thickness of bed, subject to a maximum diameter of 150 mm and graded so that when compacted, filling is dense and without voids; or

b. Gravel and stone: to BS 882 Table 4 for 20 mm nominal size.

Blinding: sand to BS 882 Table 5.

Laying and compacting:
a. spread hardcore evenly and blind top surface with sand or other approved material;
b. compact in layers until movement ceases;
c. fully compact around road gullies, manholes or the like.

Permissible deviations: devations from required levels not to exceed:
a. sub-base: +0 to -40 mm;
b. any point under a 3000 mm straight edge: 15 mm.

Method of measurement

Filling generally:
Measure as equal to the void filled.

Measure the average thickness after compaction.

Rates for the following include

Filling generally:
For compacting in layers not exceeding 150 mm thick.

Hardcore obtained from the excavations or demolitions:
For selecting for re-use and breaking to required sizes.

Item Q20	*Cubic Metre*	1 Obtained from excavations or demolitions £	2 Imported to site £
	Filling to make up levels		
032	not exceeding 0.25 m average thick	15.20	29.15
033	exceeding 0.25 m average thick	13.07	27.02

	Square Metre	£
034	Grading surface to falls, crossfalls or cambers: compacting	1.14
035	Blinding surface	1.81

CONCRETE

Reference to other Sections: the Preambles and Rates to Section E10 apply equally to this Sub-Section unless otherwise stated.

Specification

Aggregate for lean concrete bases: coarse and fine aggregates, batched separated, or an all-in aggregate, to BS 882, of nominal size 20 to 40 mm.

Lean concrete bases: cement contents to be not less than 4 per cent by weight of dry aggregate.

Laying pavings: place and compact concrete continuously to prescribed joints and:

a. spread and strike off with surcharge sufficient to obtain required compacted thickness;
b. compact with mechanical beam pattern compactors using poker vibrators at edges and ends of slabs. Obtain full slab depth compaction, uniform density, strength with appropriate number of passes of compaction equipment. Avoid contact between poker vibrators and fabric reinforcement;
c. finish concrete stopped between joints as a construction joint;
d. check surface with 3000 mm straight edge, immediately make good irregularities exceeding 6 mm;
e. complete compaction and finish to produce a surface free from laitence or excessive water.

		1	2	3	4	5	6
		Lean		Plain		Reinforced	
		10 N/mm²:		30 N/mm²:		30 N/mm²:	
		20 to 40 mm agg		20 mm agg		20 mm agg	
		Thickness					
		not exceeding 150 mm	150 to 450 mm	not exceeding 150 mm	150 to 450 mm	not exceeding 150 mm	150 to 450 mm
Item Q21	*Cubic Metre*	£	£	£	£	£	£
036	Bed	93.73	91.92	101.42	95.97	105.06	103.24

		£
	ADD where	
037	sloping not exceeding 15° from horizontal	3.63
038	laid in bays not exceeding 10 m²	2.04

Q21: IN SITU CONCRETE ROADS, PAVINGS AND BASES

FORMWORK

Reference to other Sections: the Peambles and Rates to Section E20 apply equally to this Sub-Section unless otherwise stated.

Item Q21		Metre	£
	Edge of bed: basic finish		
039	not exceeding 250 mm high		6.52
040	250 to 500 mm high		10.58
		Each	
	Mortice for road reflecting stud: basic finish		
041	225 x 175 x 50 mm		2.85
042	300 x 175 x 50 mm		3.33
	Sump: rebated all round: fine finish: extra concrete any grade		
043	225 x 225 x 150 mm		7.87
044	300 x 300 x 225 mm		12.46

REINFORCEMENT: STEEL FABRIC

Reference to other Sections: the Preambles and Rates to Section E30 apply equally to this Sub-Section unless otherwise stated.

Specification

Laying mesh reinforcement:
a. Lay sheets flat and straight;
b. Lay main reinforcement in mesh parallel to longitudinal axis of slab;
c. Lap mesh sheets transversely; no longitudinal lap;
d. Stop reinforcement short of movement joints:
   1. for slabs 150 mm or more thick: 60 mm;
   2. for slabs less than 150 mm thick: 50 mm.

Rates for the following include

Generally:
For 450 mm transverse laps.

Item		Square Metre	£
045	Fabric to BS 4483: any type: nominal mass not exceeding1 kg per m²		3.11
046	ADD *for each additional 1 kg per m²*		1.12

Q21: IN SITU CONCRETE ROADS, PAVINGS AND BASES

MOVEMENT JOINTS

Specification

Movement joint filler: knot-free softwood or waterproof compressible, non-extruding, pre-moulded filler with high recovery factor after compression at temperatures below 50°C.

Joint sealant: to BS 2499 type A2.

Preforming movement joints: prior to concreting, set rigidly in position and support to prevent displacement of joint filler, sealing groove fillet and:

a. maintain support until adjacent concrete has set before placing concrete for next slab;

b. keep sealing groove fillet in position until concrete on both sides of joint is fully cured;

c. remove fillet immediately prior to sealing joint.

Rounding on upper edges at joints: round upper edges of slabs at joints to 10 mm radius using bullnose arris trowel. Do not overwork concrete.

Placing softwood filler: immerse softwood filler in water for 48 hours before placing in joint and keep damp prior to concreting.

Sealing grooves: remove sealing groove fillet, clean out groove and fill with sealing compound.

Item Q21	*Metre*	£
	Movement joint: 25 mm thick filler: groove formwork	
047	not exceeding 150 mm deep	3.21
048	150 to 300 mm deep	5.20
049	300 to 450 mm deep	8.00
050	Sealant: 25 x 25 mm	9.06

WORKED FINISHES TO INSITU CONCRETE

	Square Metre	£
051	Tamped ribbed finish	0.73
052	Rolled pattern finish	1.21
053	Power floated finish to smooth, even surface	3.05
054	Even textured finish achieved with scraping straight edge and medium coarse fibre broom	2.91
	ADD to the foregoing Rates where	
055	sloping	0.73
056	to falls or crossfalls	0.47

Q21: IN SITU CONCRETE ROADS, PAVINGS AND BASES

REPAIRS TO CONCRETE

Specification

Joint sealant: to BS 2499, Type A2.

Rates for the following include

Re-sealing movement joint groove:
For removing hardened joint material.

For removing all dust and debris by scraping or brushing.

For priming sides and bottoms of all joints with an approved solution as recommended by the manufacturer of the joint sealant.

For re-filling groove with joint sealant.

Repairing crack:
For removing all dust and debris by scraping or brushing.

For filling crack with latex rubber bitumen emulsion.

For dusting surface with cement or fine sand.

Item Q21	Metre	£
057	Re-sealing movement joint groove: not exceeding 30 x 30 mm.	13.64
058	Repairing crack: not exceeding 10 mm wide	3.44

Q22: COATED MACADAM ROADS AND PAVINGS

GENERALLY

Method of measurement

Area:
Measure the area in contact with base. Make no deduction for voids not exceeding 0.50 m² or grounds.

Thickness:
Measure the compacted thickness exclusive of surface dressing.

Where laid over existing uneven paving, agree the average thickness with the PM before laying.

Rates for the following include

Generally:
For laying to falls, crossfalls, cambers or slopes not exceeding 15° from horizontal.

For forming or working into shallow channels and associated labours.

For laying on any new or existing base.

For preparing the base except forming key.

Work executed in small quantities

Where the total area of coated macadam surfacing executed in one location at the same time under one or more orders falls within the categories shown, multiply Rates Q20.061 to Q20.073 by the following factors:

059	not exceeding 10 m²	multiply by 3.00
060	10 to 25 m²	multiply by 1.30

Q22: COATED MACADAM ROADS AND PAVINGS

TACK COATS

Specification

Tack coat: to BS 434 Part 1.

Workmanship: comply with BS 434 Part 2 and
BS 4987 Part 2, Clause 4.5.

Note

Use tack coat only where ordered.

Item Q22	Square Metre	£
061	Generally	0.75

COATED MACADAM

Specification

Coated macadam: manufacture, transport and
lay in accordance with BS 4987 Parts 1 and 2.

Bitumen binder: penetration grade bitumen.

Coarse aggregate: crushed rock or slag.

Note

Clause references are to BS 4987 Part 1.

		1	2
	Square Metre	60 mm thick	ADD or DEDUCT *for each 5 mm variation in thickness*
		£	£
	Base course: bitumen binder		
062	20 mm size open graded base course as Clause 6.1	10.73	0.89
063	40 mm size single course as Clause 6.2	10.73	0.89
064	28 mm size dense base course as Clause 6.4	11.31	0.94
065	20 mm size dense base course as Clause 6.5	11.31	0.94

		1	2
		20 mm thick	ADD or DEDUCT *for each 5 mm variation in thickness*
		£	£
	Wearing course		
066	10 mm size close graded wearing course as Clause 7.4: bitumen binder	3.82	0.94
067	6 mm medium graded wearing course as Clause 7.6: bitumen binder	3.97	0.98

		£
068	Blinding wearing course with coated grit as Clause 7.9.	0.94

Q22: COATED MACADAM ROADS AND PAVINGS

LABOURS ON COATED MACADAM

Rates for the following include

For surfacing of any description and any thickness.

Generally:
For surfacing in any number of courses unless otherwise stated.

	Metre	£

Jointing to existing: cutting to line: coating with hot penetration grade bitumen

Item		£
069	single course	0.76
070	two course: trimming back wearing course to break joint: extra material	1.82

Each

071	Working into recessed cover and around frame: any size	3.79
072	Working around obstruction: not exceeding 0.30 m girth	1.14
073	ADD *for each additional 0.30 m of girth*	0.50

REPAIRS TO COATED MACADAM

Specification

Repairing crack:
a. Remove all dust and debris by scraping and brushing;
b. Fill crack with latex rubber bitumen emulsion;
c. Dust surface with cement or fine sand.

Filling pot hole:
a. Cut out to full depth of original layer and trim back wearing course to break joint;
b. Remove all dust and debris by scraping and brushing;

c. Score surfaces and apply tack coat to bottom and sides;
d. Fill with new material to match existing;
e. Compact thoroughly so that patch conforms to existing surface and will not be further compacted by traffic;
f. Blind with coated grit where required to match existing surface.

Note

Filling pot holes exceeding 1 m².
Pay for at the Rates for new work.

	Metre	£
074	Repairing crack: not exceeding 10 mm wide.	3.44

	1	2	3	4
	Not exceeding 0.10 m²	0.10 to 0.25 m²	0.25 to 0.50 m²	0.50 to 1.00 m²
Each	£	£	£	£
Filling pot hole: any thickness				
075 base course	3.15	5.99	10.10	17.37
076 wearing course	2.59	4.22	6.17	8.95

Q22: COATED MACADAM ROADS AND PAVINGS

ROAD AND PAVING MARKING

Specification

Thermoplastic road marking material: to BS 3262 and manufactured by a BSI Kitemark Licensee.

Glass beads: to BS 6088, Class A.

Application of thermoplastic road markings:
apply in following thicknesses:
a. synthetic hydrocarbon resin bound materials:
   1. screed lines: 2 to 5 mm;
   2. sprayed lines other than yellow: 1.5 mm;
   3. sprayed yellow edge lines: 0.8 mm.
b. gum or wood resin bound materials:
   1. screed lines: 3 to 5 mm;
   2. sprayed lines other than yellow: 2 mm;
   3. sprayed yellow edge lines: 2 to 3 mm.

Method of measurement

Markings:
Measure net area.

Rates for the following include

Generally:
For straight or curved work.

For work on new or old surfacing or paving of any description.

For tack coat where required.

For white or yellow colour.

		1	2	3	4
		New	Previously painted	Removing or obliterating existing markings	
				removing by approved method: making good road surface	painting over with black chlorinated rubber paint
Item Q22	Metre	£	£	£	£
	Thermoplastic marking				
	line				
077	not exceeding 300 mm wide	9.58	9.12	2.91	3.37
078	letter, numeral or symbol	9.81	9.35	3.48	3.83
079	ADD for incorporating glass beads as 20% of the total mix mass	1.37	1.37	-	-

Q23: GRAVEL AND HOGGIN PAVINGS

GENERALLY

Specification

Hard binding gravel: 20 mm maximum size, containing a preponderance of angular material free from an excess of clay and sufficient grit to enable adequate compaction by rolling.

Clinker: approved, well-graded clinker, 40 mm maximum size, free from deleterious substances and excess dust.

Fine hoggin: a combination of naturally occurring gravel, sand and clay with a minimum of 85 per cent by weight passing a 10 mm BS sieve.

Spreading and compacting paving: evenly spread and compact by a 1.5 tonne minimum weight roller to required compacted thickness and levels.

Edging and pegs: sawn softwood, preservative treated with creosote. Nail edging to driven pegs with galvanised nails.

Method of measurement

Generally:
Measure area in contact with base. Make no deduction for voids not exceeding 0.50 m².

Measure the compacted thickness.

Rates for the following include

Generally:
For working over and around obstructions.

Item Q23	Square Metre	1 Gravel £	2 Clinker £	3 Hoggin £
	Paving: 50 mm thick			
080	level and to falls only	3.89	2.94	3.75
081	to falls and crossfalls and to slopes not exceeding 15° from horizontal	4.22	3.26	4.07
082	ADD *for each additional 25 mm of thickness*	1.38	0.90	1.31
	ADD where in repairs			
083	not exceeding 1 m²	0.14	0.14	0.14
084	1 to 5 m²	0.07	0.07	0.07

Q23: GRAVEL AND HOGGIN PAVINGS

STONE FILLED FIREBREAKS

Specification

Broken or crushed stone chippings:
Obtain from an approved supplier.

Weedkiller: as ordered and applied strictly in accordance with the directions in Section Q30.

Notes

Supplying weedkiller:
Pay for separately

Edgings:
Pay for at the appropriate rates in Section Q10.

Rates for the following include

Generally:
For forming against buildings, fences or the like.

For disposing surplus excavated material.

Item Q23	Metre	£
	Excavating trench for firebreak 150 mm deep: trimming edges to a straight and even line: filling with stone chippings: raking surface level: applying weedkiller	
085	500 mm wide	6.33
086	1000 mm wide	11.04

WEED FREE BASE FOR COILED BARBED OR RAZOR WIRE

Specification

Gravel:
Obtain from an approved supplier.

Weedkiller: as ordered and applied strictly in accordance with the directions in Section Q30.

Notes

Supplying weedkiller:
Pay for separately

Edgings:
Pay for at the appropriate rates in Section Q10.

Rates for the following include

Generally:
For disposing surplus excavated material.

	Metre	£
	Excavating trench 225 mm deep: trimming edges to a straight or curved line: filling with gravel: raking surface level: applying weedkiller	
087	1750 mm wide	22.45
088	2000 mm wide	25.60

Q23: GRAVEL AND HOGGIN PAVINGS

COCKLESHELL PAVING

Specification

Cockleshells:
Approximately 25 mm diameter. Obtain from an approved supplier.

Spread evenly and lightly rake over to give an even finished surface.

Method of measurement

Generally:
Measure area in contact with base.

Make no deduction for voids not exceeding 0.50 m²

Measure the thickness as laid.

Rates for the following include

Generally:
For working over and around obstructions.

Item Q23	Square Metre	£
089	Paving: 50 mm thick: level and to falls only	2.80
090	ADD for each additional 25 mm of thickness	1.16
091	ADD where to falls and crossfalls not exceeding 15° from horizontal	0.06
	ADD where in repairs	
092	not exceeding 1 m²	0.12
093	1 to 5 m²	0.06

TIMBER EDGINGS AND PEGS

Specification

Sawn softwood edgings and pegs:
Sawn softwood board, preservative treated with creosote.

Cleft softwood edgings and pegs:
Softwood logs minimum 125 mm or 150 mm diameter, as ordered, cleft to half round profile, stripped of bark and pressure preservative treated. Pegs of matching profile with slightly chamfered top.

Nail edging to driven pegs with galvanised nails

Rates for the following include

For extra pegs at angles and intersections.

For cutting closely spaced vertical grooves in the back of curved boards to achieve smooth flowing lines.

Item Q23	Metre	£
	Edging: 50 x 50 mm pegs with pointed ends: at 1000 mm centres	
094	25 x 100 mm: 300 mm long pegs	4.94
095	25 x 150 mm: 300 mm long pegs	6.34
096	38 x 100 mm: 300 mm long pegs	5.78
097	38 x 150 mm: 300 mm long pegs	7.32
098	50 x 200 mm: 450 mm long pegs	8.57
099	50 x 300 mm: 450 mm long pegs	11.09
	Edging: two logs on edge high: 600 mm long pegs with pointed ends at 1200 mm centres	
100	250 mm high	8.06
101	300 mm high	9.34

Q25: SLAB, BRICK AND COBBLE PAVING

GENERALLY

Specification

Cement: to BS 12 or BS 146 and manufactured by a BSI Registered Firm.

Sand for mortar: to BS 1200 Table 1.

Mortar mix: cement and sand, 1:3 by volume.

Grout: ready mixed lime and sand, 1:3 by volume: to BS 4721, Section 2.

Sand for bedding: clean, sharp, natural silica sand containing not more than 3 per cent by weight passing a 63 micron BS sieve and not more than 10 per cent by weight retained on a 5 mm BS sieve.

Method of measurement

Generally:
Measure area of exposed face. Make no deduction for voids not exceeding 0.50 m².

Rates for the following include

Generally:
For cutting.

Fair joint to flush edge of existing paving:
For preparing edge of existing.

PRECAST CONCRETE AND STONE FLAGS

Specification

Concrete paving flags: hydraulically pressed concrete to BS 7263: Part 1, natural colour. Standard sizes as ordered.

Natural stone paving flags:
a. Stone: hard sound Yorkshire or Caithness or suitable local stone of equal quality. Prepare stone for laying on natural bed with surfaces out of winding;
b. Sizes as ordered;
c. Finish:
   1. Yorkshire and similar stones: sawn with sawn edges;
   2. Caithness and similar stones: self - faced with all irregularities dressed off: edges carefully squared.

Mortar bed: not less than 25 mm thick.

Sand bed: not less than 40 mm thick.

Lay flags to an even surface, well pressed into bed in parallel courses to break joints by minimum of 150 mm.

Joints and jointing:
a. joints to be even and approximately 10 mm wide;
b. work grout well into joints;
c. clean off surplus grout from surface of slabs.

Course and match flags with existing pavings.

Q25: SLAB, BRICK AND COBBLE PAVING

PRECAST CONCRETE AND STONE FLAGS - *continued*

		1	2	3	4	5	6	7	8
		Precast concrete				Stone			
		Supplying and laying		Laying only		Supplying and laying		Laying only	
		Thickness							
Item		50 mm	63 mm	50 mm	63 mm	50 mm	75 mm	50 mm	75 mm
Q25	*Square Metre*	£	£	£	£	£	£	£	£
	Paving: regular rectangular sizes: level and to falls only: grouting joints								
102	bedding on sand	17.12	20.06	9.23	10.04	93.74	119.66	9.56	13.27
103	bedding on mortar	18.57	21.51	10.68	11.49	95.19	121.10	11.00	14.72
	Paving: random rectangular sizes: level and to falls only: grouting joints								
104	bedding on sand	-	-	-	-	91.63	117.30	11.66	15.21
105	bedding on mortar	-	-	-	-	93.08	118.75	13.11	16.66
106	ADD where to falls and crossfalls and to slopes not exceeding 15° from horizontal	4.85	5.66	4.85	5.66	6.47	8.89	6.47	8.89
	ADD where in repairs								
107	not exceeding 1 m²	7.28	8.89	7.28	8.89	8.89	11.32	8.89	11.32
108	1 to 5 m²	3.64	4.45	3.64	4.45	4.45	5.66	4.45	5.66
	Metre								
	Jointing to existing								
109	regular size flags	7.36	8.81	3.23	3.56	7.57	9.11	3.56	4.04
110	random size flags	-	-	-	-	6.75	7.28	4.45	4.85

	1	2	3
	Precast concrete or stone		
	Thickness		
Each	50 mm	63 mm	75 mm
	£	£	£
111 Cutting and fitting around obstruction: not exceeding 0.30 m girth	3.07	3.56	4.04
112 ADD *for each additional 0.30 m of girth*	2.75	3.23	3.64

Q25: SLAB, BRICK AND COBBLE PAVING

PEDESTRIAN DETERENT PAVING

Specification

Paviors: precast concrete:
a. Pyramid pattern with smooth grey finish: size
   600 x 600 x 75 mm thick; or
b. patterned to give appearance of natural
   quarried granite setts: colour black: size
   600 x 600 x 65 mm thick.

Mortar bed: not less than 25 mm thick.

Sand bed: not less than 40 mm thick.

Joints and jointing:
a. joints to be even and approximately 3 to 4 mm
   wide;
b. work grout well into joints;
c. clean off surplus grout from surface of slabs.

Item Q25	Square Metre	1 Pyramid pattern Supplying and laying £	2 Laying only £	3 Granite sett pattern Supplying and laying £	4 Laying only £
	Paving: level and to falls only: grouting joints				
113	bedding on sand	49.88	5.45	49.88	5.45
114	bedding on mortar	50.94	6.50	50.94	6.50
115	ADD where to falls and crossfalls and to slopes not exceeding 15° from horizontal	8.11	8.11	8.11	8.11
	ADD where in repairs				
116	not exceeding 1 m²	8.57	8.57	8.57	8.57
117	1 to 5 m²	4.29	4.29	4.29	4.29
	Metre				
118	Jointing to existing	9.49	5.25	9.49	5.25

Item Q25	Each	1 Pyramid pattern £	2 Granite sett pattern £
119	Cutting and fitting around obstruction: not exceeding 0.30 m girth	3.56	3.56
120	ADD *for each additional 0.30 m of girth*	2.67	2.67

TACTILE PAVING

Specification

Tactile paving: precast concrete: colour red: top finished with 25 mm diameter domes, 6 mm high.

Mortar bed: not less than 25 mm thick.

Sand bed: not less than 40 mm thick.

Lay slabs to an even surface, and to a set pattern as ordered, well pressed into bed in parallel courses.

Joints and jointing:
a. joints to be even and close fitting;
b. work grout well into joints;
c. clean off surplus grout from surface of slabs.

Course and match flags with existing pavings.

		1	2	3	4
		Slab size			
		400 x 400 mm		450 x 450 mm	
Item		Supplying and laying	Laying only	Supplying and laying	Laying only
Q25	*Square Metre*	£	£	£	£
	Paving: 50 mm thick: level and to falls only: grouting joints				
121	bedding on sand	26.81	5.45	24.71	5.45
122	bedding on mortar	27.86	6.50	25.76	6.50
123	ADD where to falls and crossfalls and to slopes not exceeding 15° from horizontal				
	ADD where in repairs				
124	not exceeding 1 m²	8.57	8.57	8.57	8.57
125	1 to 5 m²	4.29	4.29	4.29	4.29
	Metre				
126	Jointing to existing	7.29	5.25	7.09	5.25

	Each	£
127	Cutting and fitting around obstruction: not exceeding 0.30 m girth	3.56
128	ADD *for each additional 0.30 m of girth*	2.67

Q25: SLAB, BRICK AND COBBLE PAVING

GRANITE SETTS

Specification

Setts: to BS 435:
a. size: 125 mm deep: any width: any length;
b. finish: square hammer dressed.

Lay setts on 50 mm bed of mortar with 12 mm joints and grout.

Rates for the following include

Granite sett paving in fan-shaped pattern in concentric arcs:
For all half setts to achieve pattern.

Item Q25	Square Metre	1 Supplying and laying £	2 Laying only £
	Paving: level and to falls only		
129	in parallel courses with joints alternately broken and touching	64.30	21.32
130	in fan-shaped pattern in concentric arcs	74.33	31.34
131	ADD where to falls and crossfalls and to slopes not exceeding 15° from horizontal	3.13	3.13
	ADD where in repairs		
132	not exceeding 1 m²	18.60	18.60
133	1 to 5 m²	10.19	10.19
	Metre		
134	Jointing to existing	2.51	2.51

	Each	£
135	Cutting and fitting around obstruction: not exceeding 0.30 m girth	5.34
136	ADD *for each additional 0.30 m of girth*	3.12

COBBLESTONES

Specification

Cobbles: selected hard water-smoothed stones free from deleterious substances and in the size range 50 to 75 mm.

Hoggin base: compacted and levelled fine hoggin not less than 75 mm thick.

Lean concrete base: as specified in Section Q21 not less than 75 mm thick.

Bedding cobbles: bed endwise shoulder to shoulder on base.

Laying cobbles: lay to pattern ordered. Hammer cobbles in by hand to a depth of 60 per cent of their length so that tops are level and to a uniform finish.

Joints and jointing: sprinkle a dry mix of mortar over cobbles to form a 5 mm skin over exposed base. Brush with soft brush to expose tops of cobbles to required amount and sprinkle water to set.

Item Q25	*Square Metre*	1 Supplying and laying £	2 Laying only £
	Paving: level and to falls only		
137	hoggin base	63.34	40.51
138	lean concrete base	65.94	43.12
139	ADD where to falls and crossfalls and to slopes not exceeding 15° from horizontal	3.13	3.13
	ADD where in repairs		
140	not exceeding 1 m²	29.52	29.52
141	1 to 5 m²	16.99	16.99
	Metre		
142	Jointing to existing	3.76	3.76

	Each	£
143	Cutting and fitting around obstruction: not exceeding 0.30 m girth	4.45
144	ADD *for each additional 0.30 m of girth*	2.67

Q25: SLAB, BRICK AND COBBLE PAVING

PRECAST CONCRETE BLOCK PAVIORS

Specification

Block paviors and mitre blocks: manufactured in accordance with BS 6717 Part 1: chamfered on top edges: manufacturer's standard colours
a. paviors: size 200 x 100 mm.
b. mitre blocks: triangular: size 200 x 191 mm overall.

Bed paviors and mitre blocks on sand minimum 50 mm thick.

Pattern: lay to a regular stretcher bond pattern aligned with main margins or to a regular herringbone pattern with mitre block margins.

Joints: close fitting with sand well brushed in.

Rates for the following include

Generally:
For margins.

Item Q25	*Square Metre*	1 Supplying and laying Thickness 65 mm £	2 80 mm £	3 100 mm £	4 Laying only 65 mm £	5 80 mm £	6 100 mm £
	Paving: level and to falls only						
145	stretcher bond pattern	29.18	32.56	36.25	19.93	22.36	24.78
146	herringbone pattern	32.42	35.79	39.48	23.17	25.59	28.02
147	ADD where to falls and crossfalls and to slopes not exceeding 15° from horizontal	3.13	3.13	3.13	3.13	3.13	3.13
	ADD where in repairs						
148	not exceeding 1 m²	17.55	19.25	20.95	17.55	19.25	20.95
149	1 to 5 m²	10.03	11.28	12.54	10.03	11.28	12.54
	Metre						
150	Jointing to existing	3.35	3.88	4.44	2.51	2.95	3.40

	Each	1 Thickness 65 mm £	2 80 mm £	3 100 mm £
151	Cutting and fitting around obstruction: not exceeding 0.30 m girth	2.67	3.12	3.56
152	ADD *for each additional 0.30 m of girth*	1.56	2.00	2.45

Q25: SLAB, BRICK AND COBBLE PAVING

LAYING ONLY BRICK PAVING

Specification

Bed: bricks on mortar not less than 20 mm thick.

Pattern: lay to a regular stretcher bond pattern aligned with main margins or to a regular herringbone pattern, neatly splay cut at margins.

Joints: make joints approximately 10 mm wide and fill with bedding mortar to a flush surface.

Notes

Calculate the number of bricks from the following Table:

Number of bricks per square metre including waste			
	Thickness		
Laid	35 or 50 mm	65 or 67 mm	73 mm
Flat	40	40	40
On edge	-	62	56

Rates for the following include

Generally:
For everything *except* the cost of bricks.

For laying new or old bricks of any of the following types:
a. Clay facing bricks or engineering bricks Class A or B to BS 3921; standard format work size 215 x 102.5 x 65 mm;
b. Calcium silicate facing bricks to BS 187; work size 215 x 102.5 x 65 mm;
c. Approved facing or engineering bricks as ordered; nominal size 219 x 105 x 67 or 73 mm;
d. Clay pavior bricks to BS 6677: Part 1; standard format work size 215 x 105 x 35 or 50 mm.

For plain border, one brick wide.

Item Q25			1 Clay pavior bricks £	2 Facing or engineering bricks £
	Paving: level and to falls only	*Square Metre*		
	laid flat			
153	stretcher bond pattern		22.41	22.60
154	herringbone pattern		24.92	25.10
	laid on edge			
155	stretcher bond pattern		-	33.59
156	herringbone pattern		-	37.35
157	ADD where to falls and crossfalls and to slopes not exceeding 15° from horizontal		3.23	3.23
	ADD where in repairs			
158	not exceeding 1 m²		18.59	19.40
159	1 to 5 m²		9.30	9.70

Q25: SLAB, BRICK AND COBBLE PAVING

LAYING ONLY BRICK PAVING - *continued*

Item Q25		1 Clay pavior bricks £	2 Facing or engineering bricks £
	Metre		
160	Jointing to existing	1.78	2.10
	Each		
161	Cutting and fitting around obstruction: not exceeding 0.30 m girth	3.23	4.04
162	ADD *for each additional 0.30 m of girth*	1.62	2.02

WORK TO OLD BRICK PAVING

	Square Metre	£
	Raking out decayed joints not less than 10 mm deep: repointing with a neat flush joint in mortar	
163	bricks laid flat	6.62
164	bricks laid on edge	9.26
	Metre	
165	Raking out detached joint: 10 mm deep: repointing with a neat flush joint in mortar	0.82

PERFORATED UNITS FOR PROTECTED GRASS PAVING

Specification

Precast concrete perforated blocks: 406 x 406 x 103 mm deep blocks suitable for traffic up to 3 tonnes.

Plastic perforated formers: 600 x 600 x 100 mm deep formers for in situ concrete suitable for traffic up to 10 tonnes.

Sand blinding: 10 to 20 mm thick.

Concrete: 30 N/mm² : 10 mm maximum size aggregate.

Reinforcement: mesh to BS 4483 Ref 193 weighing 3.02 kg/m².

Expansion joints: 25 x 100 mm wrought softwood at 10 m centres.

Soil filling: selected topsoil brushed into perforations.

Grass seed: selected grass seed as ordered.

Laying: lay blocks fully interconnected and to an even surface.

Note

Supplying grass seed:
Pay for separately.

Q25: SLAB, BRICK AND COBBLE PAVING

PERFORATED UNITS FOR PROTECTED GRASS PAVING - *continued*

Rates for the following include

Generally:
For laying blocks or formers on sand bed.

For burning out tops of plastic formers after 48 hours.

For brushing topsoil into perforations.

for sowing and raking grass seed.

Item Q25	Square Metre	£
166	Precast concrete perforated blocks: level and to falls only	30.27
167	100 mm thick in situ concrete laid on and worked around plastic formers: reinforcement: brushing surface of concrete: level and to falls only	26.77

TREE GRILLES

Specification

Perforated tree grille slabs: precast concrete: from an approved manufacturer

Kerbs: to match paving: "L" shaped: each 496 x 496 x 50 mm thick x 150 mm high overall, in pairs linked with galvanised staples, to form one complete square enclosure: smooth grey finish.

Sand bed: minimum 25 mm thick.

Lay grille slabs to an even surface well pressed into bed in parallel courses.

Joints and jointing:
a. close jointed and run sand into joint.
b. brush surplus sand from grilles.

	Each	£
	Tree grille slab	
168	496 x 496 x 50 mm thick: smooth grey finish	10.14
169	ADD where with exposed aggregate	2.54
170	600 x 300 50 mm thick: smooth grey or white finish	11.84
171	Kerb: pair to form square enclosure: 2000 mm girth overall	22.68

Q26: SPECIAL SURFACINGS/PAVINGS FOR SPORT

GENERALLY

Note

*Provision, maintenance and repairs and marking
out of Non-Porous Surfaces:*
Pay for at the Rates in Sections Q20, Q21, Q23
and Q25.

POROUS WATER-BOUND SURFACES

Specification

Shale or crushed rock:
Obtain from an approved manufacturer.

Lay 50 mm thick using hand implements, self
propelled or pedestrian operated self-powered
equipment.

Compact with a 2/3 tonne smooth dead-weight
roller, spray with water and roll again to achieve
approved degree of compaction and to produce
an approved playing surface.

Notes

*Excavating, filling and surface treatment of
formation:*
Pay for at the Rates in Section D20.

Supplying plastic marking tape and fixing pins:
Pay for separately.

Method of Measurement

New shale or crushed rock surfacing:
Measure area in contact with base.

Make no deduction for voids not exceeding
0.50 m²

Measure the compacted thickness.

Rates for the following include

Setting out lines:
For temporary guide lines.

For checking dimensions/layouts.

Fixing or refixing marking tape:
For laying to straight or curved lines with neatly
formed joints.

For fixing with pins.

For rolling flush to surrounding levels.

Brushing:
For removing extraneous material from marking
tapes.

POROUS WATER-BOUND SURFACES - *continued*

Item Q26	*100 Square Metres*	£
172	New shale or crushed rock surfacing: 52 mm thick: rolling: watering: re-rolling	533.48
173	Scarifying to a depth of 25 mm: disposing of arisings: scarifying formation: spreading shale or crushed rock surfacing material 25 mm thick: grading with reverse edge of a "Trulute" or other approved implement: watering: dragging mat over surface: brushing: rolling to produce an approved playing surface	281.88
174	Scarifying to a depth of 25 mm: removing and disposing of weeds or the like: levelling using the cutting edge of a "Trulute" or other approved implement: watering: dragging mat over surface: brushing: rolling to produce an approved playing surface	13.17
175	Sweeping up debris: removing and disposing arisings	3.63
176	Levelling out footprints or the like: watering: dragging mat over surface: brushing: rolling to produce an approved playing surface	5.35

	Metre	
177	Taking up marking tape fixed with pins: setting aside for re-use	0.11
178	Refixing displaced marking tape	0.11
179	Fixing marking tape	0.23
180	Setting out lines to sports areas: fixing marking tape	0.35

PREPARING SYNTHETIC SURFACED CRICKET PITCH

Note	Pay for at the appropriate Rates in Section Q35.

Adjacent grass:
Cut a strip 3m wide adjacent to the pitch using a
pedestrian operated self-powered mower fitter
with a grass box and trim edge at junction with
pitch.

	Each - per pitch	£
181	Commencing on the day before the match, sweeping surface of pitch: disposing arising. On the morning of the day of the match, rolling using hand roller or pedestrian operated self-powered roller to an approved standard of firmness: re-making creases with external quality emulsion paint.	11.85
182	Watering surface of pitch using hand held hosepipe fitted with coarse rose, without overlapping on to adjacent grass: watering clay in stump boxes.	8.43

RENOVATING SYNTHETIC SURFACED CRICKET PITCH

Item Q26	*Each - per pitch*	£

183 Removing synthetic mat, underlay and shock pads: scarifying hard porous water-bound base using the cutting edge of a 'Trulute' or other approved implement: filling depressions with hard porous water-bound material of similar type and quality to existing: watering: raking and rolling to produce an approved level surface: refixing underlay and shock pads, excavating base as necessary beneath the shock pads to produce a true and level base for the mat: refixing mat with 100 mm galvanised nails or nylon pins pulled taut to provide an approved playing surface. 210.23

Each - per patch

184 Repairing minor damage to synthetic mat by spreading contact adhesive over damage, building up in layers until flush with surrounding area: sprinkling rovings of mat material over adhesive whilst still tacky: touching up with external quality emulsion paint to match existing: removing and disposing arisings. 10.64

185 Repairing major damage to synthetic mat by cutting out rectangular patch containing the damage: applying 100 mm wide plastic adhesive tape to underside around edge of hole, leaving 50 mm wide strip exposed: patching by accurately fitting matching material, firmly fixed at edges to adhesive tape: sealing joint with contact adhesive: sprinkling rovings of mat material over adhesive whilst still tacky: touching up with external quality emulsion paint to match existing: removing and disposing arisings 38.02

RUBBER MATS AND TILES

Specification

Tiles:
Impact-absorbing, slip resistant, and non-abrasive rubber mats or tiles to BS 5696: Part 3.

Critical fall height to be tested to BS 7188.

Obtain from an approved manufacturer and lay in accordance with their instructions.

Primer/adhesive:
Obtain from tile manufacturer.

Rates for the following include

Generally:
For cleaning off surplus adhesive from face of tiling.

For all necessary cutting.

Fair joint to flush edge of existing paving:
For preparing edge of existing paving.

RUBBER MATS AND TILES - *continued*

		1	2	3	4
		Critical Fall Height			
		0.70 m	1.20 m	1.70 m	2.50 m
		Overall thickness			
Item		22 mm	43 mm	60 mm	100 mm
Q26	*Square Metre*	£	£	£	£
	Surfacing: solid: level and to falls only: black: tile size				
186	500 x 500 mm	67.14	73.51	78.29	86.25
187	600 x 600 mm	59.18	65.55	70.32	78.29
188	750 x 750 mm	52.81	55.99	62.36	70.32
189	1000 x 1000 mm	46.44	49.62	52.81	59.18
	ADD where				
190	coloured tiles	4.80	4.80	4.80	7.99
191	to falls and to crossfalls and to slopes not exceeding 15° from horizontal	1.46	1.46	1.46	1.46
	in repairs				
192	not exceeding 1 m²	8.89	12.13	15.36	19.40
193	1 to 5 m²	4.45	6.06	7.68	9.70
	Tapered edge tile				
194	100 mm wide	9.80	-	-	-
195	200 mm wide	-	13.42	-	-
196	Fair joint to flush edge of existing paving	1.46	2.22	2.98	3.74
197	Straight kerb edge tiles: 100 mm wide	-	-	14.25	19.82
198	Extra over for angle	-	-	13.19	18.06
199	Cutting and fitting around obstructions not exceeding 0.30 m of girth	0.73	1.15	1.57	1.99
200	ADD *for each additional 0.30 m of girth*	0.44	0.66	0.89	1.12

Q26: SPECIAL SURFACINGS/PAVINGS FOR SPORT

BARK/WOOD PAVINGS AND COVERINGS

Specification

Bark/wood products:
Obtain from an approved supplier.

Lay in accordance with supplier's recommendations.

Bark chips to paths:
Clean conifer or hardwood chips: particle size 5 to 30 mm.

Wood fibre to paths:
Clean pulverised softwood with a low bark content: particle size not exceeding 30 mm.

Method of measurement

Generally:
Measure area in contact with base.

Make no deduction for voids not exceeding 0.50 m²

Measure the thickness as laid.

Rates for the following include

Generally:
For working over and around obstructions.

Item Q26	Square Metre	1	2	3	4	5	6	7	8
		Conifer				Hardwood			
		Thickness							
		100 mm	150 mm	200 mm	250 mm	100 mm	150 mm	200 mm	250 mm
		£	£	£	£	£	£	£	£
201	Bark chips to path: level and to falls only	3.85	5.58	7.30	9.02	4.50	6.54	8.59	10.63
202	ADD where to falls and crossfalls and to slopes not exceeding 15° from horizontal	0.09	0.12	0.15	0.19	0.09	0.12	0.15	0.19
	ADD where in repairs								
203	not exceeding 1 m²	0.12	0.15	0.20	0.25	0.12	0.15	0.20	0.25
204	1 to 5 m²	0.06	0.08	0.09	0.13	0.06	0.08	0.09	0.13

Item		1	2	3	4	5
		Thickness				
		50 mm	100 mm	150 mm	200 mm	250 mm
		£	£	£	£	£
205	Wood-fibre to path: level and to falls only	2.70	4.20	6.09	7.99	9.89
206	ADD where to falls and crossfalls and to slopes not exceeding 15° from horizontal	0.06	0.09	0.12	0.15	0.19
	ADD where in repairs					
207	not exceeding 1 m²	0.08	0.12	0.15	0.20	0.25
208	1 to 5 m²	0.05	0.06	0.08	0.09	0.13

SAFETY SURFACINGS FOR PLAY AREAS

Specification

Bark/wood products:
Obtain from an approved supplier.

Free from dust and fines, angular fragments and sharp pieces.

Lay in accordance with supplier's recommendations.

Bark to play areas:
Clean conifer bark with wood content less than 2.5%: nominal particle size range 10 to 50 mm.

Wood chips to play areas:
Clean conifer chips with wood content greater than 2.5%: nominal particle size range 5 to 50 mm.

Sand to play areas:
Clean washed silica sand of smooth rounded particles, free from artificially crushed material, nominal particle size range 0.25 - 0.45 mm.

Method of measurement

Generally:
Measure area in contact with base.

Make no deduction for voids not exceeding 0.50 m²

Measure the thickness as laid.

Rates for the following include

Generally:
For working over and around obstructions.

Item Q26	Square Metre	1 Thickness 50 mm £	2 100 mm £	3 150 mm £	4 200 mm £	5 250 mm £	6 300 mm £
209	Bark to play area: level and to falls only	4.80	7.99	11.18	14.37	17.55	20.74
210	Woodchips to play area: level and to falls only	4.07	6.52	8.98	11.43	13.88	16.34
211	ADD where to falls and crossfalls and to slopes not exceeding 15° from horizontal	0.06	0.09	0.12	0.15	0.19	0.23
	ADD where in repairs						
212	not exceeding 1 m²	0.08	0.12	0.15	0.20	0.25	0.29
213	1 to 5 m²	0.05	0.06	0.08	0.09	0.13	0.15
214	Sand to play area: level and to falls only	6.69	11.76	16.83	21.91	26.98	32.05
215	ADD where to falls and crossfalls and to slopes not exceeding 15° from horizontal	0.09	0.14	0.18	0.23	0.28	0.35
	ADD where in repairs						
216	not exceeding 1 m²	0.12	0.18	0.23	0.30	0.37	0.44
217	1 to 5 m²	0.07	0.09	0.12	0.14	0.19	0.23

Q30: SEEDING/TURFING

GENERALLY

Specification

Final preparation of the land: carry out with cultivators, harrows and rollers to an approved firmness and grade tilth. When ordered, the final preparation and sowing of grass seed is to be carried out using a combined harrow, tilther and seeder.

Finish of beds for seeding is to:
a. Conform to the levels ordered with the surface free from large stones or the like.

b. Consist of the correct crumb structure to the full working depth with a fine tilth to a depth of 25mm to approval.

Finish of beds for turf: same as that for seeding except that the surface is to be consolidated and finished to a tilth approximately 12mm deep to approval.

APPLYING PESTICIDES/HERBICIDES/WEED KILLERS

Specification

Pesticides: comply with all statutory obligations concerning the use of pesticides.

Application of chemicals: all chemicals shall be approved for site requirements. Apply chemicals in accordance with the manufacturer's instructions and relevant Codes of Practice.

Clean equipment after use with each different type of material. Pesticides must not be applied with equipment used for fertilisers.

Application by spraying: do not spray when rain is expected or in windy conditions, which could cause drifting that would damage nearby vegetation. Do not use volatile pesticides in hot weather when vapour drift might damage susceptible plants and green house crops. Ensure that watercourses and wildlife are not damaged by leaching of chemicals. Take every precaution to ensure that spraying is confined to the area to be treated.

Wear required protective clothing when handling concentrates, washing off splashes from the skin immediately. Wash hands before meals and after work.

Keep containers tightly closed and in a safe place.

Notes

Generally:
The Contractor shall make good at his own expense any damage caused as a result of his negligence in the use of pesticides.

Cultivation: when ordered, pay for at the appropriate Rates in the Section D20.

Supplying materials:
Pay for separately.

Rates for the following include

Generally:
For any necessary mixing with water.

Spreading and applying:
For spreading and applying at the coverage rates ordered.

Applying by spraying:
For wettable powder or liquid chemicals.

Item		Hectare	£
Q30			
	Applying by		
001	vehicle-mounted or trailer boom spraying equipment: selective weedkiller, growth regulator or pesticide		7.52

Q30: SEEDING/TURFING

APPLYING PESTICIDES/HERBICIDES/WEED KILLERS - *continued*

Item Q30		£
	100 Square Metres	
	Applying by	
	knapsack or hand sprayer	
002	over grassed area or hardstanding: selective or total weedkiller, growth regulator, mosskiller or fungicide	1.05
	Square Metres	
003	over plants in shrub bed or the like (measure ground area): selective weedkiller, fungicide or pesticide	0.04
	100 Metres	
004	on construction or other joint in paving, at fence line, kerb edge or at base of building: strip not exceeding 300 mm wide: total weedkiller	0.60
	Square Metres	
005	weed-wipe: over grassed area, hardstanding or plants in shrub bed: selective or total weedkiller, growth regulator, mosskiller or fungicide	0.09
	Hectare	
	Spreading	
	granular or pelleted pesticide: over grassed area: by	
006	vehicle-mounted mechanical spreader	7.99
	100 Square Metres	
007	mechanical hand spreader	0.24
	granular selective or total weedkiller: by mechanical hand spreader	
008	over ground	0.24
	100 Metres	
009	at fence line, kerb or at base of building: strip not exceeding 300 mm wide	0.17

CULTIVATING TOPSOIL

Note

Cultivation: when ordered, pay for at the appropriate Rates in the Section D20.

Q30: SEEDING/TURFING

STONE REMOVAL

Note

Stone removal: when ordered, pay for at the appropriate Rates in the Section D20.

FINE GRADING TOPSOIL

Specification

Timing: when topsoil is reasonably dry and workable, grade to smooth, flowing contours, with falls for adequate drainage, removing all minor hollows and ridges.

Machine grading:
Finish the work so that:
a. Final levels are to the standard of accuracy ordered.
b. Work marries in to adjoining arable or grass land after settlement.
c. Finished levels after settlement are 35 mm above adjoining runways, roads, paving, kerbs, manholes and other hard surfaces.
d. The finished surface is uniformly smooth and free of sudden changes of levels, within tolerances ordered and sufficiently even to allow the range of equipment used in its main--tenance to work easily at normal operating speeds without damage to the equipment or the turf.

Hand grading:
Finish the work so that:
a. Work marries in to adjoining surfaces after settlement.
b. Finished levels after settlement are 25 mm above adjoining paving, kerbs, manholes and other hard surfaces.
c. The finished surface consists of a uniformly fine tilth, consolidated by heeling to an even degree.

Equipment:
For large areas use tractor-drawn wheeled blade graders.

For small areas use tractor-mounted blades not exceeding 1.5 m wide or other approved equipment as appropriate.

Note

The items in this Sub-section apply only where the adjustment of existing levels does not involve any increase or decrease exceeding 150 mm.

Item Q30	Hectare	£
	Grading: to general surfaces: level or not exceeding 15° from horizontal	
010	by machine: large area	169.93
	100 Square Metres	
011	by machine: small area	7.49
	ADD where	
012	15 to 30° from horizontal	0.74
013	exceeding 30° from horizontal	1.53
	Square Metres	
014	by hand: small area	0.11

Q30: SEEDING/TURFING

Specification

Generally:
Comply with BS 7370: Part 3.

Notes

Cultivation: when ordered, pay for at the appropriate Rates in Section D20.

Supplying materials:
Pay for separately.

Rates for the following include

Generally:
For any necessary mixing with water.

Spreading and applying:
For spreading and applying at the coverage rates ordered.

Item Q30		*Hectare*	£
	Spreading		
	by vehicle-mounted mechanical spreader - *per tonne per hectare*		
	over ground		
015	sand, ash or the like		14.17
016	loam, compost, peat or sewage sludge		18.03
	over sports pitch or the like		
017	sand, ash or the like		17.90
018	loam or peat		22.67

		100 Square Metres	
	by hand: over lawn - *not exceeding 100 grammes per m²*		
019	sand, ash or the like		0.85
020	loam, peat or compost		0.99

Q30: SEEDING/TURFING

FERTILISERS

Specification

Application of chemicals: apply chemicals in accordance with the manufacturer's instructions and relevant Codes of Practice.

Wear required protective clothing when handling concentrates, washing off splashes from the skin immediately. Wash hands before meals and after work.

Keep containers tightly closed and in a safe place.

Distribution: except on lawns, shrub beds or other small areas, distribute by mechanical spreader. On lawns, shrub beds or other small areas, mark out the area to be dressed to ensure even distribution and distribute by mechanical hand spreader or by hand.

Notes

Generally:
The Contractor shall make good at his own expense any damage caused as a result of his negligence in the use of fertilizers.

Cultivation: when ordered, pay for at the appropriate Rates in the Section D20.

Supplying materials:
Pay for separately.

Rates for the following include

Generally:
For any necessary mixing with water.

Spreading and applying:
For spreading and applying at the coverage rates ordered.

Applying by spraying:
For wettable powder or liquid chemicals.

Item Q30	Hectare	£
	Spreading	
	by vehicle-mounted mechanical spreader: over ground	
	granular or pelleted fertilizer	
021	spinner - *per 250 kg per hectare*	8.12
022	pneumatic - *per 250 kg per hectare*	8.63
023	manure - *per tonne per hectare*	16.49
024	lime - *per tonne per hectare*	3.50

	100 Square Metres	
025	by mechanical hand spreader or by hand: over lawn: granular or pelleted fertilizer or lawn dressing - *per kg per 100 m²*	1.05

	Square Metre	
026	by hand over shrub bed or the like: organic, granular or powdered fertilizer - *per 25 g per m²*	0.10

Q30: SEEDING/TURFING

MESH REINFORCEMENT FOR GRASS AREAS

Specification

Mesh reinforcement: high density polyethylene with securing pegs. Obtain from an approved manufacturer.
a. For foot traffic: 20 mm square mesh with extra strengthening filaments at centre and edges, securing pegs 150 mm long.
b. For vehicle traffic: 27 mm round heavy duty mesh, securing pegs 280 mm long.

Lay and secure with pegs along all edges at maximum 1500 mm centres, drive pegs well into ground so that no projections will interfere with mowing.

Supplying mesh:
Pay for separately.

Note

Cutting grassed areas prior to laying mesh: Pay for at the Rates in Section Q35.

Rates for the following include

Generally
For laps.

For cutting to shape or profile.

For removing fixing pegs when grass is well re-established.

Item Q30	*Square Metre*	1 Foot Traffic £	2 Vehicle Traffic £
	Mesh reinforcement: on grassed area:		
027	on surfaces not exceeding 30° from horizontal	0.35	0.44
028	on surfaces 30° to 50° from horizontal	0.48	0.60

Q30: SEEDING/TURFING

SEEDING AND ROLLING

Specification

Seeds: use named blue label certified seed varieties complying with EC regulations for purity and germination and also complying with the Ministry of Agriculture Fisheries and Food Higher Voluntary Standard.

Certification: supply to PM samples of mixtures as delivered to site or copy of original certificate of germination, purity and composition carried out by an Official Seed Testing Station.

Timing: sow seeds only when weather and soil conditions are approved.

Sowing: spread seed evenly at the specified rate(s) applied in two equal sowings in transverse directions.

Harrowing:
a. On large areas, lightly harrow or rake in and roll and cross roll after seeding using a light--weight roller.
b. On small areas, sow seeds evenly by hand rake in and roll after seeding using a light--weight roller.

Rollers: tractor-trailed general purpose smooth or Cambridge ring type as ordered.

Speed: operate at a speed that will produce the optimum crushing of clods and degree of consolidation ordered but not to exceed 10 km/h.

Small cultivated areas: rolling speed is not to exceed 3 km/h.

By hand: only when ordered for reinstating.

Notes

Harrowing:
Pay for at the appropriate Rates in Section D20.

Supplying grass seeds:
Pay for separately.

Rates for the following include

For sowing at the coverage rates ordered.

Item Q30		£
	Hectare	
029	Sowing approved grass seed at rate directed: using tractor-mounted combined harrow, tilther and seeder - *not exceeding 40 grammes per m²*	41.80
	Sowing grass seed	
030	in two passes using mechanical seed sower	14.01
	100 Square Metres	
031	by hand	2.54
	Hectare	
	Rolling: using	
032	Cambridge roller	9.40
033	flat roller: 3 to 4 tonnes	21.05
	100 Square Metres	
	Rolling small cultivated area: using	
034	pedestrian operated self-powered roller	1.45
035	hand roller	2.35

Q30: SEEDING/TURFING

HYDRAULIC SEEDING

Specification

Remove rubbish and stones exceeding 25 mm in any dimension.

Weed using an appropriate selective herbicide.

Grade to smooth flowing levels and ensure that the roots can penetrate into the substrate, leaving a ribbed or rough textured surface.

Item Q30	Square Metre	£
	Hydraulic seeding: coverage rate	
036	not exceeding 250 g/m²	1.51
037	250 to 500 g/m²	2.26
038	exceeding 500 g/m²	3.60

TURFING

Specification

Turf: to BS 3969 and from an approved source, free from undesirable grasses and weeds, treated with selective herbicide not more than 3 months and not less than 4 weeks before lifting.

Before turf stripping commences cut grass and roll as ordered.

Weather conditions: do not strip or lay turf when weather is exceptionally dry, when surfaces are waterlogged, when persistent cold or drying winds are likely to occur or during frost or snow.

Stripping turf: cut and strip turf with turf float or mechanical stripper to a size of 900 x 300 x 30 mm thick. Roll up remove and stack where directed not exceeding 1 m high. Box to an even thickness of 20 mm where ordered.

Re-lay turf within 7 days of stripping. Ensure that the programme of stripping is co-ordinated with that of re-laying.

Delivery and storage: take all necessary precautions to avoid drying out and deterioration of turf. Arrange supply of turf to avoid excessive stacking. Do not stack to a height of more than 1 m. Use turf which shows any signs of deterioration without delay or lay out on topsoil and keep moist.

Protection: do not drive vehicles or machines over prepared areas. Unload turf outside the area and provide access to the area being turfed by means of planked wheelbarrow runs.

Surface preparation: prepare surface including raking until ground is broken to a fine tilth 25 mm deep and uniformly firmed to finish at the correct levels. Remove all large stones.

Lay turfs:
a. within 18 hours of delivery in spring or summer and within 24 hours of delivery in autumn or winter.
b. working off planks laid on previously laid turf.
c. in consecutive rows in stretcher bond to correct levels working over turf already laid. Use whole turves at edges. Trim to a true line.
d. with closely butted joints and firm by lightly and evenly beating with wooden beaters. Do not stretch turf.
e. commencing on one side facing the unturfed area and working from the newly laid turf.

Banks exceeding 30° from horizontal: lay turves diagonally or horizontally and secure with pointed softwood pegs, 200 mm long x 25 mm square, or galvanised wire pins, bent or hairpin pattern, 200 mm long x 4 mm diameter. Remove all pegs or pins when turf is well established.

Q30: SEEDING/TURFING

TURFING - *continued*

Specification - *continued*

Adjust levels by lifting turves, raking out or infilling with finely sifted topsoil, and re-bedding turves ensuring full contact with the substrate.

Dress surface of newly laid turf with finely sifted topsoil and brush well in to completely fill all joints leaving the surface with an approved level finish.

Cut away turf to a diameter of 1000 mm around individual trees and leave soil exposed.

Water the completed turf immediately after laying, taking care that soil is not washed out of joints. Check by lifting a corner of turf that water has penetrated to the soil below.

Notes

Fertilizing:
When ordered, pay for at the appropriate Rates in the "Fertilisers" sub-section.

Grass cutting:
When ordered, pay for at the appropriate Rates in Section Q35.

Supplying new turves:
Pay for separately.

Item Q30	*Square Metre*	£
	Rolling, stripping, lifting and rolling up turf: transporting a distance not exceeding 100 m: stacking:	
039	by mechanical turf-stripping equipment	0.92
040	by hand	1.34
041	ADD *for each additional 100 m of transporting distance*	0.09
	Taking turf from stack: transporting a distance not exceeding 100 m: laying: dressing: on surface	
042	level or not exceeding 30° from horizontal	0.75
	exceeding 30° from horizontal	
043	not exceeding 2 m high	0.80
044	2 to 5 m high	1.09
045	5 to 10 m high	1.82
046	exceeding 10 m high	2.73
047	ADD *for each additional 100 m of transporting distance*	0.15
048	Boxing and cutting turf to a uniform thickness of 20 mm : removing and depositing surplus material	0.37

Q30: SEEDING/TURFING

REINSTATEMENT OF WORN OR DAMAGED TURF

Specification

Generally: re-turf to BS 7370:Part 3, Clause 12.2, using turf to match the existing in appearance and quality.

Rates for the following include

Generally:
For marking out area to be replaced in multiples of turf sizes.

For lifting old turf using a hand or mechanical turf lifter to a maximum depth of 25 mm.

For lightly forking the area to a depth of 75 mm and removing all stones over 25 mm in any dimension.

For applying a complete fertilizer, as necessary.

For building up the prepared base with soil.

Item Q30	Square Metre	£
049	Lifting damaged or worn turf in grassed area: removing and depositing arisings using wheelbarrows or the like on planked runs as directed: re-turfing: finishing level with surrounding surface after consolidation: top dressing with fine soil rubbed well in using a lute	1.54

PROTECTION

Specification

Protective fencing: protect newly seeded/turfed areas with fencing as ordered. Maintain until grass is well established then remove and reinstate ground.

Note

Protective fencing: when ordered, pay for at the appropriate Rates in Section Q40.

Q30: SEEDING/TURFING

WATERING

Definitions

Hand held watering equipment: hosepipe not exceeding 25 mm bore with spray nozzle for use on small grass or amenity planting areas where the PM decides that the use of unattended equipment is not practicable.

Perforated or trickle hose: for use in shrub beds and herbaceous borders. Lay without kinks.

Single portable rotating or oscillating sprinkler unit: for use on small grass or amenity planting areas.

Portable sprayline unit: oscillating or rain-gun type for use on large areas of grass and for hard porous recreational areas. Use in groups of three or more.

Watering cans: of adequate capacity and fitted with a rose.

Note

Number of hours of watering: rate of application (litres per unit of measurement) as ordered.

Rates for the following include

Generally:
For supplying stand-pipes, hosepipes, fittings, approved spray nozzles, sprinklers and spraylines.

For connecting to water supply and dismantling on completion.

For moving equipment around the site.

For applications either prior to or after planting.

Sprinklers and spraylines:
For erecting and re-siting where necessary.

Watering from bowser:
For collecting water and transporting any distance by towed bowser of any capacity.

Item Q30	Hour	£
	Watering	
	evenly over an area within 100 m of standpipe: using	
050	hand held watering equipment	11.36
051	perforated or trickle hose	2.08
052	single portable rotating or oscillating sprinkler unit	2.83
053	*ADD for each additional or subsequent unit*	0.83
054	group of three portable sprayline units	3.75
055	*ADD for each additional or subsequent unit*	0.87
056	evenly over an area within 25 m of water bowser: using hand held watering equipment	16.54
057	planters, window boxes, pots and hanging baskets using either hand held watering equipment from mains supply or bowser, or using watering cans	16.94
	Where work to specific soil types is ordered: multiply the Rates by the following factors:	
058	Light soils	no adjustment
059	Medium soils	multiply by 1.1
060	Heavy soils	multiply by 1.2

Q31: EXTERNAL PLANTING

GENERALLY

Specification

Standards: carry out the work to approved agricultural and horticultural standards.

Timing: time all stages of work to obtain optimum effect, giving full regard to the season, weather and soil condition.

Cultivate soil to depths stated or as otherwise ordered. Carry out the work using ploughs, disc harrows, rotary cultivators, rigid or spring tined harrows or other equipment as ordered. Produce a coarse friable soil condition to the full working depth suitable for blade grading.

Note

Clearing vegetation: when ordered, pay for at the appropriate Rates in the Section D20.

Subsoiling: when ordered, pay for at the appropriate Rates in the Section D20.

Fine grading: when ordered, pay for at the appropriate Rates in the Section Q30.

Rates for the following include

Generally:
For work executed using equipment mounted on or towed by tractor, unless otherwise stated.

For clearing obstructions to the use of equipment before commencing work.

For disposing roots and all weeds.

For stone picking except where work is paid for at Rates per 100 Square Metres or per Hectare when Items D20.065 to D20.068 shall be paid in addition.

For work on any type of soil.

Cultivating, harrowing and rolling:
For once over the area ordered.

CULTIVATING TOPSOIL

Note

Cultivation: when ordered, pay for at the appropriate Rates in the Section D20.

STONE REMOVAL

Note

Stone removal: when ordered, pay for at the appropriate Rates in the Section D20.

Q31: EXTERNAL PLANTING

PLANTS, SHRUBS, HEDGES AND TREES

GENERALLY

Scope

Work in this Section comprises the planting and maintenance of trees, hedges, shrubs including roses, herbaceous and annual bedding plants and bulbs.

Specification

Nursery stock: comply with BS 3936.

Container-grown plants:
a. do not remove from containers until planting areas have been prepared.
b. ensure minimum damage to roots.
c. remove and dispose of "bio-degradeable containers".

Handle trees and shrubs in accordance with the Joint Council of Landscape Industries "Code of Practice for Plant Handling".

Label all trees and plants in accordance with BS 3936.

Backfilling: if so directed, remove and deposit excavated material and backfill with topsoil from elsewhere on the site.

Transport all materials over grassed areas using wheelbarrows on planked runs.

Notes

Supplying trees, shrubs, plants, bulbs, etc.: Pay for separately.

Supplying mulch, fertilizers and soil ameliorants: Pay for separately.

Cultivation: when ordered, pay for at the appropriate Rates in Section D20.

Backfilling using topsoil from elsewhere on the site: pay for at the appropriate Rates in Section D20.

Rates for the following include

Planting generally:
For planting any item as ordered.

For watering-in.

Stakes, ties and buffer pads:
For supplying and fixing.

Q31: EXTERNAL PLANTING

MULCHING

Specification

Mulch: free of pests, disease, fungus and weeds. Clear all weeds, water soil thoroughly, and mulch the whole surface of planting beds.

Application: apply in thicknesses appropriate to the location and in accordance with good practice.

Item Q31	Each	1 Bed size not exceeding 10 m² £	2 10 m² to 25 m² £	3 25 m² to 50 m² £	4 50 m² to 100 m² £	5 exceeding 100 m² £
	Mulching with approved mulching material:					
061	surface of planting beds	0.65	0.99	1.49	2.78	4.36

		1 Number of trees not exceeding 10 Nr £	2 10 Nr to 25 Nr £	3 25 Nr to 50 Nr £	4 50 Nr to 100 Nr £	5 exceeding 100 Nr £
	around tree: distance in any direction					
062	not exceeding 250 m	0.55	0.45	0.40	0.37	-
063	250 m to 500 m	-	0.55	0.52	0.42	0.26

Q31: EXTERNAL PLANTING

PLANTING HERBACEOUS PLANTS AND BULBS

Specification

Herbaceous perennial plants: evenly space over the allocated area, avoiding straight lines unless otherwise ordered.

Climbing plants: plant 150 mm clear of wall/fence etc. with roots spread outward. Lightly secure branches to support. Retain canes of plants which are too small to reach supports.

After planting: water plants thoroughly immediately after planting, using a fine rose or sprinkler where necessary to avoid damaging plants. Lightly firm soil around plants and fork and/or rake soil, without damaging roots, to a fine tilth with approved gentle cambers and no hollows.

Prepared beds, containers, window boxes and the like

Set out in the order and to the spacings and depths directed.

Plant by excavating holes large enough to accommodate the full spread of the roots and with the best side of each plant to the front. Backfill planting holes and firm around the collars of the plants.

Grouped annual bedding plants: plant edges in lines or curves as appropriate and fill in the centre by planting in a random manner.

Grassed areas

Bulbs, tubers or corms: plant so that the top is at a depth of approximately twice its height with base in contact with bottom of hole. Backfill with finely broken soil and lightly firm to existing ground level.

Scatter bulbs/corms/tubers at random over the allocated area and plant where they fall.

Plant by neatly removing a plug of turf not exceeding 150 mm deep using a trowel or auger. Replace after planting and firm down.

Item Q31	Per 100	1	2	3
		Number of plants per m²		
		not exceeding 10 Nr	10 Nr 20 Nr	exceeding 20 Nr
		£	£	£
	Planting herbaceous perennials or annual bedding plants, bulbs, tuberous plants or corms in			
064	prepared beds	9.60	7.45	6.60
065	grassed areas	11.71	9.09	8.05

Square Metres

Item	Planting in prepared bed	1	2	3
066	herbaceous perennials	1.82	1.36	1.09

Item	Per 100	1	2	3	4	5
		Number of plants per container				
		not exceeding 5 Nr	5 Nr 10 Nr	10 Nr to 20 Nr	20 Nr to 50 Nr	exceeding 50 Nr
		£	£	£	£	£
067	containers, window boxes and the like	8.00	7.00	6.00	5.00	4.00
068	ADD where exceeding 4.50 m above ground level	17.00	16.00	15.00	-	-

---

PLANTING SHRUBS AND HEDGES

Specification

Planting in pits and trenches: excavate pits and trenches sufficiently wide and deep to accomm--odate the full spread of roots and to the following minimum sizes:

Hedge plants:
single row: 500 x 300 mm deep
double row: 750 x 300 mm deep

Backfill with selected excavated material to level of surrounding ground and carefully work it among the roots; firm around the plants so that they are securely anchored and with the collars at surface level.

Shrub planting pits: excavate not more than 2 days before planting and retain topsoil for re-use where specified. Break up bottoms of pits.

Hedges: as specified, consistent in species, cultivar and clone to ensure a uniform hedge. Plant shrubs in trenches large enough to take full spread of roots. Set out plants evenly as scheduled.

After planting: water plants thoroughly immediately, using a fine rose or sprinkler where necessary to avoid damaging plants. Lightly firm soil around plants and fork and/or rake soil, without damaging roots, to a fine tilth with approved gentle cambers and no hollows.

Mulching planting beds: clear all weeds, water soil thoroughly, and mulch the whole surface of planting beds.

	1	2	3
	Number of shrubs		
	not exceeding 1 Nr	2 Nr to 5 Nr	exceeding 5 Nr
Item **Q31** *Each*	£	£	£

Forming planting hole: planting in prepared bed: containerised shrub

Item		1	2	3
069	not exceeding 600 mm high	0.73	0.55	0.36
070	600 mm to 1.20 m high	1.09	0.82	0.55

	1	2
	Single row	Double row
Metre	£	£

Excavating trench: planting hedge plants: attaching stakes and ties: transplants

at 200 mm centres

Item		1	2
071	not exceeding 600 mm high	1.45	2.54
072	600 to 1200 mm high	1.82	3.09

at 300 mm centres

Item		1	2
073	not exceeding 600 mm high	1.15	1.95
074	600 to 1200 mm high	1.62	2.78

Q31: EXTERNAL PLANTING

PLANTING NURSERY STOCK AND SEMI-MATURE TREES

Specification

Trees generally: materially undamaged, sturdy, healthy, vigorous, of good shape and without elongated shoots.

Free from pests, diseases, discoloration, weeds and physiological disorders.

Root and branch systems: to be balanced and condition in accordance with the relevant part of the National Plant Specification.

Trees: to the relevant part of BS 3936, name, forms, dimensions and other criteria as ordered.

Semi-mature trees: to BS 4043, sizes and other criteria as ordered.

Planting in pits and trenches: excavate pits and trenches sufficiently wide and deep to accomm--odate the full spread of roots and to the following minimum sizes:

a. Forestry transplant
   and whip   500 x 500 x 500 mm deep

b. Feathered   1000 x 1000 x 500 mm deep

c. Standard and heavy
   standard   1250 x 1250 x 750 mm deep

d. Extra heavy
   standard   1500 x 1500 x 900 mm deep

Backfill with selected excavated material to level of surrounding ground and carefully work it among the roots; firm around the plants so that they are securely anchored and with the collars at surface level.

In grassland place excavated soil on plastic sheet to prevent damage to the turf.

Add fertilizer and/or soil ameliorants and mix into the planting soil and base of excavation as as directed.

Fork over bottom of excavation to a depth of 225 mm.

Drive stakes firmly into position after excavating and befor planting; set on the prevailing windward side of the plant.

Prune back damaged roots to sound tissue.

Prune crowns of trees at time of planting where directed.

Secure trees (other than forestry transplants and feathered trees) to stakes with approved reinforced rubber ties nailed to the stake.

Surplus arisings from planting: remove and deposit.

After planting, rake surface of soil, remove and deposit arisings and leave tidy.

Mulching trees: clear all weeds, water soil thoroughly, and mulch around each tree.

Mulching mats: fit neatly and closely around tree stem, where necessary cutting a neat slit or flap.

Tree protection: ensure that protection methods do not impede the natural movement of trees or restrict growth.

Q31: EXTERNAL PLANTING

PLANTING NURSERY STOCK AND SEMI-MATURE TREES - *continued*

Item Q31	*Each per hectare*	1 Number of trees not exceeding 10 Nr £	2 10 Nr to 25 Nr £	3 25 Nr to 100 Nr £	4 100 Nr to 500 Nr £	5 exceeding 500 Nr £
	Excavating pit: planting tree: backfilling: watering in					
075	not exceeding 600 mm high	0.44	0.37	0.34	0.29	0.25
076	600 mm to 1.00 m high	0.53	0.44	0.41	0.35	0.30
077	1.00 m to 1.50 m high	0.63	0.53	0.49	0.42	0.36

FORESTRY PLANTING

	Hectare	1 Number of trees per Hectare not exceeding 1000 Nr £	2 1000 to 2500 £	3 exceeding 2500 Nr £
	Notch planting trees			
078	conifers	109.02	181.70	290.72
079	broadleaves	163.53	272.55	436.08
080	ADD for tubes and stakes	1471.77	2452.95	3924.72

Q31: EXTERNAL PLANTING

TREE STAKES, GUARDS AND GUYS

Specification

Stakes: softwood, peeled chestnut, larch or oak, free from projections and large or edge knots with pointed lower end.

Single staking: position stake close to tree on windward side and drive vertically at least 300 mm into bottom of pit before planting. Consolidate material around stake during backfilling. Secure tree firmly but not rigidly to stake with rubber strap and collar fixed with two galvanised clout nails:

a. Long staking: cut stake off just below lowest branch of tree.

b. Short staking: cut stake to approximately 600 mm above ground level.

Double staking: drive stakes vertically at least 300 mm into bottom of pit on either side of tree position before planting. Consolidate material round stakes during backfilling. Cut stakes off just below lowest branch of tree. Firmly fix cross bar on windward side of tree and as close as possible to stem. Secure tree firmly but not rigidly to stake with rubber strap and collar fixed with two galvanised clout nails.

Item Q31	Each	1 Number of stakes, guards or guys not exceeding 5 Nr £	2 exceeding 5 Nr £
	New stake, rubber collar and strap		
	long		
081	single stake	2.92	2.33
082	double stake	3.26	2.10
	short		
083	single stake	1.66	1.08
084	double stake	2.73	1.57
	Tree guard: plastics spiral: wrapping around trunk		
085	450 mm high	2.25	0.79
086	600 mm high	2.39	0.94
087	750 mm high	2.53	1.08
	Tree guard: semi-rigid slotted polypropylene: not exceeding 75 mm diameter: fitting around trunk: base pushed slightly into ground		
088	150 mm high	1.72	0.55
089	300 mm high	2.34	0.89
090	600 mm high	3.23	1.48
091	1200 mm high	4.64	2.61
092	1800 mm high	6.05	3.73

TREE STAKES, GUARDS AND GUYS - *continued*

		1	2	3
		Diameter		
Item		200 mm	250 mm	300 mm
Q31	*Each*	£	£	£

Tree guard: circular: welded mesh: 12 gauge wire: 75 x 25 mm mesh: galvanised: supplied in two pre-shaped halves: fixing together around tree with fixing clips: adjusting height where necessary to avoid obstructing branches

Item		200 mm	250 mm	300 mm
093	525 mm high: two clips	5.60	7.90	10.21
094	825 mm high: two clips	7.91	10.71	13.51
095	1200 mm high: four clips	10.72	14.12	17.53
096	1800 mm high: four clips	14.99	19.36	23.75

		£

Tree shelter: translucent corrugated plastics: 75 x 75 mm: spot welded joints: double thickness top: fixing with one piece plastic non-slip ratchet fixing clips

		£
097	600 mm high	1.82
098	1200 mm high	2.38
099	1500 mm high	2.65
100	Tree supports: galvanised steel collar: 3 Nr galvanised steel guy cables: stays	47.09

APPLYING ANTI-DESICCANTS

	Each	£

Spraying tree with antidessicant spray

		£
101	standard	5.45
102	heavy standard	8.18
103	extra heavy standard	10.90

Q35: LANDSCAPE MANAGEMENT

GENERALLY

Specification

Applying pesticides/herbicides/weedkillers: pay for at the appropriate Rates in Section Q30.

Fine grading topsoil: pay for at the appropriate Rates in Section Q30.

Top dressing: pay for at the appropriate Rates in Section Q30.

Fertilisers: pay for at the appropriate Rates in Section Q30.

MAINTENANCE OF GRASSED AREAS

REPAIRING GRASSED AREAS

Specification

Topsoil filling: fill with imported topsoil or topsoil from elsewhere on the site.

Note

Topsoil filling: pay for at the appropriate Rates in Section D20.

Item Q35	Square Metre	£
	Digging out slurry from rut or hole in grassed area: removing and depositing arisings using wheelbarrows or the like on planked runs as directed: filling excavation with approved material to within 75 mm of surface: completing filling with approved topsoil, finishing level with surrounding surface after consolidation: raking: sowing grass seed: raking in: rolling: rut or hole	
104	not exceeding 150 mm average depth	4.15
105	150 to 300 mm average depth	6.03
106	Scarifying surface of damaged grass area: spreading approved topsoil to a consolidated average depth of 50 mm, including filling isolated hollows not exceeding 150 mm average deep: finishing level with surrounding surface: raking: sowing grass seed: raking in: rolling	2.26

Q35: LANDSCAPE MANAGEMENT

GRASS CUTTING: GENERALLY

Specification

Generally: carry out maintenance operations in accordance with BS 7370:Part 3, clause 11.

Notice: three days notice will be given for ordering the cutting of grass.

Cutters to all mowers: keep sharp and properly set to cut the sward cleanly and evenly. Set to the cutting height directed.

Avoid damage to trees etc. during current grass cutting operations. Replace at Contractor's expense all trees etc damaged by grass cutting operations.

Airfields and other large areas (excluding bird-strike deterrent areas): gang-mowing is the normal requirement for cutting grass but use multiple rotary type or flail type equipment if ordered.

Bird-strike deterrent areas: cut grass with multiple rotary type mowers minimum 3600mm wide set to a cutting height of 150mm. When ordered, bottom out.

Bottoming out grass on bird-strike deterrent areas:
a. use forage harvester or reaper with cutters set as low as possible.
b. clean out and remove arisings from grass cutting and naturally occurring thatch.
c. harrow and rake arisings into windrows and collect into trailers.

Note

Mowing out for line marking:
Pay for at the appropriate Rates multiplied by 1.25.

Rates for the following include

Generally:
For preliminary inspection of areas to be cut.

Cutting grass:
For cutting grass the whole of the area with the equipment ordered.

For cutting margins, corners, along wall and fence line bases and around obstructions using other suitable equipment if necessary, without additional payment.

For cutting on rough, sloping or uneven ground unless otherwise stated.

For cutting weeds and all growth of a non-woody nature.

For sweeping up arisings scattered on adjoining paths, roads, drives or the like and disposing.

For leaving arisings on the grass unless otherwise stated.

For disposing isolated items of obstructions e.g. stones, mole hills, rubbish or the like which might damage grass cutting equipment.

For cutting of overgrowth of grass at edges of cultivated areas, fire breaks, hard surfaces, backs of kerbs, sand play-pits or the like with edging shears to clean straight or smooth curved lines on each occasion and disposing arisings.

For cutting grass on level areas and banks within secure areas used for storing explosives or flammable fuels by means of pneumatically or hydraulically driven equipment fitted with nylon line rotary cutters, where so ordered. Non - powered equipment rates will apply.

Re-forming edges:
For re-forming edges next to cultivated areas, buildings and steps including forming V-shaped channel not exceeding 25mm wide at top next to kerbs and hard paved areas.

159

Q35: LANDSCAPE MANAGEMENT

GRASS CUTTING: TRACTOR-TRAILED OR MOUNTED EQUIPMENT

Item Q35	*Hectare*	£
	Cutting grass	
	using multiple-gang mower with cylindrical cutters	
107	3 gang	25.08
108	5 gang	15.05
109	7 gang	7.52
	using multiple-rotary motor with vertical shaft and horizontal cutters: cutting width	
110	not exceeding 2 m	45.15
111	2 to 4 m	37.62
112	exceeding 4 m	30.10
113	Cutting grass, vegetation, overgrowth or the like: using flail mower	51.29
114	Bottoming out grass on bird strike deterrent areas: removing and depositing arisings	87.61
	ADD for	
115	burning arisings	4.36
116	disposing arisings	15.27

	100 Square Metres	
	Cutting grass, vegetation, overgrowth or the like: using tractor mounted power-arm flail mower: in areas inaccessible to alternative machine: on surface	
117	not exceeding 30° from horizontal	1.28
118	30° to 50° from horizontal	2.05

GRASS CUTTING: SELF-PROPELLED EQUIPMENT

	100 Square Metres	£
	Cutting grass	
119	using multiple-cylinder mower fitted with cutting units mounted directly in such a manner as to permit one or more of the units to be disengaged and secured out of use for the purpose of working in confined or otherwise inoperable areas	0.46
120	using multiple-rotary motor with vertical shaft and horizontal cutters: cutting width	0.67
	ADD for using grass collecting box for	
121	removing and depositing arisings	0.15
122	disposing arisings	0.15

Q35: LANDSCAPE MANAGEMENT

GRASS CUTTING: PEDESTRIAN CONTROLLED EQUIPMENT

Item Q35	*100 Square Metres*	£
	Cutting grass	
123	using single cylinder mower fitted with not less than five cutting blades, front and rear rollers	0.77
	using rotary motor with vertical shaft and horizontal cutters: cutting width	
124	not exceeding 30° from horizontal	0.49
125	30° to 50° from horizontal	1.48
126	exceeding 50° from horizontal	1.96
127	Cutting bents, stalks or the like: using rotary mower	0.37
	Cutting grass using filament or cord mower: around trees, plants and street furniture	
128	not exceeding 30° from horizontal	3.38
129	30° to 50° from horizontal	4.52

GRASS CUTTING: USING NON-POWERED EQUIPMENT

---

	100 Square Metres	£
	Cutting grass	
130	using hand-propelled cylinder mower fitted with not less than seven cutting blades, front and rear rollers: removing and depositing arisings	3.63
131	ADD for disposing of arisings	0.15
	using scythe or similar hand implement: on rough area: on surface	
132	not exceeding 30° from horizontal	5.45
133	30° to 50° from horizontal	5.81
134	exceeding 50° from horizontal	6.54

	100 Metres	
	Trimming edge of grassed area: any width: using edging tool: to straight or curved line: removing and depositing arisings	
135	reforming edge of grassed area	12.72
136	where encroaching on to path	19.99
137	ADD for disposing of arisings	0.34

Q35: LANDSCAPE MANAGEMENT

GRASS CUTTING: COLLECTING ARISINGS OR THE LIKE

Item Q35	Hectare	£
138	Removing and depositing	12.65
	ADD for	
139	burning	4.36
140	disposing	15.27

	100 Square Metres	
	Hand raking: removing and depositing: on surface	
141	not exceeding 30° from horizontal	4.50
142	30° to 50° from horizontal	5.98
143	exceeding 50° from horizontal	7.46
	ADD for	
144	burning	0.08
145	disposing	0.15

HARROWING: GRASSED AREAS

Specification

Harrow with chain, spiked or drag harrow or drag mat to promote aeration and remove worm casts.

	Hectare	£
	Harrowing grassed area: removing and depositing arisings:	
	by machine	
146	chain or light flexible spiked harrow	37.42
147	drag harrow	33.68
148	ADD for disposing arisings	4.36

	100 Square Metres	
	by hand	
149	drag mat	5.81

Q35: LANDSCAPE MANAGEMENT

SCARIFYING

Specification

Scarify with tractor drawn or self-powered equipment to a suitable depth to relieve thatch conditions and remove dead grass.

Item Q35	*Hectare*	£
	Scarifying grassed area: removing and depositing arisings: using	
150	equipment mounted on or towed by tractor	53.34
151	ADD for disposing arisings	4.36

	100 Square Metres	
152	pedestrian operated self-powered equipment	0.94
153	hand implement	3.63
154	ADD to Items Q35.152 to Q35.153 for disposing arisings	0.36

ROLLING

Specification

Roll with self propelled or gang roller to consol-
-idate turf and reduce frost heave.

	Hectare	£
	Rolling grassed area: using tractor-trailed equipment: once over: using	
155	smooth three-gang roller	18.71
156	smooth single-gang roller	28.07

	100 Square Metres	
	Rolling small grassed area: once over: using	
157	self-propelled roller	1.57
158	pedestrian controlled roller	1.93
159	hand roller	2.35

Q35: LANDSCAPE MANAGEMENT

TURF AERATION

Item Q35	*Hectare*	£
	Aerating grassed area: using	
160	tractor-trailed equipment: minimum penetration of 100 mm	188.72
161	tractor-mounted equipment with power driven tines: minimum penetration of 300 mm	125.81
	100 Square Metres	
162	self-propelled hollow tine turf aerating equipment: minimum penetration of 100 mm: sweeping up: removing and depositing arisings	2.52
163	pedestrian-controlled solid or slitting tine turf aerating equipment: minimum penetration of 100 mm	2.39
164	hollow tine hand implement: minimum penetration of 100 mm: sweeping up: removing and depositing arisings	16.35
165	hand fork: minimum penetration of 100 mm: sweeping up: removing and depositing arisings	10.90
166	ADD to Items Q35.162, Q35.164 and Q35.165 for disposing arisings	0.15

LEAF CLEARANCE: GRASSED AREAS

Specification

Clear fallen leaves from grassed areas by sweeping with a motorized vacuum sweeper, rotary brush sweeper or by hand, as ordered.

	Hectare	£
	Clearing grassed area of leaves and other extraneous debris: removing and depositing arisings: using	
167	tractor-trailed or mounted equipment	33.59
	ADD for	
168	burning arisings	4.36
169	disposing arisings	15.27
	100 Square Metres	
170	pedestrian-controlled equipment	0.46
171	hand implement	1.16
	ADD to Items Q35.170 and Q35.171 for disposing arisings	
172	burning arisings	0.08
173	disposing arisings	0.15

Q35: LANDSCAPE MANAGEMENT

LITTER CLEARANCE: GRASSED AREAS

Specification

Collect and remove all extraneous rubbish detrimental to the appearance of the grassed area, including paper, packing materials, bottles, cans and the like.

Item Q35	*Hectare*	£
	Collecting litter: removing from grassed area: disposing	
174	large area	12.72
	100 Square Metres	
175	small area	0.44

BRUSHING

	100 Square Metres	£
	Brushing grassed sports areas	
176	using drag brush or net towed by tractor	0.30
177	hand brushing or switching	0.58

FOREIGN OBJECT DAMAGE CONTROL

Definition

Foreign objects: anything lying on cultivated, grassed or hard surfaces which might damage vehicle or aircraft tyres or be ingested into aircraft engines.

Rates for the following include

Generally:
For preliminary inspection.

For removing isolated foreign objects.

For removing foreign objects from any surface.

	Hectare	£
178	Collecting by hand foreign objects: disposing: where specifically ordered	14.03

GRASSED SPORTS AREAS

CRICKET PITCHES: GENERALLY

Specification

All operations must be executed in the sequence directed and in an approved manner by skilled labour.

Note

Supplying grass seed, fertilizers and weedkillers: Pay for separately.

Rates for the following include

Generally:
For supplying approved filling materials and loam.

Pitches:
For pitches size 23 x 3 m.

Patches:
For patches of any size.

Tables:
For tables size 30 x 3 m.

PREPARING CRICKET PITCH

Item Q35	*Each - per pitch*	£
179	Cutting grass using fine cut mower set to a cutting height of 4mm: raking: brushing and repeating cutting in opposite direction: disposing arisings: rolling using hand roller weighing not less than 150kg as conditions require to prepare pitch to an approved degree of firmness: marking out creases.	36.02
180	Commencing four days before day of match, selecting position of pitch parallel to line of corner pegs: scarifying using either hand implements or with two passes of pedestrian operated self-powered equipment set to operate above soil profile: brushing up: disposing arisings: cutting grass using fine cut mower set to a cutting height of 4mm: brushing and repeating cutting in opposite direction: disposing arisings: watering to provide compressible surface by allowing water to soak into surface: rolling using hand roller or pedestrian operated self-powered roller weighing not more than 1500kg to an approved standard of firmness: repeating brushing, cutting and rolling daily during the preparation. On the morning of the day of the match, cutting grass to a height of 4mm: disposing arisings: rolling using hand roller or pedestrian operated self-powered roller weighing not more than 500kg: marking cut creases.	76.66

Q35: LANDSCAPE MANAGEMENT

RENOVATING CRICKET PITCH

Item Q35	*Each - per pitch*	£
181	Sweeping up torn turf and debris: disposing arisings: aerating pitch to depth of 100mm using hand fork or pedestrian operated self-powered equipment: brushing or raking to raise nap of turf: forking over hollows: correcting levels using screened sterilised loam: compacting by treading: raking surface to form seed bed as necessary: sowing cricket table mixture grass seed at a rate of 50g per m²: raking in : rolling seeded area using hand roller: watering.	62.13

	Each - per table	
182	Scarifying with two passes using hand implement or pedestrian operated self-powered equipment set to penetrate 10 mm into the soil: sweeping up, removing and disposing arisings: aerating using hand fork or pedestrian operated self-powered solid tine aerating equipment to effect a minimum penetration of 100 mm spaced 150 mm apart: applying fine turf autumn fertiliser at a rate of 50g per m²; applying wormkiller in accordance with the manufacturer's instructions: top dressing with not exceeding 4 tonnes of screened sterilised heavy loam, filling depressions, raking and brushing in to attain smooth surface: sowing cricket table mixture grass seed at a rate of 10g per m²; raking in: rolling seeded area using hand roller: watering	731.11

REPAIRS TO GRASSED SPORTS AREAS

Note	**Rates for the following include**
Supplying grass seed: Pay for separately.	*Filling depressions or holes:* For supplying approved filling material.

	Each - per pitch	£
	Inspecting sports surface: replacing divots or filling small depressions; firming ground: re-seeding as necessary	
183	hockey pitch	16.79
184	football pitch	22.47
185	five-a-side football pitch	5.62
186	rugby pitch	34.60
187	softball pitch	11.50
188	baseball pitch	11.50
189	American football pitch	18.87
190	shot putt area	7.77
191	javelin area	11.85
192	hammer throw or discus area	8.62
193	tennis court	7.07
194	Filling holes for goal posts (any game): firming ground: re-seeding as necessary	7.90

Q35: LANDSCAPE MANAGEMENT

LINE MARKING

Specification

Marking out of sports areas, setting out and placing of equipment: conform to the current recommendations of the governing body of the relevant sport, unless otherwise directed.

Marking materials: apply approved marking materials so that lines remain clearly marked for a minimum of seven days. Add no weed killers, creosote or the like to the marking out material.

Lines: straight or to curves at the radii required.

Note

Mowing out for line marking: when ordered, pay for at the appropriate Rates in the "Maintenance of Grassed Areas" sub-section.

Rates for the following include

Generally:
For supplying marking material.

Initial marking:
For measuring and setting out.

Item Q35	Each	1 Initial marking £	2 over marking £
	Marking		
195	volleyball pitch	25.02	7.81
196	netball pitch	37.47	11.60
197	hockey pitch	57.39	15.45
198	football pitch	72.11	18.56
199	five-a-side football pitch	49.92	15.45
200	rugby pitch	98.59	29.43
201	rounders pitch	38.26	10.75
202	softball pitch	47.83	13.98
203	baseball pitch	46.35	13.98
204	American football pitch	183.94	52.98
205	cricket boundary	27.96	12.51
206	400 m running track not exceeding 8 lanes	247.22	80.93
207	shot putt area	18.39	6.17
208	javelin area	20.60	7.81
209	hammer throw or discus area	18.39	6.17
210	high jump fan	23.54	7.81
211	long jump approach	13.75	4.30
212	tennis court	36.79	10.75

Q35: LANDSCAPE MANAGEMENT

BOWLING GREENS: GENERALLY

Specification

Execute all operations in the sequence directed using skilled labour. Ensure no lift or damage is caused during maintenance operations.

Cutters to all mowers: keep sharp and properly set to cut the sward cleanly and evenly. Set to the height directed.

Cutting greens: use a fine turf cylinder lawn mower fitted with not less than ten blades, front and rear rollers and grass collection box.

Cutting perimeter banks: use suitable equipment and carry out at time of cutting the green.

Scarifying to control thatch: use approved pedestrian operated self-powered equipment. Sweep, brush up or box off all arisings. Leave a clean tidy surface.

Aeration: use approved pedestrian operated self-powered equipment to effect a minimum penetration of 100mm. Irrigation must fully penetrate the root zone. Avoid surface wetting.

Top dressing: ensure even distribution of material, using a lute, working from the undressed areas. Integrate dressing into the surface and/or aeration voids, brush or drag mat upon completion until completely worked in. Use planked wheelbarrow runs to protect the green.

Turf in repairs: of approved quality:
a. Cut and remove turf from either a nursery bed, an appointed place on the green or obtain from an approved supplier.
b. Do not strip or lay turf when weather is exceptionally dry, when surfaces are water-logged or during frost or snow.
c. Re-lay turf within seven days of stripping. Ensure that the programme of stripping is co-ordinated with that of the re-laying.
d. Ensure all repairs evenly fit without gaps and are level with adjoining areas. Adjust any deviation from specified levels by lifting, raking out or infilling with approved filling material and rolling.
e. Where turf has been removed from nursery area, make good by returning worn turf or dressing and seeding with selected grass seed of an approved quality.

f. When turf has been removed from an appointed area on the green make good with turf from either nursery area, imported turf or with selected grass seed of an approved quality.
g. Use planked wheelbarrow runs to protect the greens.

Grass seeds: use only named blue label certified seed varieties complying with EC regulations and use within the supplier's time limit. Mixture of seeds as ordered. Uncertified seeds will not be accepted.
a. Sow seeds only when whether and soil conditions are approved.
b. Sow seeds at the coverage rates directed evenly by hand, rake in and roll with light hand hand roller.

Chemicals: use only chemicals on the Ministry of Agriculture Approved Lists.

Watering: maintain adequate moisture in the greens at all times during maintenance operations.

Notes

Cutting perimeter banks: when ordered, pay for at the appropriate Rates in the "Maintenance of of Grassed Areas" sub-section.

Fertilisers: when ordered, pay for at the appropriate Rates in Section Q30.

Supplying grass seed, turf, fertilisers, top dressings or compost mix:
Pay for separately.

Rates for the following include

Generally:
For bowling greens size 38.41 x 38.41m (42 x 42 yards).

For preliminary inspection of the green to be worked on.

BOWLING GREENS: GENERALLY - *continued*

Rates for the following include - *continued*

For checking of measurements, removing strings for store and fixing where ordered prior to the commencement of the playing season.

For providing planked timber barrow runs including moving and adjusting as necessary.

For collecting and depositing all arisings from the maintenance operations, including leaves, litter etc.

For watering.

Raising levels:
For supplying approved filling materials.

Cutting grass:
For cutting straight or diagonal swards.

For cutting margins and into corners.

For sweeping up arisings scattered on adjoining paths, paved areas, perimeter ditch, drainage channels and gullies and removing and depositing.

Turf generally:
For temporary stacking.

For transporting.

Turf cut from nursery area:
For making good using worn turf from green or re-seeding.

Turf cut from appointed area on green:
For making good using imported turf or re-seeding.

BOWLING GREENS: AUTUMN MAINTENANCE

Item Q35	*Each - per green*	£
213	Switching dew from green first thing each morning and keeping grass cut to 5mm high during maintenance operations: removing and placing in store all strings and greens equipment: taking up and removing stones and filling from perimeter ditch and placing in an approved storage area: scarifying the green with the blades set so as not to penetrate the soil but to lift procumbent growth and thatch layer by 4 to 6 successive passes, each diagonally opposed to the last: overseeding with specified cultivars at the rates directed to any thin or worn areas, firstly ensuring an adequate key for grass seed by lightly pricking with a hand fork and raking.	299.52

Each - per green per occasion

Aerating using

214	spiked roller	15.69
215	solid tines	38.27
216	vertically power driven hollow tines in single pass to effect maximum penetration at 50 mm centres	47.84

Cubic Metre

217	Top dressing green with an approved compost mix or straight dressing as directed	59.95

BOWLING GREENS: WINTER MAINTENANCE

Note

This work is to commence as soon as all top dressing material has weathered into surface of green.

Item Q35	*Each - per green*	£
218	Switching or brushing dew from green first thing each morning, removing any litter or debris on and around the green and checking for any disease to the turf: as growth dictates keeping the green topped to 8mm: over a 4 week period......................	176.26

Square Metre

Cutting out and removing worn turf and laying

219	imported turf...	7.49
220	turf cut from nursery area or appointed area on the green.........................	3.63
221	Rectifying level using a straight edge to determine the extent of the depression: evenly spreading approved dressing to low areas: lightly raising level using a border/ hand fork so as not to disrupt or damage the surface or root zone: working dressing into aerated voids: applying no more material than can be integrated fully without surface damage or smothering turf...	9.60
222	Raising depressed levels to edge to green, using a border fork inserted to depth of root zone and gently easing out compaction without causing undue damage to surface or root system...	2.91
223	Raising depressed levels to green using a straight edge and levelling equipment to determine the extent of the depression: cutting, lifting and rolling back turf sufficiently to allow corrective levelling: lightly forking surface beneath turf: applying a approved pre-turfing fertiliser: integrating and raising levels with filling material consolidated by heeling and treading: re-laying turf adequately firming and working from planks: top dressing turf with approved top dressing material, spreading with a lute and well brushing in............	13.27

Q35: LANDSCAPE MANAGEMENT

BOWLING GREENS: SPRING MAINTENANCE

Item Q35	*Each - per green*	£

224   Switching or brushing dew from green first thing each morning, and removing any litter or debris on or around the green: commencing re-firming the surface by rolling with a 'Tru-level' roller or equivalent or a fine turf mower with blades disengaged passed slowly over the surface: as weather and ground conditions improve increasing the weight of the roller to 100 to 150kg and rolling in different directions to firm the green without compaction: repeating as required up to opening of the green: topping with fine turf mower gradually reducing the height of cut to 5mm: lightly scarifying the green across the two diagonals: spike rolling: over seeding any persistent weak areas with approved cutivars: lightly top dressing with approved material 0.5 to 1m³ as required, spreading with a lute and well brushing in: removing all debris: cleaning gullies: washing and replacing stone or filling to perimeter ditch: washing and cleaning area where stones were stored: removing all greens equipment from store as directed and setting in position ready for play: *over 6 to 8 week period* 905.41

BOWLING GREENS: SUMMER MAINTENANCE

Each - per green	£

225   Switching or brushing dew form green first thing each morning, and removing any litter: and debris on or around the green: brushing and keep cutting to a height of 5mm on the diagonal, the frequency and timing dependent upon weather conditions and match preparation: lightly rolling once with a 'Tru-level' smooth roller or equivalent: removing and re-laying lines during cutting operations, adjusting positions to minimise wear to greens or position of rinks all in conjunction with the match or game schedule: *over a 1 week period* 162.60

226   Aerating green with spiked roller or spike slitter 13.20

GOLF COURSES: GENERALLY

Notes

Generally:
Rates in other Sections apply to work on golf courses where Rates are not given in this Sub-Section.

Supplying grass seed:
Pay for separately.

Application of fertilizers, top dressing, etc.:
Pay for at the appropriate Rates in Section Q30.

Rates for the following include

Generally:
For preliminary inspection.

For removing and depositing arisings.

Filling depressions and holes:
For supplying approved filling material.

Q35: LANDSCAPE MANAGEMENT

GOLF COURSES: FAIRWAYS AND TEES

Item Q35		*Hectare*	£
227	Replacing divots or filling depressions: firming ground: re-seeding as necessary		22.99

GOLF COURSES: PUTTING GREENS

Notes	**Rates for the following include**
Supplying cups and flag sticks: Pay for separately.	*Cutting grass:* For the use of specialist fine turf mowers.
"Ride-on" self-powered equipment: Power unit to be fitted with flotation tyres.	

	100 Square Metres	£
	Cutting grass with mower fitted with not less than ten blades, front and rear rollers and grass collection box: using	
228	self-propelled mower	0.61
229	pedestrian controlled mower	1.05
	Aerating using	
230	spiked roller	1.18
231	solid or slit tines	2.63
232	vertically power driven hollow tines	3.35
233	Rolling: using roller of 500 kg spread over three integrated rollers	2.87
234	Hand brushing or switching	0.73
235	Repairing pitch marks: using approved repair tool	1.09

	Each	£
236	Cutting hole: using purpose made hole cutter: trimming perimeter: inserting cup and flag stick	1.82
	Filling hole: removing flag stick and cup: consolidating to level of surrounding area: re-seeding as necessary	
237	with "plug" cut from new hole	0.55
238	with approved topsoil and turf cut from nursery area or appointed area on the green	1.35

Q35: LANDSCAPE MANAGEMENT

GOLF COURSES: BUNKERS

Specification	Rates for the following include
Sand filling: Quantity and quality as ordered.	*Filling depressions:* For supplying approved filling materials.

Item **Q35**	*100 Square Metres*	£
239	Loosening sand: removing and disposing large stones, debris and weeds: filling small depressions: raking over to give an even surface	5.81
	Cubic Metres	
240	Excavating by hand to remove old sand filling	10.90
	Disposing excavated material	
241	off site	10.52
242	off site: transporting a distance not exceeding 1 km and depositing	8.30
243	ADD *for each additional 0.25 km of transporting distance*	1.04
244	Sand filling to bunker: raking over to give an even surface	34.32

GRASSED SPORTS AREAS: SUNDRIES

Specification	Rates for the following include
Sand filling to jump landing area: of type and quality ordered. *Supplying sand filling:* Pay for separately. *Supplying goal post sockets:* Pay for separately.	*Goal posts:* For fitting nets, net supports, back boards, protectors, etc. as appropriate. *Dismantling:* For taking down, cleaning loading, transporting and placing in store. *Erecting:* For removing from store, loading, transporting, cleaning out post sockets and erecting in position

Q35: LANDSCAPE MANAGEMENT

GRASSED SPORTS AREAS: SUNDRIES - *continued*

Item Q35	Each - per pitch or court	1 Dismantling £	2 Erecting £
245	Rounders posts	7.83	7.83
246	Hockey goal posts	21.81	21.81
247	Football goal posts	21.81	21.81
248	Five-a-side football goal posts	15.27	15.27
249	Rugby goal posts	31.99	31.99
250	American football goal posts	31.99	31.99
251	Volleyball net and posts	14.54	15.66
252	Tennis net and posts	14.54	16.78
253	Cricket square fencing	17.45	23.27
254	Cricket sight screens	31.99	31.99

	Each - per pitch or court	£
255	Digging holes for, and bedding in ground, goal post sockets: any game: making good ground	28.08
256	Removing from store marker posts and placing in position: tightening and adjusting goal nets: subsequently taking up marker posts and returning to store: slackening off goal nets: any game	7.66

	Each	
257	Digging out disused or damaged goal post sockets: any game: making good ground: removing and disposing arisings	7.66

	Square Metre	
	Jump landing area	
258	loosening sand: raking over to give a level, even surface	0.53
259	excavating sand 300 to 450 mm deep: brushing out: refilling with sand: raking over to give a level, even surface: removing and depositing arisings	2.31

Q35: LANDSCAPE MANAGEMENT

MAINTENANCE OF FLOWER BEDS

Specification

Lifting spring bulbs: carefully lift bulbs, clean off, treat with fungicide, store in sand filled boxes or cold frames to ripen during summer.

Lifting tubers and corms: cut down plant, carefully lift clean off and treat with fungicide and store in a frost proof shelter.

Lifting annual bedding plants: remove by hand.

Lifting established herbaceous plants: cut down; carefully lift plants, propagate by division, discarding the central woody crown. Label and heel-in offsets of divided plants in temporary location during the cultivation and preparation of beds and borders.

Temporary staking and tying in: provide softwood stakes or canes and twine to herbaceous plants as directed.

Hand weeding beds, borders and planters, etc. carefully hand weed in a way which will not damage plants, remove dead plants, spent flowers, inflorescences, discoloured leaves and stems, remove litter and leaves and erase foot-prints from beds and borders with a hand fork.

Notes

Supplying compost, mulch, processed bark and soil ameliorants:
Pay for separately.

Edging of beds and borders with edging tool:
Pay for at Rates in the "Maintenance of Grassed Areas" sub-section.

Application of fertilisers and pesticides:
Pay for at the Rates in Section Q30.

Rates for the following include

Generally:
For work to flower and shrub beds and borders, planters and the like and bases around trees.

For working carefully to avoid damage to stems, branches and roots of trees, shrubs and plants.

For removing and depositing or disposing arisings.

Temporary staking:
For additional tying in to herbaceous plants during the growing season.

Digging, hoeing and raking:
For grading cultivated surfaces to an even convex profile lightly consolidated.

Weeding, digging, hoeing, raking and cultivating:
For collecting weeds, plants, leaves, litter, stones and debris at the time of execution of the work, removing and depositing and leaving area tidy (Pay for leaf, litter and debris clearance at other times, under Rates Q35.289 to Q35.291).

Item Q35	Per 100	£
260	Dead heading bulbs: in temporary or permanent planting stations	1.12
	Lifting	
261	bulbs	10.68
262	tubers or corms	9.40
263	bedding plants	3.36
264	established herbaceous plants	70.11

MAINTENANCE OF FLOWER BEDS - *continued*

Item Q35		£
	Each	
265	Temporary staking and tying in herbaceous plant	2.19
	Cutting down spent growth of herbaceous plant	
266	unstaked	0.17
267	staked: not exceeding 4 stakes per plant: removing stakes and putting into store	0.28
	100 Square Metres	
268	Hand weeding	14.03
269	Hand digging with fork: not exceeding 150 mm deep: breaking down lumps: leaving surface with a medium tilth	28.04
270	Hand digging with fork or spade to an average depth of 230 mm: breaking down lumps: leaving surface with a medium tilth	31.54
271	ADD to Items Q35.269 and Q35.270 for incorporating soil ameliorants	9.94
272	Hand hoeing: not exceeding 50 mm deep: leaving surface with a medium tilth	21.03
273	Hand raking to remove stones, etc.: breaking down lumps: leaving surface with a fine tilth prior to planting	5.26
	Each	
	Hand weeding: planter, window box, etc.: any shape surface area of filling material	
274	not exceeding 0.25 m²	0.58
275	0.25 m² to 0.50 m²	1.16
276	0.50 m² to 0.75 m²	1.76
277	0.75 m² to 1.00 m²	2.34
278	exceeding 1.00 m²	2.92
	Hand cultivating: planter, window box, etc.: not exceeding 150 mm deep: any shape: surface area of filling material	
279	not exceeding 0.25 m²	1.16
280	0.25 m² to 0.50 m²	1.76
281	0.50 m² to 0.75 m²	2.34
282	0.75 m² to 1.00 m²	2.92
283	exceeding 1.00 m²	4.66
	Circular bed: approximately 750 mm diameter: around base of tree in grassed area	
284	maintaining by hand hoeing or digging	1.02
285	forming by hand digging	1.60
286	ADD to Items Q35.284 and Q35.285 for incorporating soil ameliorants	0.58

MAINTENANCE OF FLOWER BEDS - *continued*

Item Q35	*Square Metre*	£
	Spreading compost, mulch or processed bark to a depth of 75 mm	
287	on shrub bed	1.40
	Each	
288	on circular bed approximately 750 mm diameter: around base of isolated tree	0.60
	100 Square Metres	
	Clearing cultivated area of leaves, litter and other extraneous debris: using hand implement	
289	removing and depositing arisings	1.74
	ADD for	
290	burning arisings	0.08
291	disposing arisings	0.15

MAINTENANCE OF TREES, SHRUBS AND HEDGES

	Each	£
292	Taking up single or double tree stake and ties: removing and disposing	0.26
293	Taking off and disposing broken or decayed tie: new tie and buffer pad	1.46
294	Adjusting existing tree tie	0.15
	Taking down tree guard and stake: setting aside for re-use or disposing	
295	plastics tree shelter or spiral rabbit guard	0.66
296	galvanised wire or plastics mesh guard	0.73
	Refixing tree guard: any type: with new galvanised wire staples	
297	re-using stake previously set aside	1.31
298	providing new stake	1.79
299	Lift tree grille: remove weeds: make levels: re-lay to level: neatly refill grille interstices: lightly compact	1.82
300	Re-secure loosened guy wire	1.45
301	Replace missing guy wire	9.27
	Refirm by treading around the base	
302	tree	0.73
303	shrub	0.55

THINNING AND PRUNING SHRUBS

Specification

Generally: use only skilled labour.

Tools: keep sharp and properly set. Do not use mechanical hedge cutters or the like.

Make all cuts cleanly without tearing.

Prune all shrubs so as to maintain their shape and balance in order to produce the best decorative effect.

Cut out all dead, damaged and weak wood, tie in branches of climbing and wall plants.

Arisings: remove and deposit or dispose as directed and leave tidy.

Pruning generally: except where specified otherwise, pruning shall be undertaken following the principles of good Arboricultural practice as stated in the Arboricultural Advisory and Information Services, Arboriculture Research Note 48, A Definition of the Best Pruning Position.

Prune:
a. *Spring or early summer flowering deciduous* shrubs immediately after flowering, by pruning out all stems on which flowers have been borne, and thin out young shoots.

b. *Summer or autumn flowering deciduous shrubs* as soon as growth begins in the spring, cutting back previous year's growth to within two or three buds of the older wood.

c. *Deciduous shrubs grown for foliage or* coloured stem effect by cutting back close to ground level early in March.

d. *Evergreen shrubs* in May, early June, or September, removing dead wood and any weak or unsightly growth that spoils the natural habit of the plant.

e. *Hybrid tea and floribunda roses* in March by cutting out dead and weak growth; select strong stems to form balanced framework and prune these back to four to six buds from old wood, selecting outward facing buds.

f. *Rose stems* in Autumn by approximately one third to prevent wind rock.

g. *Climbing roses* in March by tying stems to form a balanced framework, prune sideshoots from main stem to two o four buds.

h. *Rambling roses* in July or August by removing stems that have borne flowers, space out and tie in current year's stems to form an evenly balanced framework.

i. *Shrubs massed in borders* by thinning out old wood and flower stem, and judicious pruning to reduce height and density by approximately 25%.

j. *Ground cover shrubs* such as Hypericum calycinum by cutting close to ground level in Spring.

k. *Heathers* by clipping tips of shoots that have flowered in order to maintain a compact habit.

Dead head floribunda or hybrid tea roses by cutting stems, where flowers have faded, back to within four or five buds of the previous year's wood.

Removal of excess growth, dead or diseased climbing plants or shrubs from face of building: carefully remove from walls, under tiles or slates, around windows, door, fascia boards, down pipes, gutters, etc, including removing leaves and debris form gutters and re-typing or re-wiring in as necessary.

Removal of excessive overhang: remove any growth encroaching onto grassed areas, paths, roads, signs, sightlines and light fittings.

Note

The Rates for pruning do not include for topiary work.

Rates for the following include

Generally:
For the use of steps, ladders, trestles, or tower scaffolding or the like.

For removing and depositing or disposing arisings.

THINNING AND PRUNING SHRUBS - *continued*

Item Q35	*Each - per plant*	£
	Removing excess growth from face of building or the like: height before pruning	
304	not exceeding 2 m	7.34
305	2 to 4 m	10.91
306	4 to 6 m	17.99
307	6 to 8 m	71.32
308	8 to 10 m	114.72
	Removing excess overhang: height before pruning	
309	not exceeding 2 m	4.40
310	2 to 4 m	6.54
311	4 to 6 m	10.79
312	6 to 8 m	42.79
313	8 to 10 m	68.83
	Pruning	
	ornamental shrub: height before pruning	
314	not exceeding 1 m	1.73
315	1 to 2 m	2.33
316	exceeding 2 m	2.93
317	bush or standard rose	1.16
318	climbing rose or rambling rose	7.00

	Square Metre	
319	Trimming ground cover planting	0.47
320	Pruning massed shrub border	0.58

	Each - per plant	
	Cutting off dead heads	
321	bush or standard rose	0.35
322	climbing rose or rambling rose	1.73

323   When pruning has not been executed during the previous two years, multiply the Rates for Items Q35.314 to Q35.316 by 1.50.

Q35: LANDSCAPE MANAGEMENT

HEDGE WORK : GENERALLY

Specification

Generally: use only skilled labour.

Tools: keep sharp and properly set.

Use lines and canes to obtain even height and line of hedge where directed.

Collect, remove and deposit all arisings and leave tidy.

CUTTING FIELD AND ORNAMENTAL HEDGES

Specification

Field hedges: trim to specified height and profile using suitable hand tools, hand held mechanical cutters or tractor mounted hedge cutting equip--ment, as directed.

Ornamental hedges: trim carefully and neatly to regular line and shape, using hand tools or hand held mechanical cutters. Do not use flail cutters. Remove current growth rather than old wood.

Reducing width or height of overgrown hedges: cut back to an even sight line.

Removing dead plant material: at the end of the growing season, check all shrubs and remove all dead foliage, dead wood, and broken or dam--aged branches and stems.

Definitions

Trimming sides and top of field hedge:
Cutting not exceeding 2 years' growth since last cut.

Trimming sides and top of ornamental hedge:
Cutting not exceeding 1 years' growth since last cut.

Cutting to reduce width or height of overgrown hedge:
Cutting back field hedge exceeding 2 years' growth since last cut.

Cutting back ornamental hedge exceeding 1 years' growth since last cut.

Method of measurement

Trimming sides and top of field hedge:
Measure the girth by the length after the work has been executed.

Cutting to reduce width or height of overgrown hedge:
Measure the average depth of cut from the original side or top to the finished side or top.

Measure the area after the work has been executed.

CUTTING FIELD AND ORNAMENTAL HEDGES - *continued*

Item Q35	Square Metre	1 Using hand tool or hand held mechanical tools	2 Using tractor-mounted hedge cutting equipment	3 ADD for burning arisings	4 ADD for disposing arisings
		£	£	£	£
	Trimming sides and top of hedge				
	field hedge				
324	not exceeding 2 m high	0.18	0.13	0.06	0.11
325	2 to 4 m high	0.30	0.17	0.06	0.11
	ornamental hedge				
326	not exceeding 2 m high	0.12	-	0.06	0.11
327	2 to 4 m high	0.18	-	0.06	0.11

	Square Metre	1 Using hand tools or hand held mechanical tools	2	3	4 Using tractor-mounted hedge cutting equipment	5	6
		Average depth of cut					
		not exceeding 300 mm	300 to 600 mm	600 to 900 mm	not exceeding 300 mm	300 to 600 mm	600 to 900 mm
		£	£	£	£	£	£
	Cutting to reduce						
	width of overgrown hedge						
	field hedge - *per side*						
328	not exceeding 2 m high	0.88	1.26	1.63	0.17	0.33	0.48
329	2 to 4 m high	1.14	1.51	1.89	0.26	0.41	0.57
330	4 to 6 m high	1.39	1.77	2.02	0.34	0.48	0.65
	ADD for						
331	burning arisings	0.06	0.11	0.17	0.06	0.11	0.17
332	disposing of arisings	0.17	0.22	0.28	0.17	0.22	0.28
	ornamental hedge - *per side*						
333	not exceeding 2 m high	0.63	1.00	1.39	-	-	-
334	2 to 4 m high	0.88	1.26	1.63	-	-	-
335	4 to 6 m high	1.14	1.51	1.89	-	-	-
	ADD for						
336	burning arisings	0.06	0.11	0.17	-	-	-
337	disposing of arisings	0.17	0.22	0.28	-	-	-

CUTTING FIELD AND ORNAMENTAL HEDGES - *continued*

		1	2	3	4	5	6
		Using hand tools or hand held mechanical tools			Using tractor-mounted hedge cutting equipment		
		Average depth of cut					
		not exceeding 300 mm	300 to 600 mm	600 to 900 mm	not exceeding 300 mm	300 to 600 mm	600 to 900 mm
Item Q35	*Square Metre*	£	£	£	£	£	£
	Cutting to reduce						
	height of overgrown hedge						
	field hedge						
338	not exceeding 2 m high	1.14	1.51	1.89	0.26	0.41	0.57
339	2 to 4 m high	1.39	1.77	2.02	0.34	0.48	0.65
340	4 to 6 m high	1.63	2.02	2.40	0.41	0.57	0.73
	ADD for						
341	burning arisings	0.06	0.11	0.17	0.06	0.11	0.17
342	disposing of arisings	0.17	0.22	0.28	0.17	0.22	0.28
	ornamental hedge						
343	not exceeding 2 m high	0.88	1.26	1.63	-	-	-
344	2 to 4 m high	1.14	1.51	1.89	-	-	-
345	4 to 6 m high	1.39	1.77	2.02	-	-	-
	ADD for						
346	burning arisings	0.06	0.11	0.17	-	-	-
347	disposing of arisings	0.17	0.22	0.28	-	-	-

CUTTING AND LAYING FIELD HEDGES

Specification

Cutting and laying hedges:
a. Lay the branches to an angle slightly above the horizontal and make the cuts in the stems at such an angle that they will shed water.
b. Make stakes and binders from material cut out of the hedge.
c. Drive stakes into the centre of the hedgerow line at 1 m centres and intertwine the branches in such a way as to form a strong stock-proof barrier with no gaps.
d. Neatly finish the laid hedge with binders woven between the tops of the stakes.

Cut away branches and twigs in the hedgerow that are not required for laying, clean out base of hedge and leave tidy.

Hedgerow trees: leave standing in the hedgerow those trees selected and marked by the PM.

Rates for the following include

Generally:
For providing any additional stakes that may be required.

Item **Q35**	*Metre*	1	2 ADD for burning arisings	3 ADD for disposing arisings
		£	£	£
	Cutting and laying field hedge: any sectional area: cutting all growth not exceeding 600 mm girth: depositing arisings: average width			
348	not exceeding 2 m	7.93	0.17	1.02
349	2 to 4 m	11.30	0.28	1.36

TREE WORK

Specification

Generally: comply with BS 3998.

Comply with Forestry and Arboriculture Training and Safety Coucil Safety Guides. Tree work must be carried out by a member of the Arboricultural Association.

Before starting work verify with PM which trees, shrubs and hedges are to be removed or pruned. Avoid damage to neighbouring trees, plants and property.

When removing branches, cut as shown in Arboricultural Association Leaflet No 8 'Mature tree maintenance'. Leave trees with a well balanced natural appearance.

Cut vertical branches similarly, with no more slope on the cut surface than is necessary to shed rainwater. Remove branches without damaging or tearing the stem.

Cut cleanly back to sound wood leaving a smooth surface, keeping wounds as small as possible, and angled so that water will not collect on the cut area. Cut at a fork or at the main stem to avoid stumps wherever possible. Do not cut into live wood when removing dead branches and stubs.

Tools: use appropriate well maintained sharp tools. Work involving chain saws must by carried out by holders of a Certificate of Competence. Do not use chainsaws on branches of less than 50 mm diameter. When using hand saws, cut in one continuous operation to form a smooth cut surface. Do not use anvil type secateurs.

Definitions

Detailed inspection: an inspection using a check-list in accordance with Appendix C of BS 7370: Part 1, recording and reporting significant defects which may necessitate climbing the tree as recommended in BS 3998.

Epicormic growth removal: remove adventitious growth from the base of the tree, the main stem or limbs. Cut back to the collar using a handsaw.

Crown reduction and/or shaping: cut back selectively to side buds or branches to retain a flowing branch line without leaving stumps.

Crown lifting: remove whole branches back to the stem, or cut lower portions of branches back to buds or branches without leaving stumps.

Crown thinning: selectively remove secondary and small live branch growth evenly throughout the crown. Cut portions of branches back to buds or branches without leaving stumps. Remove inward growing, crossing, rubbing, dead and damaged branches. Leave a uniform and well balanced structure of branches and foliage.

Method of measurement

Diameter of branch:
Measure at the final cut point.

Removing deadwood:
Measure as removing isolated branch or part branch.

Pollarding:
Measure only branches exceeding 50mm diameter.

Height above ground level:
a. Removing isolated branch or part branch: measure to the final cut point.
b. Pollarding: measure to the highest cut point.

Rates for the following include

Generally:
For the use of hand tools or hand held power equipment.

For removing branches of any length.

For removing heavy branches in sections.

For lowering cut branches or sections with ropes.

For cutting material into manageable lengths and stacking.

Pollarding:
For removing all growths not exceeding 50 mm diameter.

TREE WORK - *continued*

Item Q35	Each - per tree	1	2	3
		Number of trees		
		not exceeding 1 Nr	2 to 5	exceeding 5 Nr
		£	£	£
	Carrying out detailed inspection: total height of tree			
350	not exceeding 6.00 m	26.45	21.16	15.87
351	6.00 to 9.00 m	33.06	27.77	22.48
352	9.00 to 15.00 m	39.68	34.39	29.10
353	15.00 to 20.00 m	46.29	41.00	35.71
354	20.00 to 25.00 m	52.90	47.61	42.32
355	exceeding 25.00 m	59.51	54.22	48.93

Item	Each - per tree	1	2	3	4
		Diameter of tree			
		not exceeding 150 mm	150 mm to 300 mm	300 mm to 600 mm	exceeding 600 mm
		£	£	£	£
	Removing epicormic growth by cutting back to the main stem: total height of tree				
356	not exceeding 6.00 m	1.65	2.48	3.72	-
357	6.00 to 9.00 m	2.07	2.89	4.13	-
358	9.00 to 15.00 m	-	3.31	4.96	9.92
359	15.00 to 20.00 m	-	-	6.61	13.23
360	20.00 to 25.00 m	-	-	8.27	19.84
361	exceeding 25.00 m	-	-	-	26.45

TREE WORK - *continued*

Item Q35	Each	1	2	3
		Diameter of branch		
		not exceeding 100 mm	100 mm to 300 mm	300 mm to 600 mm
		£	£	£

Removing or reducing isolated branch or part branch: removing and depositing arisings: height above ground level

		1	2	3
362	ground level	6.70	8.90	13.20
	height above ground level			
363	not exceeding 6.00 m	15.13	18.07	20.30
364	6.00 to 9.00 m	21.42	22.40	24.20
365	9.00 to 15.00 m	24.72	27.30	31.30
366	15.00 to 20.00 m	25.60	29.40	33.20
367	20.00 to 25.00 m	27.60	31.50	36.90
368	exceeding 25.00 m	28.40	32.60	38.40

369 Work carried out on 2 to 5 branches consecutively: price at the foregoing Rates for Items Q35.362 to Q35.368 multiplied by 0.50.

370 Work carried out on exceeding 5 branches consecutively: price at the foregoing Rates for Items Q35.362 to Q35.368 multiplied by 0.40.

371 Work carried out under restrictions imposed by overhead/underground services, busy roads, adjacent structures, poor access or surrounding trees: price at the foregoing Rates for Items Q35.362 to Q35.368 multiplied by 1.05.

	Each - per stem removed	1	2	3	4
		Diameter of tree			
		not exceeding 150 mm	150 mm to 300 mm	300 mm to 600 mm	exceeding 600 mm
		£	£	£	£

Selecting a single healthy stem to be retained: removing all other stems back to the stock: total height of tree

		1	2	3	4
372	not exceeding 6.00 m	8.24	9.89	13.18	-
373	6.00 to 9.00 m	9.06	10.71	14.83	-
374	9.00 to 15.00 m	-	11.54	16.48	25.42
375	15.00 to 20.00 m	-	-	22.13	29.07
376	20.00 to 25.00 m	-	-	25.78	33.72
377	exceeding 25.00 m	-	-	-	39.37

TREE WORK - *continued*

Item Q35	Each - per tree	1	2	3	4
		Diameter of tree			
		not exceeding 150 mm	150 mm to 300 mm	300 mm to 600 mm	exceeding 600 mm
		£	£	£	£
	Crown reduction: re-shaping tree: average 15%: removing and depositing arisings: total height of tree				
378	not exceeding 6.00 m	32.96	45.32	53.56	-
379	6.00 to 9.00 m	49.44	64.80	89.51	-
380	9.00 to 15.00 m	-	153.03	177.75	190.71
381	15.00 to 20.00 m	-	-	205.99	227.19
382	20.00 to 25.00 m	-	-	214.23	263.67
383	exceeding 25.00 m	-	-	-	296.63

	Each - per branch	1	2	3
		Diameter of branch		
		not exceeding 100 mm	100 mm to 300 mm	300 mm to 600 mm
		£	£	£
	Crown lifting: removing lower branches or part branches			
384	for pedestrian clearance and the like not exceeding 2.50 m	8.70	11.90	17.20
385	for signage and overhead cable clearance and the like not exceeding 4.00 m	12.13	16.24	26.00
386	for vehicle and roofline clearance and the like not exceeding 5.60 m	12.96	18.37	32.96

387   Work carried out on 2 to 5 trees consecutively: price at the foregoing Rates for Items Q35.378 to Q35.386 multiplied by 0.80.

388   Work carried out on exceeding 5 trees consecutively: price at the foregoing Rates for Items Q35.378 to Q35.386 multiplied by 0.60.

389   Work carried out under restrictions imposed by overhead/underground services, busy roads, adjacent structures, poor access or surrounding trees: price at the foregoing Rates for Items Q35.378 to Q35.386 multiplied by 1.05

TREE WORK - *continued*

Item Q35	*Each - per tree*	1 Diameter of tree not exceeding 150 mm £	2 150 mm to 300 mm £	3 300 mm to 600 mm £	4 exceeding 600 mm £
	Crown thinning: even density of foliage: not exceeding 10 %: removing and depositing arisings: total height of tree				
390	not exceeding 6.00 m	23.30	29.24	33.54	-
391	6.00 to 9.00 m	34.94	40.71	44.83	46.60
392	9.00 to 15.00 m	-	53.18	58.13	61.20
393	15.00 to 20.00 m	-	-	63.42	69.44
394	20.00 to 25.00 m	-	-	74.72	85.92
395	exceeding 25.00 m	-	-	-	96.40

396   Work carried out to remove 10 to 20% of the leaf area: price at the foregoing Rates for Items Q35.390 to Q35.395 multiplied by 1.10.

397   Work carried out to remove 20 to 30% of the leaf area: price at the foregoing Rates for Items Q35.390 to Q35.395 multiplied by 1.20.

398   Work carried out on 2 to 5 trees consecutively: price at the foregoing Rates for Items Q35.390 to Q35.395 multiplied by 0.80.

399   Work carried out on exceeding 5 trees consecutively: price at the foregoing Rates for Items Q35.390 to Q35.395 multiplied by 0.60.

400   Work carried out under restrictions imposed by overhead/underground services, busy roads, adjacent structures, poor access or surrounding trees: price at the foregoing Rates for Items Q35.390 to Q35.395 multiplied by 1.05

Q35: LANDSCAPE MANAGEMENT

TREE WORK - *continued*

	1	2	3	4
	Pollard height			
	not exceeding 4.00 m	4.00 m to 7.00 m	7.00 m to 10.00 m	10.00 m to 15.00 m
Item Q35	£	£	£	£

Each - per tree

Pollarding: branches or part branches: any diameter exceeding 50 mm: re-shaping tree: removing and depositing arisings: total height of tree

		1	2	3	4
401	not exceeding 6.00 m	25.00	-	-	-
402	6.00 to 9.00 m	45.00	-	-	-
403	9.00 to 15.00 m	-	70.00	60.00	-
404	15.00 to 20.00 m	-	85.00	75.00	65.00
405	20.00 to 25.00 m	-	95.00	85.00	75.00
406	exceeding 25.00 m	-	110.00	100.00	90.00

	1	2	3
	Diameter of wound / tear		
	not exceeding 100 mm	100 mm to 150 mm	150 mm to 300 mm
	£	£	£

Each - per wound

Treating wound: to aid effective callous formation: height above ground level

		1	2	3
407	not exceeding 2.50 m	6.00	6.90	7.20
408	2.50 to 5.00 m	15.00	17.80	19.25
409	5.00 to 10.00 m	17.20	19.25	23.86
410	10.00 to 15.00 m	22.98	27.60	33.20
411	15.00 to 20.00 m	31.90	33.80	37.90

412   Work carried out on 2 to 5 trees consecutively: price at the foregoing Rates for Items Q35.401 to Q35.411 multiplied by 0.80.

413   Work carried out on exceeding 5 trees consecutively: price at the foregoing Rates for Items Q35.401 to Q35.411 multiplied by 0.60.

Q35: LANDSCAPE MANAGEMENT

TREE WORK: REMOVING TREES SHRUBS AND HEDGES

Specification

Removing trees, shrubs and hedges: before starting work verify which trees, shrubs and hedges are to be removed.

Services: check for below and above ground services in the vicinity. Inform PM if they may be affected and obtain instructions before proceeding.

Tree felling:
a. Comply with BS 3998 and current Forestry and Arboriculture Safety and Training Council Safety Guides.

b. Trees not exceeding 250 mm girth: remove complete with roots.

c. Trees exceeding 250 mm girth: Fell as close to the ground as possible.

Ensure that all operatives are adequately trained and are working under direct instruction and close supervision of a person who is competent to give both instruction and supervision.

d. Trees in confined spaces: take down carefully in small sections using ropes, crane or hydraulic platform to avoid damage to adjacent trees that are to be retained, where tree canopies overlap and in confined spaces generally.

Stack cordwood and felled timber (where to be retained) in neat piles where directed on the site.

Kill stumps with chemicals applied in accordance with the manufacturers recommendations.

Fill voids left .by removal of trees or stump grinding and consolidate to level of adjacent adjacent ground.

Rates for the following include

Cutting down hedges:
For trees and saplings not exceeding 150 mm girth in the run of the hedge.

		1	2	3	4
		Diameter of tree			
		not exceeding 150 mm	150 mm to 300 mm	300 mm to 600 mm	exceeding 600 mm
Item Q35	*Each - per tree*	£	£	£	£
	Clear felling tree: removing and depositing arisings: total height of tree				
414	not exceeding 6.00 m	6.59	32.96	58.88	-
415	6.00 to 9.00 m	8.24	59.44	115.36	-
416	9.00 to 15.00 m	-	65.92	131.84	205.99
417	15.00 to 20.00 m	-	-	148.32	247.19
418	20.00 to 25.00 m	-	-	164.80	288.39
419	exceeding 25.00 m	-	-	-	329.59

191

Q35: LANDSCAPE MANAGEMENT

TREE WORK: REMOVING TREES SHRUBS AND HEDGES - *continued*

Item Q35	*Each - per tree*	1	2	3	4
		Diameter of tree			
		not exceeding 150 mm	150 mm to 300 mm	300 mm to 600 mm	exceeding 600 mm
		£	£	£	£
	Felling tree in sections: removing and depositing arisings: total height of tree				
420	not exceeding 6.00 m	7.42	34.61	65.92	-
421	6.00 to 9.00 m	9.89	49.44	98.88	-
422	9.00 to 15.00 m	-	57.68	131.84	280.15
423	15.00 to 20.00 m	-	-	181.27	313.11
424	20.00 to 25.00 m	-	-	230.71	346.07
425	exceeding 25.00 m	-	-	-	395.51

Item	*Each*	1	2	3	4
		Girth			
		250 to 600 mm	600 to 900 mm	900 to 1200 mm	1200 to 1500 mm
		£	£	£	£
426	Killing tree stump by chemical treatment	2.91	4.36	5.82	7.27
427	Destroying tree stump: with stump chipping machine: to 150 mm below ground level: filling void: removing and depositing arisings	21.80	25.44	29.07	32.71
	ADD for				
428	burning arisings	0.58	0.87	1.16	1.45
429	disposing of arisings	1.16	1.60	1.89	2.33
430	Grubbing up stump and roots of tree: filling void: removing and depositing arisings	60.04	81.99	103.94	125.89
	ADD for				
431	burning arisings	0.73	1.02	1.31	1.74
432	disposing of arisings	1.31	1.74	2.18	2.76

TREE WORK: REMOVING TREES SHRUBS AND HEDGES - *continued*

		1	2	3
		Height of hedge		
		not exceeding 1.50 m	1.50 to 2.00 m	2.00 to 3.00 m
Item **Q35**	*Metre*	£	£	£
433	Cutting down hedge: grubbing up roots: filling voids: not exceeding 5.00 m: removing and depositing arisings	14.39	16.90	19.41

435 Work carried out on hedges 5.00 to 10.00 m long consecutively: price at the foregoing Rates for Item Q35.433 multiplied by 0.50.

435 Work carried out on hedges exceeding 10.00 m long consecutively: price at the foregoing Rates for Item Q35.433 multiplied by 0.40.

DISPOSAL OF ARISINGS

		1	2	3
			ADD for burning arisings	ADD for disposing arisings
	Cubic Metre	£	£	£
436	Collecting branches: removing and depositing	9.91	-	16.72
437	Woodchipping branches on site: removing and depositing	13.96	-	-

				£
	Each			
438	Cutting up fallen tree: moving to prevent obstruction: removing and depositing			68.95

MAINTENANCE OF DOMESTIC GARDENS

Scope

The work in this Section comprises the maintenance of enclosed domestic gardens and typically includes grass cutting, clearing weeds, maintenance of beds and borders, hedge trimming, etc.,or other work as ordered.

Note

Where a number of similar domestic gardens are to be maintained under the same order, the Contractor and the PM will agree on the work to be carried out in a typical garden.

Pay for all similar gardens as for the typical garden.

Item
Q35

Maintenance of domestic gardens

pay for at the appropriate Rates in other Sections multiplied by the following factors

garden

439	not exceeding 250 m²	multiply by 1.70
440	250 to 500 m²	multiply by 1.60
441	500 to 1000 m²	multiply by 1.50
442	exceeding 1000 m²	no adjustment

CEMETERY WORK

GENERALLY

Scope

The Contractor's attention is drawn to the sensitive nature of the work and he must ensure noise levels are kept to a minimum. Under no circumstances will the use of radios, audio equipment, etc. be permitted.

Ensure no damage is caused to monumental masonry, trees, shrubs, paths and grassed areas during the execution of the works.

Make good any damage caused at the Contractors expense.

GRAVE DIGGING

Specification

Notice: normally three to five days will be given prior to commencement of the works.

Turf: cut and lift turf and stack in neat piles adjacent to the work ready for re-laying.

Excavate grave 100 mm wider and longer than the size of the coffin.

Erect earthwork support around grave area to protect adjacent graves.

Supply and place in position grave shields, landing boards and jacks to stabilise grave sides.

On completion of excavation supply and lay artificial grass over the excavated soil.

On completion of funeral service:
a. Carefully backfill and pack evenly.
b. Dispose of surplus excavated material.
c. Re-lay turf to marry in with existing ground levels.
d. Leave the area clean and tidy on completion.

GRAVE DIGGING - *continued*

Rates for the following include

Generally:
For executing work by hand.

For using skilled labour and supervision.

For providing earthwork support, grave shields, landing boards, jacks and artificial grass and removing on completion.

Item Q35	*Each - per grave*	£
	Stripping turf, excavating grave, backfilling, removing and disposing surplus excavated material: re-laying turf	
443	single grave 1.95 m deep	202.73
444	double grave 2.55 m deep	248.18

MAINTENANCE OF GRAVES

Specification

Erecting headstone: collect from store, carefully load and transport to graveside. Excavate for base, set and surround base with concrete (20 N/mm²: 20 mm aggregate), ensure that it is set true and level and remove and dispose of surplus excavated material and reinstate turf.

General maintenance to individual graves: cut grass or weed areas by hand and prune any shrubs, bushes or perennial flowers as necessary.

Wash down and carefully clean monumental masonry and surround.

Dispose of all arisings and leave area tidy.

Notes

Headstones:
Supplied by others.

Supplying cleaning materials:
Pay for separately.

Cutting general grassed areas within cemetery:
Pay for at the Rates in the "Maintenance of Grassed Areas" sub-section.

Rates for the following include

Generally:
For any double handling of monumental masonry from transport vehicle to graveside.

	Each - per headstone	£
445	Erecting headstone	58.88

	Each - per grave	
446	General maintenance to grave	8.30

	Square Metre	
447	Washing down and cleaning monumental masonry and surround	1.74

Q35: LANDSCAPE MANAGEMENT

MAINTENANCE OF HARD LANDSCAPE

GRAVEL OR COCKLESHELL PAVING

Rates for the following include

Generally:
For collecting weeds and debris, removing and depositing and leaving tidy.

Item Q35	100 Square Metres	£
448	Raking over surface	3.52
449	Hand weeding	21.03
450	Hand hoeing: not exceeding 25 mm deep	14.04

SNOW AND ICE CLEARANCE

Specification

Comply with BS 7370: Part 2: Section 4.

Rock salt: from an approved supplier.

Store salt in containers which allow no percol--ation or seepage, at least 15 m away from cultivated, planted or grassed areas.

Spread evenly, at the rate ordered, and keep off adjacent cultivated, planted or grassed areas. Replace at own expense all grass, plants, etc. damaged by salt application.

Definitions

Precautionary treatment:
Treatment of surfaces prior to frost or snow-fall.

Clearance treatment
Treatment of surfaces after snow-fall.

Note

Supplying rock salt:
Pay for separately.

Rates for the following include

Generally:
For transporting salt from site storage.

For spreading to paths, paved areas, ramps, steps or landings.

For spreading by mechanical means or by hand implements where this is impracticable.

For spreading at the coverage rates ordered.

	100 Square Metres	£
451	Precautionary treatment - *per kilogramme per 100 m²*	0.51
	Clearance treatment - *per kilogramme per 100 m²*	
452	ice and light snow not exceeding 20 mm deep	0.58
453	snow 20 to 40 mm deep: plough: then salt	3.26
454	snow exceeding 40 mm: plough: then salt	5.01

Q35: LANDSCAPE MANAGEMENT

LEAF CLEARANCE: HARD LANDSCAPE

Specification

Comply with BS 7370: Part 2: Section 4.

Item Q35	*100 Square Metres*	£
	Clearing hard landscape area of leaves and other extraneous debris: removing and depositing arisings: using	
455	tractor-trailed or mounted equipment	0.34
456	self-propelled motorized vacuum or rotary brush sweeper	0.39
457	pedestrian-controlled equipment	0.46
458	hand implement	0.73
	ADD for	
459	burning arisings	0.08
460	disposing arisings	0.15

LITTER CLEARANCE: HARD LANDSCAPE

Specification

Collect and remove all extraneous rubbish detrimental to the appearance of the grassed area, including paper, packing materials, bottles, cans and the like.

	100 Square Metres	£
461	Collecting litter: removing from hard landscape area: disposing	
	small area	0.36

Q35: LANDSCAPE MANAGEMENT

POND MAINTENANCE: SPRING

Specification

Draining: carry out partial water change by drain-
-ing off half the water into a drain or soakaway
using a pump and hose.

Item Q35	Square Metre	£
462	Removing all decaying vegetation, deleterious matter and general litter	0.58
463	Partly draining pond and refilling: regulating the flow of water to gentle trickle	1.09
464	Removing netting: clearing debris: replacing	0.44

POND MAINTENANCE: SUMMER

Specification

Thinning: thin out plants to prevent overcrowding.
Lift baskets and cut back side shoots to the crown
of the plant using sharp secateurs. Minimise
disturbance to pond life.

	Square Metre	£
465	Thinning plants: lifting baskets: cutting back side shoots	1.45
466	Removing invasive weeds: disposing all arisings	0.73
467	Feeding plants with aquatic fertiliser pellets: inserting into soil around crown	0.65

POND MAINTENANCE: AUTUMN / WINTER

Specification

Removing ice: melt ice in several places over
the surface to allow gaseous exchange. Do not
smash with a heavy implement. Remove some
from under the ice to facilitate oxygen circulation.

	Square Metre	£
468	Removing dead withering leaves and seed heads: cutting back leaves under water: disposing arisings	0.58
469	Covering pond with strong nylon medium gauge net: preventing leaves from falling into water.	1.82
470	Removing ice from pond	0.40

Q40: FENCING

GENERALLY

Specification

Approved firms: employ an approved specialist firm for fencing. Removal of old fencing and sundry repairs may be carried out by the Contractor where permitted by the PM.

Concrete post hole filling and fence sills: 10 N/mm²: 40 mm maximum aggregate, as specified in Section E10.

Preservative treatment for softwood: water borne copper chrome arsenic preservative by full-cell pressure treatment to BS 4072. The treatment to be carried out and certified by an approved licensed processor.

Cutting treated timber: re-treat all surfaces to treated timber exposed by cutting, boring etc with matching preservatives applied in two coats by brush.

Holes for supports:
a. excavate and support earth as necessary;
b. surround fence support with concrete for half the depth of the hole unless otherwise stated;
c. backfill to ground level after concrete has hardened with selected excavated material well compacted unless otherwise stated;
d. dispose of surplus materials.

Definition of terms

Supports: posts, struts or the like.

Straining posts: include end posts and angle posts.

Notes

Components of fences:
Sizes and materials are stated only where the BS gives alternatives.

Existing holes for supports:
Where existing holes are used no adjustment is to be made to the Rates.

Method of measurement

Height of fence:
Measure vertically from surface of ground to top of infilling or to top wire if higher.

Length of fence:
Measure over supports.

Rates for the following include

Generally:
For excavating and filling holes for supports.

For supports.

For all cutting including cutting to profile necessary to follow contour of ground.

Setting out to curve:
For setting out to curve straight between posts.

For curve of any radius.

Softwood fencing components and softwood gates:
For preservative treatment.

Taking off, resecuring and fixing only generally:
For component parts of fence of any size or description.

Taking down fence complete:
For excavating.

For removing concrete surround to posts and struts and concrete sill.

For reinstating ground with selected excavated material.

Work to old fencing and gates generally:
For taking down supports including excavating, breaking out concrete surround and reinstating ground with selected excavated material.

For excavating and filling holes for supports.

For component parts of fence of any size or description unless otherwise stated.

For removing fixings and fittings.

For providing and fixing nails, staples, stirrups, ties or the like.

For fixing fittings and bolts.

For straining or re-straining.

For cutting, shaping, housing or the like of timber components.

Q40: FENCING

CHAIN LINK FENCING

Specification

Standard chain link fencing: to BS 1722 Part 1.

Length of side of mesh: 50 mm.

Line wire: mild steel.

Steel supports: rolled steel angle: galvanised.

Erection: comply with BS 1722 Part 1, Section 3

Item Q40	Metre	1 Concrete supports Height 900 mm £	2 1200 mm £	3 1400 mm £	4 1800 mm £	5 Steel supports 900 mm £	6 1200 mm £	7 1400 mm £	8 1800 mm £
001	Fence: wire diameter of mesh 3.00 mm: mesh and all wire galvanised	12.78	14.65	15.96	19.17	12.07	13.83	14.91	17.74
002	ADD where wire diameter of mesh 3.55 mm	1.63	2.24	2.57	2.92	1.63	2.24	2.57	2.92
003	Fence: wire diameter of mesh 3.55 mm overall: mesh and all wire galvanised and plastics coated Grade A	13.33	15.63	17.08	20.12	12.61	14.81	16.03	18.68
004	ADD where wire diameter of mesh 4.00 mm overall	1.33	1.57	1.59	1.59	1.33	1.57	1.59	1.59
	ADD to Items Q40.001 and Q40.004 where								
005	setting out to curve	0.66	0.71	0.74	0.82	0.66	0.71	0.74	0.82
006	ground sloping exceeding 15° from horizontal	0.66	0.71	0.74	0.82	0.66	0.71	0.74	0.82
007	length not exceeding 3 m	0.66	0.71	0.74	0.82	0.66	0.71	0.74	0.82
	Each								
	Extra for straining post								
008	one strut	28.98	35.80	38.07	43.43	41.54	51.27	53.69	66.55
009	two struts	48.75	59.41	63.36	71.66	67.23	83.18	87.41	105.27

Q40: FENCING

CHAIN LINK FENCING - *continued*

Work to old fencing

Item Q40	*Metre*	1 Height not exceeding 1200 mm £	2 1200 to 1800 mm £
	Taking down		
010	chain link mesh and line wire	1.32	1.76
011	fence complete	4.10	4.61
	Fixing only		
012	chain link mesh: providing line wire: galvanised or plastics coated	3.90	4.39
013	fence complete	9.19	10.61
014	Resecuring chain link mesh	2.32	3.47

Item		1 Height 900 mm £	2 1200 mm £	3 1400 mm £	4 1800 mm £
	Supplying only chain link mesh				
015	galvanised: 3.00 mm diameter wire	2.58	3.27	3.80	5.07
016	galvanised: 3.55 mm diameter wire	4.21	5.50	6.37	7.99
017	plastics coated Grade A: 3.55 mm overall diameter wire	3.12	4.24	4.92	6.01
018	plastics coated Grade A: 4.00 mm overall diameter wire	4.46	5.81	6.51	7.60
	Each				
	Supplying only				
019	stretcher bar complete with bolts and cleats	6.56	9.18	9.61	10.26
020	winding bracket	2.07	2.07	2.07	2.07
021	eye bolt: nuts and washers	1.06	1.06	1.06	1.06

Item		1 Intermediate post £	2 Straining post One strut £	3 Two struts £	4 Strut £
022	Taking down support	8.35	15.80	23.25	7.26
023	Fixing only support	10.13	16.63	24.73	8.13

Q40: FENCING

CHAIN LINK FENCING - *continued*

Item Q40	**Work to old fencing - continued**	1	2	3	4
		Height			
		900 mm	1200 mm	1400 mm	1800 mm
	Each	£	£	£	£
	Supplying only				
024	concrete intermediate post	5.92	7.02	8.05	10.71
025	concrete straining post	7.26	11.01	12.29	14.84
026	concrete strut	5.77	6.66	7.58	9.22
027	steel intermediate post	3.89	4.67	5.06	6.61
028	steel straining post	12.19	16.15	17.00	23.86
029	steel strut including brace as required	12.02	15.30	16.33	20.21

Item		1	2
		Galvanised	Plastics coated Grade A
	Per 10 metres	£	£
	Line wire		
030	taking off	1.45	1.45
031	re-straining	2.54	2.54
032	fixing only	5.81	5.81
033	supplying only	3.68	4.49

WOVEN WIRE FENCING

Specification

Fence filling:
Galvanised wire: 31 mm mesh size: lightly strained fixed to posts and strainers with galvanised staples and to line wires with proprietary fixing clips.

Turn bottom 150 mm of mesh at right angles to filling and secure on ground with 300 x 300 x 75 mm thick turves (cut from fience base) at 1000 mm centres.

Softwood round, bark stripped posts:
75 mm minimum diameter x 1520 mm long, peeled and pointed: preservative treated: driven 430 mm into ground at 3000 mm centres.

Line and jumper wire:
3.15 mm galvanised mild steel.

WOVEN WIRE FENCING - *continued*

Item Q40		*Metre*	£
034	Fence: 1080 mm high		5.22
	ADD where		
035	setting out to curve		0.66
036	ground sloping exceeding 15° from horizontal		0.66
037	length not exceeding 3 m		0.66

		Each	
	Extra for straining post		
038	one strut		26.21
039	two struts		40.44

Work to old fencing

		Metre	
	Fence complete: height not exceeding 1200 mm		
040	taking down		4.10
041	fixing only		7.86
042	Resecuring mesh: height not exceeding 1200 mm		2.32

STRAINED WIRE FENCING

Specification

Standard strained wire fencing: General Pattern to BS 1722 Part 3.

Steel supports: rolled steel angle: galvanised.

Wood supports: sawn softwood: square section.

Line wire: 5 mm diameter galvanised mild steel.

Number of line wires:
a. 3 for 900 mm high fence;
b. 5 for 1050 mm high fence.

Oak gate post: 100 x 50 mm nominal wrought oak post and 40 x 20 mm nominal wrought oak stop. Countersunk bolt to end post with two black bolts 10 mm diameter with washers. Hole through fence end post and gate post.

Erection: comply with BS 1722 Part 3, Section 3.

Q40: FENCING

STRAINED WIRE FENCING - *continued*

		1	2	3	4	5	6
		Concrete supports		Steel supports		Wood supports	
		Height					
Item		900 mm	1050 mm	900 mm	1050 mm	900 mm	1050 mm
Q40	*Metre*	£	£	£	£	£	£
043	Fence	7.45	8.79	5.38	6.59	4.68	5.73
	ADD where						
044	setting out to curve	0.66	0.66	0.66	0.66	0.66	0.66
045	ground sloping exceeding 15° from horizontal	0.66	0.66	0.66	0.66	0.66	0.66
046	length not exceeding 3 m	0.66	0.66	0.66	0.66	0.66	0.66
	Each						
	Extra for						
047	straining post: one strut	25.59	33.25	35.11	43.16	20.68	23.68
048	straining post: two struts	41.98	52.97	57.75	71.52	33.11	38.80
049	oak gate post	17.62	18.73	17.62	18.73	17.62	18.73

Work to old fencing

		Metre	£
050	Taking down fence complete		2.54
051	Fixing only fence complete		5.26

		1	2	3	4
		Inter-mediate post	Straining post		Strut
			One strut	Two struts	
	Each	£	£	£	£
052	Taking down support	5.45	11.80	17.42	5.81
053	Fixing only support	8.75	21.27	34.33	9.58

		£
054	Taking down oak gate post	2.72
	Fixing only oak gate post and stop: providing bolts	
055	900 mm high	14.40
056	1050 mm high	15.24

STRAINED WIRE FENCING - *continued*

Work to old fencing - *continued*

Item Q40	Each	1 Concrete supports Height 900 mm £	2 1050 mm £	3 Steel supports 900 mm £	4 1050 mm £	5 Wood supports 900 mm £	6 1050 mm £
	Supplying only						
057	intermediate post	5.93	6.73	5.22	6.11	2.90	3.27
058	straining post	7.26	12.05	9.82	12.71	3.27	3.62
059	strut	5.77	6.66	12.02	15.30	1.82	2.06
060	oak gate post: oak stop	3.22	3.50	3.22	3.50	3.22	3.50

Per 10 metres   £

Line wire

061	taking off	1.09
062	re-straining	0.99
063	fixing only	2.63
064	supplying only	2.88

Each

065	Supplying only eye bolt: nuts and washers	1.06

Q40: FENCING

CLEFT CHESTNUT PALE FENCING

Specification

Standard cleft chestnut pale fencing: to BS 1722 Part 4.

Spacing between pales:
a. 75 mm for 1050 to 1350 mm high fences;
b. 50 mm for 1500 mm high fence.

Erection: comply with BS 1722 Part 4, Section 3.

		1	2	3	4	5	6	7	8
		Concrete supports				Wood supports			
		Height							
Item		1050 mm	1200 mm	1350 mm	1500 mm	1050 mm	1200 mm	1350 mm	1500 mm
Q40	*Metre*	£	£	£	£	£	£	£	£
066	Fence: posts set in concrete	10.04	11.80	13.12	15.95	9.74	11.65	13.21	17.33
	ADD where								
067	setting out to curve	0.66	0.66	0.66	0.66	0.66	0.66	0.66	0.66
068	ground sloping exceeding 15° from horizontal	0.66	0.66	0.66	0.66	0.66	0.66	0.66	0.66
069	length not exceeding 3 m	0.66	0.66	0.66	0.66	0.66	0.66	0.66	0.66
070	DEDUCT where wood supports pointed and driven	-	-	-	-	2.34	2.92	3.19	3.60
	Each								
	Extra for								
071	straining post: one strut: pointed and driven	-	-	-	-	16.76	20.92	22.94	24.66
072	straining post: two struts: pointed and driven	-	-	-	-	26.88	33.62	36.85	40.31
073	straining post: one strut: set in concrete	24.87	31.54	33.26	34.40	22.08	24.17	25.75	27.03
074	straining post: two struts: set in concrete	40.23	48.97	51.37	53.83	34.61	38.24	40.84	43.60

CLEFT CHESTNUT PALE FENCING - *continued*

		1	2
Work to old fencing		Support set in concrete	Support driven
Item Q40	*Metre*	£	£
	Taking down		
075	fence complete	3.69	2.51
076	chestnut paling	1.03	1.03

		1	2	3	4
		Concrete supports		Wood supports	
		Height			
		1050 and 1200 mm	1350 and 1500 mm	1050 and 1200 mm	1350 and 1500 mm
		£	£	£	£
	Fixing only				
077	fence complete	4.21	5.64	5.24	6.55
078	DEDUCT where wood supports pointed and driven	-	-	2.92	3.60
079	chestnut paling	1.73	2.96	2.25	3.51

		£
	Supplying only chestnut paling	
080	1050 mm high	4.35
081	1200 mm high	4.81
082	1350 mm high	5.41
083	1500 mm high	6.22

		1	2	3	4
		Inter-mediate post	Straining post		Strut
			One strut	Two struts	
	Each	£	£	£	£
	Taking down support				
084	set in concrete	8.35	15.80	23.25	7.26
085	driven	5.08	9.26	13.44	4.54
	Fixing only support				
086	concrete: set in concrete	7.24	16.63	24.73	8.13
087	wood: pointed and driven	5.12	13.74	20.65	6.91
088	wood: set in concrete	7.24	16.63	24.73	8.13

CLEFT CHESTNUT PALE FENCING - *continued*

Item Q40	**Work to old fencing - *continued***	1 Height 1050 mm £	2 1200 mm £	3 1350 mm £	4 1500 mm £
	Each				
	Supplying only				
089	concrete intermediate post	6.59	7.00	7.76	8.49
090	concrete straining post	8.06	12.82	14.47	14.75
091	concrete strut	5.64	6.41	6.83	7.99
092	wood intermediate post	2.81	3.05	3.82	5.14
093	wood straining post	4.31	4.85	6.03	6.89
094	wood strut	2.81	3.05	3.82	5.14

		£
095	Supplying only eye bolt: nuts and washers	1.06

CLOSE BOARDED FENCING

Specification

Standard close boarded fencing: to BS 1722 Part 5.

Concrete posts: mortised for arris rails.

Timber posts: for 1800 mm high fence: 100 x 125 x 2550 mm long.

Arris rails: two cut from minimum 75 x 75 mm section.

Wood gravel boards: 32 x 150 mm.

Erection: comply with BS 1722 Part 5, Section 3

		1 Softwood boards Height 1200 mm £	2 1650 mm £	3 1800 mm £	4 Oak pales 1200 mm £	5 1650 mm £	6 1800 mm £
	Metre						
	Fence: oak posts: concrete gravel board						
096	softwood rails	43.82	54.36	57.98	-	-	-
097	oak rails	49.98	63.59	67.21	66.04	86.78	92.22
	ADD where						
098	with capping and counter rail	3.52	3.52	3.57	7.53	7.53	7.53
099	setting out to curve	0.66	0.66	0.66	0.66	0.66	0.66
100	ground sloping exceeding 15° from horizontal	0.66	0.66	0.66	0.66	0.66	0.66

Q40: FENCING

CLOSE BOARDED FENCING - *continued*

		1	2	3	4	5	6
		Softwood boards			Oak pales		
		Height					
Item		1200 mm	1650 mm	1800 mm	1200 mm	1650 mm	1800 mm
Q40	*Metre*	£	£	£	£	£	£
	ADD where						
101	length not exceeding 3 m	0.66	0.66	0.66	0.66	0.66	0.66
102	DEDUCT where timber gravel board	2.34	2.34	2.34	1.28	1.28	1.28
	Fence: concrete posts and gravel board						
103	softwood rails	41.49	47.99	52.82	-	-	-
104	oak rails	47.65	58.87	62.08	63.72	82.05	87.09
	ADD where						
105	with capping and counter rail	3.52	3.52	3.57	7.53	7.53	7.53
106	setting out to curve	0.66	0.66	0.66	0.66	0.66	0.66
107	ground sloping exceeding 15° from horizontal	0.66	0.66	0.66	0.66	0.66	0.66
108	length not exceeding 3 m	0.66	0.66	0.66	0.66	0.66	0.66
109	DEDUCT where timber gravel board	2.34	2.34	2.34	1.28	1.28	1.28

		1	2
Work to old fencing		Taking down	Fixing only
	Metre	£	£
	Fence complete		
110	1200 mm high	5.74	19.63
111	1650 mm high	6.94	22.28
112	1800 mm high	7.63	24.11
	Fence excluding posts		
113	1200 mm high	4.28	14.41
114	1650 mm high	5.34	16.78
115	1800 mm high	5.88	18.62
116	Arris rail: detaching or refixing pales	1.09	6.71
117	Capping	0.27	0.69
118	Counter rail	0.64	2.00
119	Gravel board	1.13	5.66

CLOSE BOARDED FENCING - *continued*

	1 Taking down £	2 Fixing only £
Work to old fencing - *continued*		
Item Q40 *Metre*		
Pale or board: exceeding five pales or boards in groups (measure fence length)		
120 1200 mm high	1.82	8.49
121 1650 or 1800 mm high	2.18	11.09
Each		
Pale or board: isolated or in group not exceeding five pales or boards		
122 1200 mm high	0.36	1.99
123 1650 or 1800 mm high	0.44	2.50

	1 Softwood £	2 Oak £
Metre		
Supplying only		
124 arris rail	1.84	4.38
125 capping	1.09	2.98
126 counter rail	0.72	1.99
127 gravel board	1.73	2.61
128 pale or board	0.61	1.58

	£
129 Supplying only concrete gravel board	3.11

	£
Each	
130 Taking down post	5.90
131 Fixing only post	9.60

	1 Height 1200 mm £	2 1650 mm £	3 1800 mm £
Supplying only post			
132 concrete	19.31	20.80	21.45
133 oak	27.17	36.23	38.64

	£
134 Supplying only bolt: nuts and washers	0.66

Q40: FENCING

WOODEN PALISADE FENCING

Specification

Standard wooden palisade fencing: to BS 1722 Part 6.

Oak posts: 125 x 100 mm.

Arris rails: oak: two cut from minimum 75 x 75 mm section.

Oak palisades:
a. for 1200 mm high fence: 65 x 20 mm rectangular: pointed tops;
b. for 1650 and 1800 mm high fence: triangular: two cut from 50 x 50 mm section: weathered tops.

Erection: comply with BS 1722 Part 6, Section 3.

Item		1	2	3
		Height		
Q40	Metre	1200 mm	1650 mm	1800 mm
		£	£	£
	Fence			
135	concrete posts	28.32	36.54	39.53
136	oak posts	25.01	32.10	38.04
	ADD where			
137	setting out to curve	0.66	0.66	0.66
138	ground sloping exceeding 15° from horizontal	0.66	0.66	0.66
139	length not exceeding 3 m	0.66	0.66	0.66

		1	2
Work to old fencing		Taking down	Fixing only
	Metre	£	£
	Fence complete		
140	1200 mm high	4.27	14.69
141	1650 mm high	5.36	17.29
142	1800 mm high	6.45	18.93
	Fence excluding posts		
143	1200 mm high	2.81	9.48
144	1650 mm high	3.36	11.30
145	1800 mm high	3.90	12.29
146	Arris rail: detaching or refixing palisades	0.94	5.44
	Palisades: exceeding five palisades in groups (measure fence length)		
147	1200 mm high	1.09	6.94
148	1650 or 1800 mm high	1.63	9.91

WOODEN PALISADE FENCING - *continued*

		1	2
Work to old fencing - *continued*		Taking down	Fixing only
Item **Q40**	*Each*	£	£

Palisade: isolated or in group not exceeding five palisades

149	1200 mm high	0.36	2.02
150	1650 or 1800 mm high	0.44	2.50

	Metre	£
	Supplying only	
151	arris rail	1.29
152	palisade	0.55

	Each	£
153	Taking down post	5.90
154	Fixing only post	9.60

		1	2	3
		Height		
		1200 mm	1650 mm	1800 mm
		£	£	£
	Supplying only post			
155	concrete	15.97	21.06	22.91
156	oak	8.98	12.10	22.56

		£
157	Supplying only bolt: nuts and washers	0.66

WOODEN POST AND RAIL FENCING

Specification

Standard wooden post and rail fencing: to BS 1722 Part 7.

Erection: comply with BS 1722 Part 7, Section 3.

WOODEN POST AND RAIL FENCING - *continued*

Item Q40		1	2	3	4
		Nailed type		Mortised type	
		Softwood	Oak	Softwood	Oak
	Metre	£	£	£	£
	Fence: 1100 mm high: three rails				
158	main posts pointed and driven	12.24	16.27	11.58	15.73
159	main posts set in concrete	14.43	18.40	12.65	17.69
	ADD where				
160	with four rails	2.43	3.42	2.38	3.37
161	setting out to curve	0.66	0.66	0.66	0.66
162	ground sloping exceeding 15° from horizontal	0.66	0.66	0.66	0.66
163	length not exceeding 3 m	0.66	0.66	0.66	0.66

Work to old fencing

		1	2	3	4	5	6	7	8
		Taking down				Fixing only			
		Softwood		Oak		Softwood		Oak	
		Nailed	Mortised	Nailed	Mortised	Nailed	Mortised	Nailed	Mortised
	Metre	£	£	£	£	£	£	£	£
	Fence complete								
164	three rails	3.54	3.18	3.54	3.18	6.20	4.97	6.86	5.62
165	four rails	4.08	4.08	4.08	4.08	7.11	5.82	7.93	6.64
166	Rail	0.54	0.91	0.54	0.91	1.73	2.01	2.05	2.42
	Each								
167	Prick post: pointed and driven	-	0.91	-	0.91	-	2.16	-	2.58
	Main post								
168	pointed and driven	1.82	1.82	1.82	1.82	5.38	6.57	6.36	7.88
169	set in concrete	5.45	5.45	5.45	5.45	10.34	11.54	11.33	12.85

		1	2	3	4
		Supplying only			
		Softwood		Oak	
		Nailed	Mortised	Nailed	Mortised
	Metre	£	£	£	£
170	Rail	1.45	1.45	2.24	2.24
	Each				
171	Prick post: 1600 mm long: pointed for driving	-	1.85	-	4.19
172	Main post: 1800 mm long	6.43	6.81	7.85	9.73
173	ADD where pointed for driving	1.07	1.76	1.13	1.14

Q40: FENCING

WOVEN WOOD AND LAP BOARDED PANEL FENCING

Specification

Standard woven wood and lap boarded panel fencing to BS 1722 Part 11.

Lap boarded panels: any type

Erection: comply with BS 1722 Part 11, Section 3.

		1	2	3	4	5	6
		Woven wood panels			Lap boarded panels		
		Height					
Item		1200 mm	1500 mm	1800 mm	1200 mm	1500 mm	1800 mm
Q40	*Metre*	£	£	£	£	£	£
	Fence: softwood panels and capping						
174	softwood posts	20.92	23.25	24.92	23.59	25.79	28.16
175	oak posts	23.32	25.97	27.95	25.98	28.52	31.19
176	concrete posts: rectangular or slotted	24.37	27.28	29.52	27.04	29.82	32.76
	ADD where						
177	with cedar panels and capping	14.83	16.07	18.81	9.01	9.51	10.29
178	setting out to curve	0.66	0.66	0.66	0.66	0.66	0.66
	ADD where						
179	ground sloping exceeding 15° from horizontal	0.66	0.66	0.66	0.66	0.66	0.66
180	length not exceeding 3 m	0.66	0.66	0.66	0.66	0.66	0.66

		1	2
Work to old fencing		Taking down	Fixing only: any height
	Metre	£	£
181	Fence complete	5.45	9.55
	Each		
182	Fence panel	2.72	8.47
183	Capping	0.54	1.38
184	Post	5.45	11.02

		£
	Metre	
	Supplying only capping	
185	softwood	1.73
186	cedar	3.74

WOVEN WOOD AND LAP BOARDED PANEL FENCING - *continued*

Item Q40	**Work to old fencing - *continued***	1 Height 1200 mm £	2 1500 mm £	3 1800 mm £
	Each			
	Supplying only panel			
	softwood			
187	woven wood	17.12	20.11	21.61
188	lap boarded	21.97	24.73	27.49
	cedar			
189	woven wood	44.02	49.27	55.74
190	lap boarded	38.31	41.98	46.15
	Supplying only new post			
191	softwood	3.44	4.01	4.59
192	oak	7.42	8.59	9.73
193	concrete: rectangular or slotted	8.15	9.52	10.88
194	Supplying only bolt: nuts and washers	0.44	0.44	0.44

FENCE CLADDING

Specification

Fence cladding: polyethylene mesh: from an approved manufacturer:
a. high density: black or green: 25 x 5 mm mesh apertures.
b. medium density: black: 4 mm diamond mesh apertures.

Rates fo the following include

Generally:
For fixing to wooden fences with galvanised tying wire.

For fixing to wire or metal fences with galvanised tying wire.

	Square Metre	£
	Fence cladding	
195	high density	5.13
196	medium density	4.65

Q40: FENCING

TEMPORARY WINDBREAKS

Specification

Netting: high density polyethylene mesh: from an approved manufacturer:
a. 7 mm round mesh: protection factor of 60%.
b. 30 x 2 mm mesh: protection factor of 55%.

Supports: softwood: maximum 75 mm diameter at approximately 1500 mm centres, driven 450 mm into ground.

Fixing: wiring or stapling to supports.

Rates fo the following include

Generally:
For extra supports at intersections.

Item Q40		Metre	1 7 mm round mesh Height 1500 mm £	2 30 x 2 mm mesh 2000 mm £
197	Windbreak		9.46	14.16
	ADD where			
198	setting out to curve		0.66	0.66
199	ground sloping exceeding 15° from horizontal		0.66	0.66
200	length not exceeding 3 m		0.66	0.66
201	Taking down windbreak complete		1.23	1.40

STEEL PALISADE SECURITY FENCING

Specification

Standard steel palisade security fencing:
to BS 1722 Part 12, galvanised to BS 729.

Erection: comply with BS 1722 Part 7, Section 3.6.

Rates for the following include

Generally:
For filling holes for posts with concrete to the full depth.

		Metre	1 Height 2400 mm £	2 3000 mm £
202	Fence: corrugated pales: pointed tops		102.47	126.88
	ADD where			
203	setting out to curve		1.07	1.07
204	ground sloping exceeding 15° from horizontal		1.07	1.07
205	length not exceeding 3 m		1.07	1.07

Q40: FENCING

STEEL PALISADE SECURITY FENCING - *continued*

Item Q40	Work to old fencing	1 Taking down £	2 Fixing only £
	Metre		
	Fence complete		
206	2400 mm high	6.72	31.09
207	3000 mm high	7.90	37.93
	Fence excluding posts		
208	2400 mm high	3.63	17.24
209	3000 mm high	4.43	19.29
210	Rail: detaching or fixing pales	1.36	6.27
	Pales: exceeding five pales in groups (measure fence length)		
211	2400 mm high	1.82	11.20
212	3000 mm high	2.36	12.84
	Each		
	Pale: isolated or in group not exceeding five palisades		
213	2400 mm high	0.98	2.57
214	3000 mm high	1.08	2.77

Item Q40		£
	Metre	
	Supplying only	
215	rail: 45 x 45 mm	4.03
216	rail: 50 x 50 mm	4.51
217	pale	3.19
	Each	
218	Taking down post	12.35
219	Fixing only post	34.38
	Supplying only post	
220	2400 mm high	28.16
221	3000 mm high	36.59

Q40: FENCING

ISOLATED TIMBER POSTS TO PREVENT VEHICLE ACCESS

Rates for the following include

Generally:
For filling holes for posts with concrete to the full depth.

Item Q40	Each	£
222	Oak post: 150 x 100 mm: 1200 mm long overall: weathered top: setting 750 mm in ground	24.72

GATES AND POSTS FOR CHAIN LINK FENCING

Specification

Gates and posts generally: to BS 1722 Part 1.

Steel gates:
a. steel formed with rectangular hollow section outside frame members and braces, size 40 x 40 x 3 mm; galvanised to BS 729 after manufacture;
b. chain link mesh infill to match fencing fixed with stretcher bars and bolts;
c. complete with fittings for hanging and securing.

Steel gate posts: rectangular hollow section galvanised to BS 729 after manufacture, complete with fittings for hanging and securing.

Rates for the following include

Generally:
For filling holes for posts with concrete to the full depth.

	1	2	3
	Width		
Each	1000 mm	1500 mm	2000 mm
	£	£	£
Steel gate: any type of mesh: single or double			
223 900 mm high	169.67	202.64	229.47
224 1200 mm high	181.80	217.10	245.57
225 1400 mm high	204.62	228.12	256.41
226 1800 mm high	221.95	238.78	283.80

	1	2	3	4
	Concrete		Steel	
	125 x 125 mm	150 x 150 mm	80 x 80 x 3.6 mm	100 x 100 x 4 mm
	£	£	£	£
Post: hanging or shutting: fence height				
227 900 mm	32.71	-	45.64	-
228 1200 mm	36.59	42.30	50.75	58.18
229 1400 mm	40.23	46.78	67.00	75.79
230 1800 mm	47.46	56.70	83.01	94.26

Q40: FENCING

CLOSE BOARDED GATES

Specification

Timber: wrought softwood or sawn oak.

Stiles, rails and braces: size 65 x 65 mm. Gates exceeding 1200 mm high to have a centre rail.

Board/pale filling: size 90 x 13 mm tapered to 6 mm. Lap 13 mm and nail to rails and braces with rose-headed composition nails.

Item Q40	*Each*	1 Softwood £	2 Oak £
231	Framed and braced gate: not exceeding 1.00 m²	51.66	65.82
232	ADD *for each additional 0.30 m²*	6.91	10.85

WOODEN PALISADE GATES

Specification

Timber: wrought softwood or sawn oak.

Nails: galvanised.

Nominal sizes of timber members:

Member	Width of gate	
	not exceeding 900 mm	exceeding 900 mm
Stile	50 x 75	65 x 75
Rail	32 x 75	45 x 75
Brace	32 x 83	45 x 83
Pale - pointed	20 x 90	20 x 90

Fix: pales to rails and braces with nails. Space pales 75 mm apart.

	Each	1 Softwood £	2 Oak £
233	Framed and braced gate: not exceeding 1.00 m²	45.54	60.23
234	ADD *for each additional 0.30 m²*	7.34	10.51

FIELD GATES AND POSTS

Specification

Field gates and posts generally: to BS 3470.

Timber gates: framed, braced and bolted. Bolts, nuts and washers galvanised to BS 729.

Steel gates: framed, braced and welded, heavy duty. Galvanised to BS 729 after manufacture. Complete with fittings for hanging and securing.

Timber posts: weathered tops. Holes for ironmongery.

Steel posts: capped tops. Complete with fittings for hanging and securing.

Rates for the following include

Generally:
For filling holes for posts with concrete to the full depth.

Item Q40	Each	1 Wrought softwood £	2 Sawn oak £	3 Steel £
	Gate			
235	2400 x 1100 mm	127.14	175.04	78.73
236	3000 x 1100 mm	138.32	190.19	103.91
237	3600 x 1100 mm	149.76	205.73	118.55

		1 Wrought softwood £	2 Sawn oak £	3 Concrete £	4 Circular hollow section steel £
	Gate post				
238	175 x 175 x 2100 mm long	53.64	53.19	47.81	-
239	200 x 200 x 2100 mm long	51.89	66.23	61.87	-
240	89 mm diameter x 2100 long	-	-	-	52.29
241	114 mm diameter x 2100 long	-	-	-	65.29
242	Gate stop: 100 x 125 x 600 mm: mortice for bolt socket	7.17	10.03	-	-

Q40: FENCING

IRONMONGERY FOR GATES

Specification

Ironmongery: steel, galvanised to BS 729.

Notes

Ironmongery fixed partly to softwood and partly hardwood:
Measure as fixed to hardwood.

Rates for the following include

Generally:
For providing ironmongery complete with screws, bolts, nuts and washers.

For holes and mortices in timber.

Item Q40	Each	1 Fixing to Softwood £	2 Hardwood £
	Pair hook and band hinges		
243	300 mm: bolting hook through post	13.54	14.36
244	450 mm: building in hook to brickwork	18.41	19.23
245	450 mm: heavy pattern: building in hook to brickwork	22.72	23.54
246	Set of double strap hinges for field gate: to BS 3470	36.57	39.03
247	Barrel bolt: 150 mm	4.37	4.78
248	Gate latch: 50 mm: automatic pattern	4.06	4.47
249	Gate spring catch and hook plate: 500 mm	20.89	22.53
250	Cabin hook and eye: 150 mm	6.09	6.50

WORK TO OLD GATES AND POSTS

	Each	£
	Taking down	
251	gate: not exceeding 1 m²	2.27
252	ADD *for each additional m²*	1.36
253	gate post	5.45
	Fixing only	
254	gate: not exceeding 1 m²	5.00
255	ADD *for each additional m²*	3.36
256	gate post: filling hole completely with concrete	17.56

Q40: FENCING

CLEARING FENCE LINE

Item Q40		Metre	£
257	Clearing areas not exceeding 1.00 m wide, to each side of fence line, of bushes, scrub or undergrowth: cutting long grass, weeds, brambles, saplings not exceeding 150 mm girth or the like: disposing of arisings		2.72

PERGOLAS AND ARCHES

Specification

Softwood round or square bark-stripped members:
Butt jointed and fixed together with galvanised nails or bolts.

Rates for the following include

Generally:
For setting support posts into ground at depth ordered.

For filling holes for support posts with hardcore well packed and consolidated to half the full depth and backfilling the remainder with selected excavated material to the full depth.

For all in-line and corner bracings.

For all cuttings and notchings.

For treating cut timber and ends of support posts with preservative.

		Each	£
	Softwood: 100 mm diameter or 100 x 100 mm square		
	support post		
258	not exceeding 2000 mm long		15.35
259	2000 to 4000 mm long		19.32
		Metre	
260	vertical, horizontal or diagonal member		6.75

BREAKING THROUGH PAVINGS

		Each	£
	Extra over excavating for support for breaking through existing paving not exceeding 150 mm thick and reinstating		
261	concrete		6.05
262	reinforced concrete		9.68
263	brick, block or stone or concrete flag		2.27
264	coated macadam or asphalt		4.84

Q50: SITE/STREET FURNITURE/EQUIPMENT

GENERALLY

Notes

Ground-fixed and floor mounted items:
Heights stated are the overall heights above ground.

Free-standing items:
Heights stated are the overall heights above ground (including plinths where applicable).

Rates for the following include

Generally:
For moving items from delivery point or existing location and re-siting as ordered within the site.

For assembling (where appropriate) and fixing in accordance with manufacturer's instructions.

Ground-fixed items:
For excavating holes for supports, bases, etc. and disposing of arisings.

For breaking through existing hard surfacings.

For setting into ground at depth recommended by the manufacturer or as ordered.

For filling holes for supports, bases, etc. with concrete (10 N/mm²: 40 mm maximum size aggregate) to the full depth.

Floor or wall-mounted items:
For fixing with bolts to any background.

For grouting holding down bolts with cement mortar.

Free-standing items:
For plinth units where applicable.

For placing in position as ordered.

BOLLARDS: FIXING ONLY

		1	2
		Maximum diameter	
Item		200 to	300 to
Q50	*Each*	300 mm	400 mm
		£	£
Bollard: straight or tapered: ground fixed			
	precast concrete: any finish: height		
001	not exceeding 500 mm	14.68	19.30
002	500 to 750 mm	16.29	21.72
003	750 to 1000 mm	17.91	24.15
	ductile or cast iron: any finish: height		
004	not exceeding 500 mm	13.06	17.68
005	500 to 750 mm	14.68	20.11
006	750 to 1000 mm	16.29	22.53

Q50: SITE/STREET FURNITURE/EQUIPMENT

PLANT CONTAINERS: FIXING ONLY

Notes

Supplying filling materials:
Pay for separately

Planting:
Pay for at the appropriate Rates in Section Q31.

Rates for the following include

Filling containers:
For filling with drainage material, soil, compost or other approved material and preparing for planting

Method of measurement

Planting area:
Measure as the surface area of the filling materia

Item Q50	Each	1 Planting area not exceeding 0.50 m² £	2 0.50 to 1.00 m² £	3 1.00 to 1.50 m² £	4 1.50 to 2.00 m² £
	Plant container: any shape: free standing				
	precast concrete: height				
007	not exceeding 500 mm	5.45	6.90	9.81	14.17
008	500 to 750 mm	7.27	9.09	12.36	17.08
009	*ADD for each additional 250 mm of height*	1.45	1.74	2.04	2.33
	glass reinforced cement: height				
010	not exceeding 500 mm	4.09	5.18	7.36	10.63
011	500 to 750 mm	5.45	6.81	9.27	12.81
012	*ADD for each additional 250 mm of height*	1.09	1.31	1.53	1.74
	glass reinforced plastics: height				
013	not exceeding 500 mm	2.74	3.47	4.93	7.12
014	500 to 750 mm	3.65	4.57	6.21	8.58
015	*ADD for each additional 250 mm of height*	0.73	0.88	1.02	1.17

	Cubic Metre	£
016	Filling containers	9.17

Q50: SITE/STREET FURNITURE/EQUIPMENT

SEATS, BENCHES AND TABLES: FIXING ONLY

Item Q50	*Each*	1 Seat Free-standing £	2 Seat Ground-fixed £	3 Bench Free-standing £	4 Bench Ground-fixed £
	Hardwood				
017	1200 mm	3.63	6.99	3.63	6.99
018	1500 mm	5.09	8.81	5.09	8.81
019	1800 mm	6.54	10.63	6.54	10.63
020	2000 mm	7.27	11.53	7.27	11.53
	Composite concrete/hardwood				
021	1200 mm	15.99	26.64	8.72	14.23
022	1500 mm	17.44	28.45	10.18	16.04
023	1800 mm	18.90	30.27	11.63	17.86
024	2000 mm	20.35	32.09	13.08	19.68
	Composite cast iron/hardwood				
025	1200 mm	14.39	24.64	7.85	13.14
026	1500 mm	15.70	26.27	9.16	14.77
027	1800 mm	17.01	27.91	10.47	16.41
028	2000 mm	18.32	29.55	11.77	18.04
	Steel: 2000 mm long				
029	1200 mm	12.79	22.64	6.98	12.05
030	1500 mm	13.95	24.09	8.14	13.50
031	1800 mm	15.12	25.55	9.30	14.95
032	2000 mm	16.28	27.00	10.47	16.41

£

033	Picnic table/bench: softwood or hardwood: not exceeding 2000 mm long	8.72

Q50: SITE/STREET FURNITURE/EQUIPMENT

LITTER BINS: FIXING ONLY

Definition	**Rates for the following include**
Capacity (precast concrete units): Manufacturer's specified capacity.	*Generally:* For inserting inner basket or liner (where applicable)

Item **Q50**	Each	£
	Litter bin	
	precast concrete: any shape: freestanding: capacity	
034	not exceeding 100 litres	3.52
035	100 to 200 litres	4.68
036	exceeding 200 litres	7.01
037	hardwood: floor mounted: not exceeding 500 x 500 x800 mm high	5.15

		1 Ground- fixed £	2 Floor- mounted £
	mild steel: pedestal type: not exceeding 500 mm diameter overall		
	two-piece: lockable top section: padlock: hand two keys to PM		
	medium duty: height		
038	not exceeding 750 mm	8.05	5.70
039	750 to 900 mm	9.96	7.05
040	heavy duty: height not exceeding 750 mm	12.04	8.52
041	one-piece: heavy duty: height not exceeding 750 mm	11.75	8.32

Q50: SITE/STREET FURNITURE/EQUIPMENT

CYCLE STANDS: FIXING ONLY

Rates for the following include

Paving type cycle blocks:
For any additional filling under to bring flush with surrounding paving.

Free-standing type cycle blocks:
For bedding in cement and sand (1:3).

Item Q50	*Each*	£
	Cycle block: precast concrete	
	paving type: 100 mm thick	
042	600 x 300 mm	5.53
043	500 x 500 mm	6.22
044	free-standing type: 590 x 210 x 280 mm	8.21

		1 Ground-fixed £	2 Floor-mounted £	3 Wall-mounted £
045	Cycle parking stand: galvanised mild steel: 915 mm high: not exceeding 1500 mm long: two fixing points	13.29	-	-
	Front wheel support: galvanised mild steel			
046	275 mm high: single sided for one bicycle	-	-	5.59
	515 mm high			
047	single sided for one bicycle	8.20	6.31	-
048	double sided for two bicycles	8.93	7.04	-
	Range of front wheel supports: 3000 mm long: galvanised mild steel frame			
049	330 mm high: single sided for five bicycles	-	-	20.62
	515 mm high			
050	single sided for six bicycle	23.47	15.76	-
051	double sided for twelve bicycles	24.92	17.21	-

Q50: SITE/STREET FURNITURE/EQUIPMENT

SPORTS AND PLAYGROUND EQUIPMENT: FIXING ONLY

Specification

Generally:
Assemble, erect and test strictly in accordance with the manufacturer's instructions.

Note

Ground-fixed items:
Heights stated are heights above ground.

Rates for the following include

Ground-fixed items:
For excavating holes for supports, bases, etc. and disposing of arisings.

For breaking through existing hard surfacings.

For setting into ground at depth recommended by the manufacturer or as ordered.

For setting horizontally, vertically or raking as appropriate or as ordered.

For filling holes for supports, bases, etc. with concrete (20N/mm²: 20 mm aggregate) to the full depth.

				1	2
				Height	
Item				2400 mm	3000 mm
Q50		*Each*		£	£

Swing: any type

	Number of seats	*Number of ground fixing points*			
052	1	2	. . . .	20.84	23.02
053	1	4	. . . .	35.87	38.05
054	2	4	. . . .	38.05	40.23
055	3	4	. . . .	40.96	43.14
056	4	6	. . . .	59.62	61.80
057	5	6	. . . .	63.25	65.43
058	6	6	. . . .	66.89	69.07

		£
059	Swing area safety barrier: 1250 mm wide: 900 mm high: two ground fixing points	16.48

Slide: steps, deck and handrails: six ground fixing points

	Overall length	*Overall height*	*Deck height*		
060	3350 mm	1600 mm	1000 mm	. . . .	75.61
061	4150 mm	2400 mm	1500 mm	. . . .	82.88

R12: DRAINAGE BELOW GROUND

GENERALLY

Reference to other Sections: the Preambles to Sections D20, E10, E20, E30 and F10 apply equally to this Section unless otherwise stated.

Specification

Jointing pipes of dissimilar materials: ensure that
a. pipe materials are compatible ; or
b. a suitable adaptor is used.

Connection to Local Authority's and Water Company's sewers: make arrangements with the Local Authority/Water Company for connections to be made.

Interim and final pipeline tests: either water or air test:
a. water test as follows:
   1. effectively temporarily plug drain under test;
   2. connect standpipe to head of drain under test;
   3. fill pipes with water approximately one hour before starting test;
   4. apply a test pressure of not less than 1200 mm head of water above crown of the pipes at the high end of the section being tested but not more than 6000 mm above the low end;
   5. non-absorbent pipes: make good after 10 minutes loss of water indicated by a fall in level. After 30 minutes, no further measurable loss to be evident;
   6. absorbent pipes: make good loss of water indicated by a fall in level and measure over a period of 30 minutes by adding water from a measuring vessel at regular intervals of 10 minutes. Record the quantity required to maintain the original water level. In interim test the average quantity added must not exceed one litre per hour per metre diameter of pipe. eg:
      0.05 litre per metre of 100 mm diameter pipe in 30 minutes;
      0.08 litre per metre of 150 mm diameter pipe in 30 minutes;
      0.12 litre per metre of 225 mm diameter pipe in 30 minutes;

0.15 litre per metre of 300 mm diameter pipe in 30 minutes;
0.19 litre per metre of 375 mm diameter pipe in 30 minutes;
0.22 litre per metre of 450 mm diameter pipe in 30 minutes;
In final tests pipelines will be considered satisfactory if, after stabilisation, water level shows no appreciable fall after 30 minutes.

b. air test as follows:
   1. effectively temporarily plug drain under test;
   2. connect glass `U' tube gauge to drain plug in length of drain under test at a convenient position;
   3. pump or blow air into test section until pressure equivalent to 100 mm head of water in indicated;
   4. where gullies and ground floor appliances are connected, pump or blow air into test section until pressure equivalent to 50 mm head of water only is indicated;
   5. without further air being added, the pressure must not fall below 75 mm after a period of 5 minutes. Where gullies and ground floor appliances are connected, pressure must not fall below 38 mm after a period of 5 minutes.
If pipeline fails this test, apply water test as (a).

Interim test of underground chambers: apply interim test for watertightness before backfilling and before surrounding precast manholes with concrete as follows:
a. keep external faces of chambers clear of backfill for inspection until approved;
b. temporarily seal all pipe openings in chambers;
c. fill chambers less than 1.5 m in depth to invert to the underside of the cover and deeper chambers to a minimum depth of 1.5 m with clean water and allow up to 8 hours for initial absorption. Top up before starting test;
d. the water level should not drop over a period of 30 minutes in excess of figures in the following table:

R12: DRAINAGE BELOW GROUND

GENERALLY - *continued*

Age of chamber construction up to Water Test Level	Method of Construction		
	Brickwork	Concrete sections	Clayware, plastics or any "One Piece" Chambers
	Maximum permissible drop in water level (mm)		
3 to 7 days only	40	10	5
over 31 days	5	5	5

Where the drop in level during a water test on a brick manhole or inspection chamber exceeds 40 mm but does not exceed 60 mm, the test may be repeated at 31 days, when the criteria of acceptance for that period shall apply.

Final test of underground chambers: apply final test as specified for interim test except that external faces will not be exposed for inspection.

Definition of terms

Manhole: includes manholes, catchpits, soakaways and petrol/mud/oil interceptors.

Notes

Generally:
Rates in other Sections apply to drainage below ground where Rates are not given in this Section.

Method of measurement

Pipework:
Measure over all fittings and branches.

Reducing fittings:
Measure extra over the largest pipe in which they occur.

Rates for the following include

Generally:
For testing new drainage work.

Pipe:
For horizontal or vertical pipe in trench.

For joints in the running length.

For work in runs of any length unless otherwise stated.

Pipe fitting:
For cutting and jointing pipes to fitting.

Taper or the like:
For socket at small end.

Screwed or bolted access door:
For all bolts, screws, washers and drilling and tapping required.

Accessory:
For jointing to drain.

For jointing as pipework unless otherwise stated.

For setting on and surrounding with 150 mm concrete grade 20 N/mm²: 20 mm aggregate including formwork.

For extra excavation, disposal and earthwork support.

Work to existing pipework and manholes:
For removing and replacing gratings, manhole covers or the like.

For temporarily stopping drains.

EXCAVATING TRENCHES

Specification

Excavation: excavate to required levels with accurate and even gradients restricting trench widths to either 450 mm or 1.5 times external diameter of pipe to be laid plus 250 mm, whichever is the greater.

Selected backfill: backfill and compact by hand in 100 mm layers to 300 mm above pipes not requiring a surround with approved selected fill fill readily compacted, free from roots, vegetable matter, building rubbish, frozen soil, clay lumps retained on a 75 mm sieve and stones retained on a 25 mm sieve.

Main backfill: backfill with previously excavated material excluding boulders, timber, vegetable matter and waste material in layers not exceeding 300 mm thick and compact each layer.

Method of measurement

Excavating trench:
Measure uninterrupted line of excavating between manholes or between an accessory and a manhole or between accessories.

Rates for the following include

Generally:
For earthwork support.

For consolidating trench bottom.

For trimming excavations.

For forming handholes.

For backfilling and compacting.

For setting aside and replacing topsoil.

For disposing of surplus excavated materials off site.

Item R12	Metre	1	2	3	4	5
		Nominal size of pipe not exceeding				
		200 mm	225 mm	300 mm	375 mm	450 mm
		£	£	£	£	£
	Excavating trench: for pipe: average depth					
001	not exceeding 0.25 m	4.33	-	-	-	-
002	0.25 to 0.50 m	9.03	9.39	10.48	-	-
003	0.50 to 0.75 m	13.73	14.34	16.18	17.93	19.81
004	0.75 to 1.00 m	18.43	19.29	21.89	24.39	27.03
005	1.00 to 1.25 m	23.13	24.24	27.60	30.86	34.24
006	1.25 to 1.50 m	27.82	29.19	33.30	37.32	41.46
007	1.50 to 1.75 m	32.52	34.14	39.01	43.78	48.68
008	1.75 to 2.00 m	37.22	39.09	44.71	50.24	55.89
009	2.00 to 2.25 m	41.92	44.04	50.42	56.70	63.11
010	2.25 to 2.50 m	46.62	48.99	56.13	63.16	70.33
011	2.50 to 2.75 m	51.32	53.94	61.83	69.63	77.55
012	2.75 to 3.00 m	56.02	58.89	67.54	76.09	84.76
013	3.00 to 3.25 m	60.72	63.85	73.25	82.55	91.98
014	3.25 to 3.50 m	65.42	68.80	78.95	89.01	99.20

R12: DRAINAGE BELOW GROUND

EXCAVATING TRENCHES - *continued*

Item **R12**	*Metre*	1	2	3	4	5
		Nominal size of pipe not exceeding				
		200 mm	225 mm	300 mm	375 mm	450 mm
		£	£	£	£	£
	Excavating trench: for pipe: average depth					
015	3.50 to 3.75 m	70.12	73.75	84.66	95.47	106.41
016	3.75 to 4.00 m	74.82	78.70	90.36	101.93	113.63
017	4.00 to 4.25 m	79.51	83.65	96.07	108.40	120.85
018	4.25 to 4.50 m	84.21	88.60	101.78	114.86	128.06

019 Where hand excavation is specifically ordered, price at the foregoing Rates multiplied by 2.00.

GRANULAR MATERIAL

Specification

Granular material: coarse aggregate to BS 882 Part 4, single size or graded.

Lay granular material and compact in 100 mm layers. Do not lay granular material within 24 hours of the completion of concrete beds.

Beds: full width of trench: 100 mm thick.

Haunching: side fill half way up the pipe.

Surrounds: thickness above pipe equal to nominal pipe size.

	Metre	1	2	3
		Bed	Bed and haunching	Bed and surround
		£	£	£
	For pipe: nominal size			
020	not exceeding 200 mm	3.61	5.68	10.39
021	225 mm	3.82	6.14	11.97
022	300 mm	4.29	7.70	17.40
023	375 mm	4.70	9.71	25.43
024	450 mm	5.11	12.74	34.77

	Cubic Metre	£
025	Thickening to bed or surround	49.31

PLAIN IN SITU CONCRETE

Specification

Concrete mix: grade 20 N/mm²: 20 mm aggregate.

Beds: 300 wider than external diameter of pipe: 150 mm thick.

Haunching: side fill half way up the pipe and slope off to the crown.

Surrounds: 150 mm thick above pipe.

Vertical casing: 150 mm thick.

Compressible joint filler: bitumen impregnated insulating board to BS 1142 Part 3, 18 mm minimum thick, cut to finished profile of concrete and pipe.

Construction joints: form at intervals not exceeding 5000 mm coinciding with pipe joints.

Rates for the following include

Generally:
For formwork.

Pipes with flexible joints:
For construction joints through concrete.

		1	2	3	4	5	6
		Pipes with rigid joints			Pipes with flexible joints		
		Bed and haunching	Bed and surround	Vertical casing	Bed and haunching	Bed and surround	Vertical casing
Item R12	*Metre*	£	£	£	£	£	£
	For pipe: nominal size						
026	80 mm	9.81	15.78	20.81	10.83	17.31	22.84
027	100 mm	11.07	17.63	23.12	12.09	19.15	25.15
028	150 mm	13.14	20.66	26.75	14.15	22.19	28.79
029	200 mm	15.20	23.76	30.45	16.22	25.28	32.49
030	225mm	16.60	25.87	33.45	17.61	27.40	35.49
031	300 mm	19.33	30.14	38.44	20.35	31.67	40.48
032	375 mm	22.06	34.55	43.97	23.08	36.07	46.01
033	450 mm	24.79	39.10	49.25	25.81	40.63	51.29
	Cubic Metre						
034	Thickening to bed or surround	102.13	122.00	149.64	106.20	128.11	157.78

CONCRETE PIPEWORK

Specification

Pipes and fittings: to BS 5911 and manufactured by a BSI Kitemark Licensee:
a. pipe class: M;
b. cement type: Ordinary Portland;
c. ogee rigid joint type: cement-sand mortar (1:2);
d. spigot and socket joint type: in accordance with the pipe manufacturer's recommendations.

CONCRETE PIPEWORK - *continued*

Item R12	*Metre*	1	2	3	4	5	6
		Ogee joints			Spigot and socket flexible joints		
		Nominal size					
		300 mm	375 mm	450 mm	300 mm	375 mm	450 mm
		£	£	£	£	£	£
035	Pipe	25.08	32.70	38.35	34.53	41.79	47.60
	Each						
	Extra for						
036	taper: any size socket	-	-	-	119.87	199.48	199.94
037	bend	105.08	158.52	184.28	175.62	238.77	260.35
	junction: any type						
038	100 mm branch	47.60	47.60	47.60	47.60	47.60	47.60
039	150 mm branch	69.14	69.14	69.14	69.14	69.14	69.14
040	225 mm branch	97.16	97.16	97.16	97.16	97.16	97.16
041	300 mm branch	132.83	132.83	132.83	132.83	132.83	132.83

CLAY PIPEWORK: RIGID JOINTS

Specification

Spigot and socket pipes and fittings: to BS 65
and manufactured by a BSI Kitemark Licensee:
a. type: normal or surface water;
b. joint type: cement-sand mortar (1:2).

Item	*Metre*	1	2	3	4	5	6
		British Standard Surface Water Extra Strength			British Standard Normal Super Strength		
		100 mm	150 mm	225 mm	100 mm	150 mm	225 mm
		£	£	£	£	£	£
042	Pipe	10.05	14.88	28.54	11.04	15.47	26.84
	Each						
	Extra for						
043	pipe stopper: setting in mortar	6.26	10.46	20.00	6.26	10.46	20.00
044	taper	-	19.49	38.00	-	27.31	39.52
045	level invert taper	-	18.74	36.12	-	26.08	37.57
046	bend	4.81	7.03	18.39	10.45	15.91	30.52
047	rest bend	9.83	14.75	-	13.37	21.23	46.01
048	junction: any type: any size branch	10.36	15.60	-	14.76	23.11	41.83
049	double junction: any type: any size branches	-	-	-	33.89	48.49	93.42

CLAY PIPEWORK: FLEXIBLE JOINTS

Specification

Pipes and fittings: to BS EN 295 and manufactured by a BSI Kitemark Licensee:
a. type: normal;
b. joint type: in accordance with the pipe manufacturer's recommendations;
c. strength class: super strength.

		1	2	3	4	5	6
		Plain ended pipes			Spigot and socket pipes		
		Nominal size					
Item		100 mm	150 mm	225 mm	100 mm	150 mm	225 mm
R12	*Metre*	£	£	£	£	£	£
050	Pipe	8.89	14.03	24.98	12.85	16.37	29.20
	Each						
	Extra for						
051	adaptor to plastics soil pipe	7.73	9.02	-	7.15	8.24	-
052	pipe stopper: setting in mortar	9.45	11.71	-	9.45	11.71	-
053	taper	-	11.93	38.81	-	36.72	53.15
054	bend	7.64	12.58	35.41	16.29	24.58	45.37
055	rest bend	14.60	15.85	38.86	19.06	29.29	64.89
056	junction: any type: any size branch	14.07	17.94	54.23	22.01	32.02	70.39
057	double junction: any type: any size branches	-	-	-	29.43	65.25	140.82

PLASTICS PIPEWORK

Specification

UPVC pipes and fittings: to BS 4660 and manufactured by a BSI Kitemark Licensee: joint type: ring seal.

		1	2
		Nominal size	
		110 mm	160 mm
	Metre	£	£
058	Pipe	8.25	16.72
	Each		
	Extra for		
059	taper	-	22.95
060	bend	16.64	34.79
061	junction: any type: any size branch	23.66	68.96
062	double junction: any type: any size branches	26.52	72.79

R12: DRAINAGE BELOW GROUND

CAST IRON PIPEWORK: SPIGOT ENDED

Specification

Pipes and fittings: to BS 437 with joint couplings to BS 6087:
a. joint type: in accordance with the pipe manufacturer's recommendations;
b. coating: as BS 437 Clause 9;
c. pipes, fittings and couplings manufactured by a BSI Kitemark Licensee.

Item R12		1	2	3
		Nominal size		
		75 mm	100 mm	150 mm
	Metre	£	£	£
	Pipe			
063	in run exceeding 3 m long	50.08	54.89	89.39
064	in run not exceeding 3 m long	58.58	65.52	105.34
	ADD where			
065	on piers	1.70	2.13	3.19
066	suspended (measure supports separately)	2.55	3.19	4.78
	Each			
	Extra for			
067	cement joint to clay	-	32.45	-
068	piece: rectangular access door bolted and sealed	-	116.41	195.58
069	level invert taper	-	60.00	86.54
070	bend	47.08	58.89	95.61
071	bend: rectangular access door bolted and sealed	-	87.43	174.52
072	long radius bend	-	74.55	132.40
073	rest bend	-	71.46	119.29
	oblique junction			
074	100 mm branch	72.44	88.19	-
075	150 mm branch	-	140.47	155.79

CAST IRON PIPEWORK: SPIGOT AND SOCKET

Specification

Pipes and fittings: to BS 437 and manufactured to BS 437 and manufactured by a BSI Kitemark Licensee:
a. joint type: hempen yarn with run lead and/or with lead wool where approved;
b. coating: as BS 437 Clause 9.

R12: DRAINAGE BELOW GROUND

CAST IRON PIPEWORK: SPIGOT AND SOCKET - *continued*

Item R12	*Metre*	1	2	3	4
		Nominal size			
		75 mm	100 mm	150 mm	225 mm
		£	£	£	£
	Pipe				
076	in run exceeding 3 m long	48.91	66.08	95.69	314.30
077	in run not exceeding 3 m long	59.54	79.37	113.41	340.88
	ADD where				
078	on piers	2.66	3.31	5.32	7.97
079	suspended (measure supports separately)	4.66	5.79	7.97	15.95
	Each				
	Extra for				
080	large socket for clay	-	44.85	65.70	187.38
081	loose collar	51.64	76.34	121.88	226.11
082	socket plug	29.37	40.29	66.01	108.79
083	blank cap	29.92	40.75	67.63	-
084	piece: rectangular access door bolted and sealed	95.71	122.64	229.50	403.00
085	socket reducer	33.21	52.34	70.90	143.92
086	socket ferrule with brass screw cap	55.97	71.77	116.81	307.48
087	level invert taper	50.13	68.85	104.16	115.96
088	bend	39.40	57.04	107.33	267.22
089	bend: rectangular access door bolted and sealed	-	102.97	202.83	-
090	long radius bend	40.78	67.37	106.77	-
091	rest bend	-	87.13	153.96	-
092	long radius rest bend	-	84.94	-	-
	oblique junction				
093	75 mm branch	72.20	86.74	-	-
094	100 mm branch	-	80.25	145.96	274.08
095	150 mm branch	-	-	170.78	313.86
096	225 mm branch	-	-	-	397.99
	oblique junction: rectangular access door bolted and sealed				
097	100 mm branch	-	162.66	309.97	-
098	150 mm branch	-	-	306.26	-

DUCTILE IRON PIPEWORK

Specification

Spigot ended pipes and fittings: to dimensions of BS 437 with joint couplings to BS 6087. Joint type: in accordance with the pipe manufacturer's recommendations.

Spigot and socket pipes and fittings: to BS 4772, manufactured by a BSI Kitemark Licensee and:
a. pipe strength class: K9;

b. fittings strength class: K12 for fittings other than branches, K14 for branches.
c. joint type: in accordance with the pipe manufacturer's recommendations.

Rates for the following include

Generally:
For spigot ended or spigot and socket pipes and fittings.

		1	2	3	4
		Nominal size			
Item		80 mm	100 mm	150 mm	200 mm
R12	*Metre*	£	£	£	£
	Pipe				
099	in run exceeding 3 m long	38.21	42.40	58.82	91.96
100	in run not exceeding 3 m long	46.72	53.03	78.31	118.54
	ADD where				
101	on piers	1.70	2.13	2.84	3.72
102	suspended (measure supports separately)	2.55	3.19	4.78	6.38
	Each				
	Extra for				
103	piece: large socket for clay or cast iron	-	47.04	-	-
	level invert taper				
104	80 mm	-	49.55	-	-
105	100 mm	-	-	63.19	-
106	150 mm	-	-	-	106.96
107	bend	55.93	64.88	99.91	192.37
	tee				
108	80 mm branch	72.53	83.54	134.22	205.77
109	100 mm branch	-	86.46	138.10	211.41
110	150 mm branch	-	-	162.82	300.24
111	200 mm branch	-	-	-	315.66

DUCTILE IRON PIPEWORK - *continued*

Item R12	*Each*	1 Nominal size 80 mm £	2 100 mm £	3 150 mm £	4 200 mm £
	Extra for ductile iron change fitting to cast iron pipework				
	change collar				
112	to 100 mm pipe	-	62.24	-	-
113	to 150 mm pipe	-	-	91.45	-
	change piece				
114	to 100 mm pipe	-	53.74	-	-
115	to 150 mm pipe	-	-	68.97	-

WORK TO EXISTING PIPEWORK: CONCRETE

	Each	1 Nominal size 300 mm £	2 375 mm £	3 450 mm £
116	Connecting new pipe to existing pipe end: cement joint	19.48	28.30	41.06

		1 Nominal size 100 mm £	2 150 mm £	3 225 mm £	4 300 mm £
117	Connecting new pipe to existing pipe: cutting away concrete bed and haunching: cutting aperture: saddle connector: cement joints: making good concrete bed and haunching	53.36	73.17	116.21	192.78

WORK TO EXISTING PIPEWORK: CLAY

	Each	1 Nominal size 100 mm £	2 150 mm £	3 225 mm £	4 300 mm £
	Connecting new pipe to existing pipe end				
118	cement joint	6.29	8.63	12.94	18.87
119	double socket: cement joints	15.82	23.72	35.58	52.30
120	Cutting out short length of existing pipe and concrete bed and haunching: inserting new oblique branch (British Standard Super Strength): loose collar: cement joints: making good concrete bed and haunching	38.61	54.19	100.80	177.02
121	Connecting new pipe to existing pipe: cutting away concrete bed and haunching: cutting aperture: saddle connector: cement joints: making good concrete bed and haunching	56.33	73.59	115.36	181.87

R12: DRAINAGE BELOW GROUND

WORK TO EXISTING PIPEWORK: CAST IRON

Item R12	Each	1	2	3	4
		Nominal size			
		75 mm	100 mm	150 mm	225 mm
		£	£	£	£
122	Cutting out and remaking caulked lead joint: providing new lead	23.53	29.60	39.97	59.90
	Connecting new pipe to existing pipe end				
123	caulked lead joints	27.78	34.91	47.05	70.54
124	change fitting: flexible joints	52.49	63.78	86.44	116.76
125	change fitting: flexible joint: caulked lead joint	41.27	50.85	66.35	97.02
126	Cutting out short length of existing pipe: inserting new oblique branch with loose collar: caulked lead joints	118.11	175.87	277.87	815.71

CONCRETE ACCESSORIES

Specification

Street gullies: to BS 5911 Part 2 and manufactured by a BSI Kitemark Licensee.

	Each	1	2
		Untrapped	Trapped
		£	£
	Gully: outlet 100 or 150 mm nominal size		
127	375 mm diameter x 750 mm deep	107.25	112.69
128	375 mm diameter x 900 mm deep	117.28	122.72
129	450 mm diameter x 750 mm deep	122.49	127.35
130	450 mm diameter x 900 mm deep	131.34	136.80
131	ADD for rodding eye, stopper and chain	9.16	9.16

CLAY ACCESSORIES

Specification

Terminal fittings: to BS 65 and manufactured by a BSI Kitemark Licensee.

	Each	£
	Gully: outlet 100 mm nominal size	
132	225 mm diameter	67.57
133	150 x 150 mm	54.50
134	230 x 230 mm	65.45

CLAY ACCESSORIES - *continued*

Item R12	*Each*	£
	ADD to Items R12.133 and R12.134 for	
135	horizontal inlet	14.41
136	vertical inlet	20.34
137	Trap: for use with raising piece: 100 mm diameter: outlet 100 mm nominal size	29.56
138	Raising piece: 225 mm diameter: 150, 230 or 305 mm high	21.77
139	Trapless yard gully: 225 mm diameter x 380 mm deep: outlet 100 mm nominal size	61.82
140	Hopper: 225 to 100 mm diameter: 230 mm high	33.51
	ADD to Items R12.138 to R12.140 for	
141	horizontal inlet	12.86
142	vertical inlet	12.86
143	Rainwater shoe: horizontal or vertical inlet: 100 mm nominal size	44.96
144	ADD for horizontal side inlet	2.59
145	Raising piece: rectangular: for use with rainwater shoe: 255 x 150 x 150 mm high	21.77
	Road gully: trapped: outlet 100 or 150 mm nominal size	
146	300 mm diameter x 610 mm deep	136.66
147	300 mm diameter x 760 mm deep	144.61
148	375 mm diameter x 760 mm deep	166.32
149	375 mm diameter x 915 mm deep	173.69
150	450 mm diameter x 915 mm deep	214.68
151	ADD for rodding eye and stopper	10.59
	Grease or mud intercepting gully: outlet 100 nominal size	
152	225 mm diameter x 550 mm deep	97.12
153	225 mm diameter x 610 mm deep: galvanised perforated bucket	134.76
154	300 mm diameter x 610 mm deep: galvanised perforated bucket	173.75
155	ADD for horizontal inlet	20.15
156	ADD for rodding eye and stopper	14.22

R12: DRAINAGE BELOW GROUND

PLASTICS ACCESSORIES

Specification

UPVC terminal fittings: in accordance with pipe manufacturer's recommendations.

Item R12	*Each*	£
	Gully: plastics grating: outlet 110 mm nominal size	
157	180 mm diameter: roddable	56.22
158	180 mm diameter: roddable: 110 mm diameter back inlet	61.52
159	ADD for back inlet bend	32.65
160	Trap: for use with raising piece: 110 mm diameter: outlet 110 mm nominal size	37.01
	Raising piece: 110 mm diameter	
161	155 mm high: two 82 mm boss upstands	28.71
162	180 mm high: four 50 mm boss upstands	32.98
	Hopper: 140 mm high: four back inlet upstands: plastics gratings	
163	160 x 160 mm to 110 mm diameter	30.08
164	230 x 160 mm to 110 mm diameter	34.37

CAST IRON ACCESSORIES

Specification

Terminal fittings: to BS 437 unless otherwise stated.

Road gully gratings and frames: to BS 437 Part 1 and manufactured by a BSI Kitemark Licensee.

Rates for the following include

Generally:
For coated fittings unless otherwise stated.

		1	2	3	4
		Coated		Galvanised	
		Nominal size			
		100 mm	150 mm	100 mm	150 mm
	Each	£	£	£	£
165	Vertical pattern fresh air inlet with lock: caulked lead joint	92.03	131.59	98.27	139.20
	Ground level pattern fresh air inlet: grating flush with surface				
166	cement joint	104.10	151.09	110.72	162.50
167	caulked lead joint	136.05	185.85	141.12	197.26

CAST IRON ACCESSORIES - *continued*

Item R12		1 Low invert £	2 High invert £
	Each		
	Trap: P type outlet: nominal size		
168	75 mm	65.89	91.26
169	100 mm	78.04	107.02
170	150 mm	115.69	180.28

Item		£
	Trapless gully: 225 mm diameter	
171	225 mm deep: outlet 100 mm nominal size	133.18
172	560 mm deep: outlet 100 mm nominal size	218.36
173	Rainwater shoe: 100 mm nominal size	116.28
	Grease or mud intercepting gully: outlet 100 mm nominal size: internal access fitted with screwed brass cap: heavy grating: galvanised perforated bucket	
174	300 mm diameter x 610 mm deep	580.49
175	300 mm diameter x 760 mm deep	690.86
176	ADD to Items R12.174 and R12.175 for 100 mm nominal size branch inlet cast on	20.82

Item		1 Cement joint £	2 Caulked lead joint £
	Plain raising piece: 225 mm diameter		
177	75 mm high	47.05	72.81
178	150 mm high	57.92	84.94
179	225 mm high	68.80	97.07
180	300 mm high	79.67	109.19
181	Tapered gully inlet: outlet 100 mm nominal size: 225 mm high	63.31	85.19
	ADD to Items R12.177 to R12.181 for horizontal branch inlet cast on		
182	75 mm nominal size	39.94	39.94
183	100 mm nominal size	44.79	44.79
	Plain raising piece: 300 mm diameter		
184	75 mm high	117.59	151.94
185	150 mm high	149.83	179.17
186	225 mm high	188.33	218.93
187	300 mm high	226.85	258.69

CAST IRON ACCESSORIES - *continued*

Item R12	*Each*	1 Cement joint £	2 Caulked lead joint £
	Raising piece: for rainwater shoe: rectangular		
188	75 mm high	37.88	63.65
189	150 mm high	48.76	75.78
190	225 mm high	59.64	87.91
191	300 mm high	70.52	100.04
192	Urinal connector: 75 mm nominal size: 300 mm long: screwed inlet	26.12	38.26

		1 Coated	2	3 Galvanised	4
		Joint to frame			
		Cement £	Caulked lead £	Cement £	Caulked lead £
	Sealing plate and frame: cover plain or recessed: brass screws: sealing cover in grease				
193	to suit 225 mm diameter gully or raising piece	45.79	75.31	48.87	78.39
194	to suit 300 mm diameter gully or raising piece	59.30	91.14	64.26	96.10
195	240 x 140 mm: for rainwater shoe	40.87	70.40	41.58	71.11
196	Sealing plate and frame: to suit 225 mm diameter gully or raising piece: washer: brass screws	49.55	79.08	53.56	83.09

		1 Coated £	2 Galvanised £
	Grating		
197	40 mm thick: to suit 225 mm diameter gully or raising piece	13.00	12.50
198	55 mm thick: to suit 300 mm diameter gully or raising piece	21.50	27.27
199	150 x 150 mm	3.61	5.64
200	230 x 230 mm	8.78	15.03
201	240 x 240 mm	6.98	11.29

		1	2	3
		Diameter of sleeve		
		100 mm £	150 mm £	225 mm £
202	Uncoated socketed sleeve with puddle flange: 3 mm mild steel ring: not exceeding 600 mm long: caulked lead joint at socket end: pointing with bituminous compound at other end: (measure building in separately)	122.03	186.11	422.78

CAST IRON ACCESSORIES - *continued*

Item R12		*Each*	£

Road gully grating and frame: bedding and flaunching in cement-sand mortar

203	heavy duty non-rock type: BS Ref. GA1-450: wheel load 11.50 tonnes: minimum waterway area 900 cm²	184.06
204	heavy duty hinged type: BS Ref. GA2-325: wheel load 11.50 tonnes: minimum waterway area 650 cm²	163.51
205	medium duty hinged type: BS Ref. GB-325: wheel load 5.00 tonnes: minimum waterway area 650 cm²	125.83
206	kerb-type for use in kerbs of half or full batter profile: BS Ref. GK-115: weir depth 115 mm	173.41

ACCESSORIES: SUNDRIES

Specification

Engineering bricks: imperforate clay bricks to BS 3921 Class B.

		1	2
		100 x 100 mm	100 x 150 mm
	Metre	£	£
207	Plain concrete: grade 20 N/mm²: 20 mm aggregate: kerb to gully top: trowelled finish: rounded top: angles: dishing to grating: formwork	14.50	14.92

		£
208	Brick seating to frame of road gully: engineering bricks in cement-sand (1:3): half brick thick: two courses high: facework one side: (including the cost of bricks)	17.17

WORK TO EXISTING ACCESSORIES

Rates for the following include

Raising or lowering gully grating and frame:
For taking off and resetting grating and frame.

For any excavation, etc. in lowering level.

For any materials, etc. in raising level.

WORK TO EXISTING ACCESSORIES - *continued*

Item R12	*Each*	£
209	Raising or lowering gully grating and frame: any size - *per 75 mm of level difference*	18.82
210	Taking up and replacing grating: not exceeding 350 mm diameter or 250 x 250 mm	2.19
211	ADD where fixed with screws	1.28
212	Taking up grating: cutting away bedding mortar and taking up frame: not exceeding 350 mm diameter or 250 x 250 mm	3.74
213	Fixing only frame: bedding in cement-sand mortar (1:3): replacing grating: not exceeding 350 mm diameter or 250 x 250 mm	7.71
214	Taking up grating: burning or cutting out joint and removing frame: not exceeding 350 mm diameter or 250 x 250 mm	8.78
215	Fixing only frame: caulked lead joint: replacing grating: not exceeding 350 mm diameter or 250 x 250 mm	26.46
	Taking up road gully grating and frame: cutting away mortar: overall area	
216	not exceeding 0.10 m²	8.59
217	0.10 to 0.25 m²	13.51
218	0.25 to 0.50 m²	21.73
	Fixing only road gully grating and frame: bedding and flaunching in approved quickset resin mortar: overall area	
219	not exceeding 0.10 m²	8.16
220	0.10 to 0.25 m²	13.81
221	0.25 to 0.50 m²	23.24

MANHOLES: EXCAVATING

Rates for the following include

Generally:
For forming sides curved on plan if ordered.

For setting aside and replacing topsoil.

For backfilling with and compacting selected excavated material in layers not exceeding 150 mm thick.

For disposing of surplus excavated materials off site.

		1	2	3
		Maximum depth not exceeding		
		1.00 m	2.00 m	4.00 m
	Cubic Metre	£	£	£
222	Pit	32.15	38.62	45.82

	Square Metre	£
223	Levelling bottom of excavation: compacting	0.73

R12: DRAINAGE BELOW GROUND

MANHOLES: EARTHWORK SUPPORT

Item R12	*Square Metre*	1	2	3
		Maximum depth not exceeding		
		1.00 m	2.00 m	4.00 m
		£	£	£
	To face of excavation: distance between opposing faces			
224	not exceeding 2 m	3.41	3.97	4.67
225	2 to 4 m	3.66	4.46	5.95
226	exceeding 4 m	6.34	8.18	10.75
227	ADD where curved	1.99	2.28	2.63

MANHOLES: HARDCORE

Specification

Hardcore for soakaways: broken brick, stone or crushed concrete 150 to 75 mm gauge, containing no fines.

	Cubic Metre	£
228	Filling to or around soakaway: exceeding 0.25 m average thick	28.32

MANHOLES: IN SITU CONCRETE: PLAIN: GRADE 20 N/mm²: 20 mm AGGREGATE

	Cubic Metre	£
229	Backfilling around manhole or the like	109.68

MANHOLES: IN SITU CONCRETE: PLAIN: GRADE 20 N/mm²: 14 mm AGGREGATE

	Square Metre	£
	Benching in bottom: trowelled finish: average thickness	
230	225 mm	43.08
231	300 mm	57.11
232	375 mm	71.14

R12: DRAINAGE BELOW GROUND

MANHOLES: IN SITU CONCRETE: SULPHATE RESISTING: PLAIN: GRADE 30 N/mm²: 20 mm AGGREGATE

Item R12	*Cubic Metre*	£
	Bed	
233	not exceeding 150 mm thick	96.33
234	150 to 450 mm thick	92.70

MANHOLES: IN SITU CONCRETE: SULPHATE RESISTING: REINFORCED: GRADE 30 N/mm²: 20 mm AGGREGATE

	Cubic Metre	£
	Suspended slab: tamped finish (measure reinforcement separately)	
235	not exceeding 150 mm thick	110.87
236	150 to 450 mm thick	107.23
237	exceeding 450 mm thick	103.60

MANHOLES: FORMWORK

	Square Metre	£
238	Soffit of slab: any height: basic finish: not exceeding 200 mm thick	29.62
239	ADD *for each additional 100 mm of thickness*	2.50

	Metre	£
	Edge of suspended slab: basic finish	
240	not exceeding 250 mm high	10.03
241	250 to 500 mm high	16.08
242	Extra for rebate: basic finish - *per 25 mm of girth*	1.00

		1	2	3
		Diameter		
		300 mm	375 mm	450 mm
		£	£	£
243	Half-round channel: fine finish: to falls	11.60	18.22	24.66
244	ADD where curved on plan	3.66	5.49	7.32
	Each			
245	Extra for junction between branch channel and main channel	3.20	3.89	4.58

R12: DRAINAGE BELOW GROUND

MANHOLES: PRECAST CONCRETE: SULPHATE RESISTING

Item R12	*Square Metre*	1 20 N/mm²: 20 mm aggregate £	2 30 N/mm²: 20 mm aggregate £
246	Cover slab: 100 mm thick (measure reinforcement separately)	35.17	36.88
247	ADD *for each additional 25 mm of thickness*	6.40	6.83

	Each	£
248	Extra for rebated opening for manhole cover and frame: any size: any thickness	20.25

MANHOLES: PRECAST CONCRETE UNITS

Specification

Manholes: to BS 5911 and manufactured by a BSI Kitemark Licensee; joints for watertight construction in accordance with manufacturer's recommendations.

Step irons: to BS 1247, fixed in manhole components before delivery.

Soakaways: perforated concrete to BS 5911 and manufactured by a BSI Kitemark Licensee; joints in accordance with manufacturer's recommendations.

Rates for the following include

Generally:
For bedding and pointing in cement-sand mortar (1:3).

For manhole or soakaway units (measure soakaway perforations separately).

Cover slab:
For reinforcement.

Shaft, chamber and taper rings:
For un-reinforced units not exceeding 1200 mm.

For reinforcement in units 1350 mm diameter.

		1	2	3	4	5
		\multicolumn{5}{l}{Internal diameter}				
	Each	675 mm £	900 mm £	1050 mm £	1200 mm £	1350 mm £
	Cover slab: opening 525 mm minimum diameter					
249	75 mm thick	39.21	62.19	121.31	171.95	248.99
250	88 mm thick	40.83	64.65	125.69	177.80	257.44
251	125mm thick	46.43	72.57	139.04	195.89	282.43
	Shaft ring					
252	300 mm high	27.13	-	-	-	-
253	600 mm high	40.54	-	-	-	-
	Chamber ring					
254	300 mm high	-	53.01	69.32	87.15	-
255	600 mm high	-	102.50	131.99	164.66	226.39
256	900 mm high	-	128.80	193.03	241.81	285.92
	Taper ring: 675 mm minimum diameter					
257	600 mm high	-	66.63	82.89	105.18	-
258	900 mm high	-	-	-	-	242.81

MANHOLES: PRECAST CONCRETE UNITS - *continued*

Item R12	*Each*	1 Height 150 mm £	2 Height 230 mm £	3 Height 300 mm £
	Rectangular shaft section: internal size			
259	600 x 450 mm	51.44	66.56	77.36
260	750 x 600 mm	67.94	87.24	99.56
261	1000 x 675 mm	109.08	137.00	148.30

		£
262	Reducing unit: internal size 1000 x 675 mm reducing to 750 x 600 mm	251.92
	Cover slab: 75 mm thick: minimum clear opening 600 x 450 mm: to suit shaft section	
263	600 x 450 mm	50.57
264	750 x 600 mm	70.62

		1 Diameter 60 mm £	2 Diameter 80 mm £	3 Diameter 100 mm £	4 Diameter 150 mm £	5 Diameter 200 mm £	6 Diameter 225 mm £	7 Diameter 300 mm £	8 Diameter 375 mm £	9 Diameter 450 mm £
265	Perforation through shaft, chamber ring or the like: for pipe or as soakaway perforation	2.40	3.84	4.80	7.19	9.59	10.79	14.39	17.98	21.58

		£
266	Step iron: cast into concrete during manufacture.	8.84

MANHOLES: PLASTICS UNITS

Specification

Inspection chambers: polypropylene, compatible with the pipe system.

Rates for the following include

Generally:
For jointing to drains.

For fixing blanking plugs.

For setting on and surrounding with 150 mm concrete grade 20 N/mm²: 20 mm aggregate including formwork.

For extra excavation, disposal and earthwork support.

R12: DRAINAGE BELOW GROUND

MANHOLES: PLASTICS UNITS - *continued*

Item R12	*Each*	£

Inspection chamber: 450 mm diameter: 110 mm nominal size channels and side inlets: blanking plugs: cast iron cover Grade C light duty single seal type and plastics frame: depth to invert

267	230 mm	164.14
268	600 mm	193.49
269	1000 mm	225.04

MANHOLE: LAYING ONLY BRICKWORK

Specification

Clay common bricks: solid bricks to BS 3921, durability designation FL.

Engineering bricks: imperforate clay bricks to BS 3921 Class B and manufactured by a BSI Kitemark Licensee.

Mortar: cement-sand (1:3)

Notes

Number of bricks:
Calculate from the Tables in Section F10.

Rates for the following include

Building in end of pipe:
For cutting pipe.

For turning single half-brick ring arch over pipes 225 to 300 mm nominal size.

For turning double half-brick ring arch over pipes 375 to 450 mm nominal size.

		1	2
		Common bricks	Engineering bricks
	Square Metre	£	£
	Wall: bedding in mortar with open vertical joints		
270	half-brick thick	22.51	-
271	one-brick thick	41.25	-
	Wall		
272	half-brick thick	22.98	29.65
273	one-brick thick	42.41	52.35
274	one-and-a-half-brick thick	52.44	73.62
275	one-brick thick: curved on plan not exceeding 2 m radius	67.63	77.35
276	one-brick thick: curved on plan not exceeding 2 m radius: 35 mm open vertical joints in alternate courses	59.45	-
	Extra for facework		
277	exceeding half-brick wide	5.03	5.49
278	exceeding half-brick wide: curved on plan not exceeding 2 m radius	7.65	8.11

R12: DRAINAGE BELOW GROUND

MANHOLE: BRICKWORK SUNDRIES

		1	2	3	4	5	6	7	8
		Nominal size							
Item		80 mm	100 mm	150 mm	200 mm	225 mm	300 mm	375 mm	450 mm
R12	*Each*	£	£	£	£	£	£	£	£
	Building in end of pipe: common brickwork: making good facework one side								
279	half-brick thick	2.12	2.65	3.97	5.29	8.86	11.81	19.85	23.82
280	one-brick thick	3.23	4.03	6.05	8.07	11.98	15.97	25.41	30.50
281	one-and-a-half-brick thick	4.33	5.42	8.13	10.84	15.09	20.12	30.96	37.15

282   Building into engineering brickwork: price at the foregoing Rates for common brickwork multiplied by 2.00.

	Metre	£
	Brick seating to frame of manhole cover: in cement-sand mortar (1:3): facework one side (including the cost of bricks)	
	half-brick thick: two courses high	
283	common bricks	10.83
284	engineering bricks	14.16
	one-brick thick: one course high	
285	common bricks	15.96
286	engineering bricks	18.94

MANHOLES: CHANNELWORK

Specification

Vitrified clay channels and bends: to BS 65 and manufactured by a BSI Kitemark Licensee:
a. type: normal;
b. bed and joint type: cement-sand mortar (1:2).

UPVC channels and bends: to BS 4660 and manufactured by a BSI Kitemark Licensee:
a. joint type: ring seal;
b. bed: cement-sand mortar (1:2).

MANHOLES: CHANNELWORK - *continued*

Item		1	2	3	4	5
		Clay			UPVC	
		100 mm	150 mm	225 mm	110 mm	160 mm
		Nominal size				
R12	*Each*	£	£	£	£	£

Half-round section: not exceeding 600 mm effective length

Item		1	2	3	4	5
287	straight	6.85	10.07	21.40	37.39	62.87
288	ADD *for each additional 150 mm of effective length*	1.57	2.52	1.87	13.68	15.67
289	curved	12.97	20.05	57.58	49.42	89.85
290	ADD *for each additional 150 mm of effective length*	0.25	0.45	-0.23	13.68	15.67
	tapering to smaller size					
291	straight	21.83	45.15	86.27	-	-
292	curved	31.18	83.21	165.80	-	-
293	Half section branch bend	12.97	20.05	56.87	17.88	47.26
294	Three quarter section branch bend	13.90	22.06	68.74	-	-

MANHOLES: CAST IRON PIPEWORK

Specification

Petrol trapping bends and inspection chambers: to BS 437.

Rates for the following include

Generally:
For coated fittings.

For caulked lead joints.

Inspection chamber:
For bedding in cement-sand mortar (1:2).

	Each	£
295	Petrol trapping bend: 380 x 760 x 100 mm nominal size	241.86
296	ADD where cut to length - *per cut*	8.86

MANHOLES: CAST IRON PIPEWORK - *continued*

Item R12	*Each*	1 Nominal size 100 x 100 mm £	2 150 x 100 mm £	3 150 x 150 mm £
	Inspection chamber with bolted cover			
297	no branches	204.05	-	278.58
298	one branch one side	262.73	294.68	441.92
299	one branch each side	338.80	389.91	547.44
300	two branches one side	444.11	529.89	761.91
301	two branches each side	537.86	674.06	875.04
302	three branches one side	535.57	731.81	896.08
303	three branches each side	726.95	809.82	1004.96
304	four branches one side	645.64	835.37	991.05
305	four branches each side	901.93	945.59	1134.88

MANHOLES: CAST IRON

Specification

Covers and frames: to BS 497 and manufactured by a BSI Kitemark Licensee.

Step irons for brick manholes: to BS 1247 and manufactured by a BSI Kitemark Licensee.

Rates for the following include

Access covers and frames: For coated units.

For rectangular overall shape to medium and heavy duty frames.

	Each	£
	Access cover and frame: bedding frame in cement-sand mortar (1:3): bedding cover in grease and sand	
	Grade A: heavy duty non-rock type: minimum clear opening	
306	550 mm diameter	213.34
307	600 mm diameter	175.56
	Grade B: Class 1: medium duty non-rock type: minimum clear opening	
308	550 mm diameter	176.27
309	600 mm diameter	135.14
	Grade B: Class 2: medium duty single seal type: minimum clear opening	
310	550 mm diameter	133.58
311	600 x 450 mm	124.12
312	600 x 600 mm	148.57

R12: DRAINAGE BELOW GROUND

MANHOLES: CAST IRON - *continued*

Item R12	Each	£

Grade B: Class 2: medium duty single seal recessed top type: min. clear opening

| 313 | 600 x 450 mm | 170.45 |
| 314 | 600 x 600 mm | 197.64 |

Grade C: light duty single seal type: minimum clear opening

| 315 | 600 x 450 mm | 66.54 |
| 316 | 600 x 600 mm | 131.02 |

Grade C: light duty single seal recessed top type: minimum clear opening

317	600 x 450 mm	121.69
318	600 x 600 mm	165.77
319	ADD to Items R12.306 to R12.318 for ventilated cover	18.21

Set of malleable lifting keys

| 320 | for heavy or medium duty covers | 10.06 |
| 321 | for light duty covers | 6.40 |

Step iron: building into joints of brickwork

general purpose pattern

322	115 mm tail	9.56
323	230 mm tail	11.36
324	corner pattern: 25 mm diameter: 595 mm long	10.33

MANHOLES: STEEL

Specification

Covers and frames: zinc coated steel, suitable for wheel loadings not exceeding 5 tonnes.

Rates for the following include

Concrete filling to skeleton type manhole covers: For all necessary formwork.

	1	2
	Clear opening	
Each	450 x 600 mm	600 x 600 mm
	£	£

Access cover and frame: bedding frame in cement-sand mortar (1:3): bedding cover in grease and sand

floor plate type

| 325 | single seal | 31.78 | 43.73 |
| 326 | double seal | 47.51 | 67.34 |

MANHOLES: STEEL - *continued*

Item R12	Each	1 Clear opening 450 x 600 mm £	2 600 x 600 mm £
	Access cover and frame: bedding frame in cement-sand mortar (1:3): bedding cover in grease and sand		
327	recessed skeleton, non-locking type...............................	39.04	54.63
	ADD where		
328	locking type...............................	9.85	14.78
329	locking type with rubber seals...............................	13.75	20.64
330	ADD for filling with 25 N/mm² concrete trowelled smooth................	8.40	11.10

MANHOLES: CLAY ACCESSORIES

Specification

Intercepting traps: to BS 65 and manufactured by a BSI Kitemark Licensee.

	Each	£
	Intercepting trap or reverse action intercepting trap: with or without fresh air inlet socket: clearing arm with stopper: nominal size	
331	100 mm...............................	57.28
332	150 mm...............................	82.79
333	225 mm...............................	242.31
334	ADD to 100 mm nominal size trap for lever locking stopper, chain and staple: cutting and pinning staple to masonry...............................	29.38

MANHOLES: CAST IRON ACCESSORIES

Specification

Disconnecting traps: to BS 437.

	Each	£
	Disconnecting trap: inlet for cast iron pipe: clearing arm with bridle plate and screw	
335	100 mm nominal size...............................	220.10
336	ADD where reverse action...............................	56.58
337	150 mm nominal size...............................	341.46
338	ADD where reverse action...............................	85.93
	ADD for lever locking stopper, chain and staple: cutting and pinning staple to masonry	
339	for 100 mm nominal size trap...............................	26.78
340	for 150 mm nominal size trap...............................	38.07

R12: DRAINAGE BELOW GROUND

WORK TO EXISTING MANHOLES

Rates for the following include

Raising or lowering cover and frame:
For any excavation etc in lowering level.

For any materials etc in raising level.

Item R12	*Metre*	£

Preparing top of existing brick wall for raising

341	half-brick thick	1.83
342	one-brick thick	3.20
343	one-and-a-half-brick thick	4.58

		1	2	3	4	5	6	7	8
		Nominal size							
		100 mm	110 mm	150 mm	160 mm	225 mm	300 mm	375 mm	450 mm
Each		£	£	£	£	£	£	£	£

Cutting out short length of existing pipe and concrete bed and haunching or surround: providing and inserting connector to receive half-round section channel (measure channel separately): jointing to pipe in cement-sand mortar (1:2)

		100 mm	110 mm	150 mm	160 mm	225 mm	300 mm	375 mm	450 mm
344	concrete pipe	66.92	-	85.23	-	107.12	152.60	199.34	253.65
345	plastics pipe	-	61.06	-	75.93	-	-	-	-
346	clay pipe	62.39	-	74.76	-	111.38	162.27	-	-
347	iron pipe	73.08	-	103.81	-	183.15	303.61	-	-

		1	2	3	4
		Nominal size			
		100 mm	150 mm	225 mm	300 mm
Each		£	£	£	£
348	Cutting out existing branch drain and branch channel from existing manhole: making good brickwork, rendering and benching	38.09	43.75	51.58	67.25
349	Connecting new branch drain to existing manhole: cutting hole in wall one-brick thick: cutting away existing benching as necessary: inserting new clay branch bend: bedding and jointing in cement-sand mortar (1:2): making good all work disturbed	64.71	78.54	110.59	180.99

WORK TO EXISTING MANHOLES - *continued*

		1	2
		Cover and frame: any type: any size: total weight	
Item **R12**	*Each*	not exceeding 150 kg £	150 to 230 kg £
350	Taking up and replacing cover: sealing cover in grease	4.75	6.03
351	Taking up cover: cutting away bedding mortar and taking up frame	8.59	12.06
352	Fixing only cover and frame: bedding frame in approved quickset resin mortar: bedding cover in grease and sand	14.36	24.65
			£
353	Raising or lowering cover and frame: any size - *per 75 mm of level difference*		25.58

TESTING EXISTING DRAINS

Rates for the following include

Generally:
For taking up and replacing in position gratings, manhole covers or the like.

For carrying out final test in accordance with the requirements for new work.

	Metre	£
	Testing with water or air: existing drain: diameter	
354	not exceeding 200 mm	1.74
355	200 to 350 mm	2.60
356	300 to 500 mm	3.47

	Each	
357	Testing with air: existing soil, waste or ventilating pipe: any height: any diameter: together with length of drain connecting soil pipe with nearest manhole	10.42

R12: DRAINAGE BELOW GROUND

CLEARING EXISTING DRAINS

Item R12	*Each*	1 Distance between access points not exceeding 30 m £	2 30 to 50 m £
	Rodding drain from manhole or clearing eye: cleaning out and removing all matter: flushing with water and leaving clear: removing and replacing in position manhole covers or the like: diameter		
358	not exceeding 200 mm	24.63	32.84
359	200 to 350 mm	28.74	41.06

		£
	Cleaning out and removing all mud and rubbish	
360	from gully: any type	5.09
361	from catchpit	6.54
362	ADD to Items R12.360 and R12.361 where mud bucket taken out and cleaned and replaced in position	2.18

R13: LAND DRAINAGE

GENERALLY

Reference to other Sections: the Preambles to Sections D20 and R12 apply equally to this Section unless otherwise stated.

Notes

Generally:
Rates in other Sections apply to land drainage where Rates are not given in this Section.

EXCAVATING TRENCHES

Rates for the following include

Generally:
For backfilling with hard rubble, gravel, broken stone or clinker graded 75 to 40 mm wide to within 150 mm of ground level and covering with selected topsoil.

R13: LAND DRAINAGE

EXCAVATING TRENCHES - *continued*

		1	2	3
		Nominal size of pipe		
		not exceeding 200 mm	225 mm	300 mm
Item R13	*Metre*	£	£	£
	Excavating trench: for pipe: average depth			
363	0.25 to 0.50 m	14.93	15.59	16.76
364	0.50 to 0.75 m	23.39	24.37	26.13
365	0.75 to 1.00 m	31.85	33.16	35.50
366	1.00 to 1.25 m	39.51	41.55	44.88
367	1.25 to 1.50 m	47.18	49.94	54.25

CONCRETE PIPEWORK

Specification

Pipes: to BS 1194: plain ended, unjointed.

		1	2	3
		Nominal size		
		100 mm	150 mm	225 mm
	Metre	£	£	£
	Pipe			
368	non-porous inverts	5.36	8.13	13.17
369	porous inverts	6.01	8.85	14.48

CLAY PIPEWORK

Specification

Pipes: to BS 1196: plain ended, unjointed.

		1	2	3	4
		Nominal size			
		75 mm	100 mm	150 mm	225 mm
	Metre	£	£	£	£
370	Pipe	5.21	6.01	8.85	14.48

R13: LAND DRAINAGE

PLASTICS PIPEWORK

Specification

Pipes: to BS 4962 and manufactured by a BSI Kitemark Licensee. Joint in accordance with pipe manufacturer's recommendations.

Rates for the following include

Pipe:
For junctions and fittings.

Item R13	*Metre*		1	2
			Nominal size	
			110 mm	160 mm
			£	£
371	Pipe: smooth, perforated, plain ended and unjointed		10.50	19.32

	1	2	3	4	5
	Nominal size				
	60 mm	80 mm	100 mm	125 mm	160 mm
	£	£	£	£	£
372 Pipe: flexible, corrugated, perforated and jointed	1.13	1.48	2.12	2.95	4.11

RUBBLE DRAINS

	Metre	£
373	Excavating open channel in short lengths: 150 to 250 mm wide x 300 mm deep to follow fall of ground: filling to within 50 mm of surface with approved hardcore and top 50 mm with approved fine gravel	3.59

MOLE DRAINS

Specification

Mole drain areas at depths, spacings and directions ordered.

Implements: use a mole plough with expander drawn by a tractor, fitted with tracks if so directed. Set plough to provide a smooth channel of circular cross section at the required depth.

Timing: carry out the work only when subsoil is moist enough to enable a smooth channel to be formed and when the surface is dry enough to avoid damage to the soil structure.

Rolling: on completion of the work roll the surface with a tractor-drawn roller, or run the tracks of the tractor drawing the plough along the surface slit so as to press back the soil.

	100 Metres	£
374	Forming mole drain: not exceeding 75 mm diameter x 500 mm deep	18.00

R13: LAND DRAINAGE

DITCHES

GENERALLY

Specification

Spoil: throw well clear of ditch and spread and level either by grading out into the adjoining land or forming a bank with smooth even sides and top as directed.

Work to bottoms: commence from the outfall and work upstream so that the bottom falls to an even gradient and is 75 mm below the invert of all pipes and culverts.

EXCAVATING AND RE-GRADING DITCHES

Specification

Excavate to re-form ditches and re-grade bottoms to falls as directed. Finish work 75 mm below and 75 mm clear on either side of culverts or pipes in the ditch's course.

Courses: to be of even width and even grade and as straight as possible. Any curves to be smooth and free flowing.

Drains: bring in other open drains discharging into the ditch so as to give the minimum resistance to the flow. Clear ends of drain pipes discharging into the ditch and make good any damage.

Channel spaces: leave channel spaces to allow surface water from the adjoining land to reach the ditch where required.

Notes

Actual volume for excavating:
Agree with the SO before work commences.

Item R13	Cubic Metre	£
375	Excavating to re-form ditch: re-grading bottom: removing, spreading and levelling spoil: including work to drains and channel spaces: removing and disposing all vegetation and rubbish: leaving waterway clear	10.76
376	Excavating to form ditch: grading bottom: removing, spreading and levelling spoil: including work to drains and channel spaces:	6.87

R13: LAND DRAINAGE

CLEARING WATERWAYS

Note

Where silt has accumulated to a greater depth than 150 mm, or falls of earth have occurred, obstructing the course of the ditch, measure clearance in accordance with Item R13.375.

Item R13	*Metre*	£
	Clearing bottoms: removing all silt not exceeding 150 mm deep, vegetation and rubbish: disposing arisings: leaving waterway clear	
377	channel: not exceeding 610 mm girth	1.16
378	culvert: not exceeding 1200 mm girth	3.85
	Each	
379	Cleaning grating to culvert mouth: not exceeding 1200 mm diameter: disposing arisings: leaving waterway clear	6.03

CLEARING DITCH SIDES

Notes

Protection of habitats:
Carry out with due regard to the protection of wild life habitat. To satisfy this requirement, clear only one bank side per annum, the other side being cleared in alternate years.

Vegetation traps:
Where vegetation is being cut on the banks or weeds removed from the bottom, erect vegetation traps just upstream of the next culvert or pipe below the work to collect all vegetation floating downstream. Clear traps frequently to prevent backing up.

	Square Metre	£
380	Cutting all vegetation other than trees on banks of ditch: removing and depositing arisings	0.29
	ADD for	
381	burning arisings	0.07
382	disposing arisings	0.15

R13: LAND DRAINAGE

OUTFALLS

Notes

Brick headwalls:
Calculate the number of bricks from the Table in Section F10.

Concrete work:
Pay for the Rates for in situ concrete in the Section E.

Item R13	Each	£
	Excavating for land drain outfall headwall and 1 m of pipe not exceeding 150 mm diameter: backfilling: headwall size	
383	500 x 800 mm	7.36
384	600 x 1000 mm	8.97
385	750 x 600 mm	8.17
386	900 x 750 mm	10.59
	Outfall comprising glass reinforced cement headwall with rot proof netting anchor and 1 m rigid polythene pipe: cutting hole in headwall: jointing pipe to headwall and land drain pipe	
	500 x 800 mm headwall: pipe diameter	
387	80 mm	27.32
388	100 mm	28.59
389	150 mm	33.66
	600 x 1000 mm headwall: pipe diameter	
390	100 mm	41.27
391	150 mm	46.34
392	200 mm	52.68
	Outfall comprising one brick headwall in any type of bricks in cement and sand mortar (1:3): brick on edge coping: facework to face, two returns and top: cutting and fitting around and building in pipe end: *excluding cost of bricks*	
	750 x 600 mm headwall: pipe diameter	
393	80 mm	53.07
394	100 mm	54.90
395	150 mm	59.48
396	200 mm	64.06
397	225 mm	66.35
	900 x 750 mm headwall: pipe diameter	
398	80 mm	62.93
399	100 mm	64.76
400	150 mm	69.34
401	200 mm	73.91
402	225 mm	76.20

Index